THE THREE LOVES

PHILOSOPHY, THEOLOGY, AND WORLD RELIGIONS

McGill Studies in Religion
McGill University

Edited by
Arvind Sharma

Volume 2
THE THREE LOVES
PHILOSOPHY, THEOLOGY, AND WORLD RELIGIONS
Essays in Honour of
Joseph C. McLelland
edited by
Robert C. Culley
William Klempa

The Three Loves

PHILOSOPHY, THEOLOGY, AND WORLD RELIGIONS

Essays in Honour of
Joseph C. McLelland

edited by

Robert C. Culley
William Klempa

Scholars Press
Atlanta, Georgia

THE THREE LOVES
PHILOSOPHY, THEOLOGY, AND WORLD RELIGIONS

Essays in Honour of
Joseph C. McLelland

edited by
Robert C. Culley
William Klempa

cover design by Ian Culley

Library of Congress Cataloging-in-Publication Data
The three loves : philosophy, theology, and world religions : essays
    in honour of Joseph C. McLelland ; edited by Robert C. Culley,
    William Klempa.
       p.   cm. — (McGill studies in religion ; v. 2)
    Includes bibliographical references.
    ISBN 0-7885-0029-5 (paper : alk. paper)
    1. Religions. 2. Reformation. 3. Faith. I. McLelland, Joseph C.
II. Culley, Robert C. III. Klempa, William. IV. Series.
BL50.T47   1994
200—dc20   94-30658
                                          CIP

Printed in the United States of America
on acid-free paper

To Joseph C. McLelland

Socrates*: "... wonder is the feeling of a philosopher,*
*and philosophy begins in wonder." (*Plato, *Theaetetus)*

CONTENTS

Preface ix

A Biographical Note: Joseph C. McLelland xiii

Publications of Joseph C. McLelland xv

Conceiving the Invisible: Joseph C. McLelland's
Modal Approach to Theological and Religious Pluralism
Maurice Boutin 1

I. PHILOSOPHY

Incomplete Rationality and Religious Faith
Bruce Alton 21

Kierkegaard's Unfolding of Faith:
The Initiation of "My Reader"
Alastair McKinnon 39

Happy Falls: A Philosophical Account of Evil
Donald Evans 63

Reflections on Ricoeur's *Soi-Même comme unn autre*
Morny Joy 79

Emmanuel Lévinas and the Irony of A/theism
Richard Cooper 93

II. REFORMATION STUDIES

The Reformation: A Paradigm for Christian Theology
Alister McGrath 107

For and Against John Milbank
Gregory Baum 123

Reformation Studies and Christian Theology
Douglas John Hall 141

Iconoclast or Regenerator? The Work of Andreas Bodenstein
in Reforming the Church of the Sixteenth Century
Edward J. Furcha 159

III. WORLD RELIGIONS

Religious Pluralism in its Relation to Theology
and Philosophy—and of These Two to Each Other
Wilfred Cantwell Smith 173

Towards a Dialogical Theology:
Some Methodological Considerations
David Lochhead 185

The Epistemological Foundations of Hindu Religious Tolerance
Arvind Sharma 199

Contributors 205

PREFACE

This collection of papers given at a symposium in honour of Professor Joseph C. McLelland, Professor Emeritus of the Philosophy of Religion at McGill University and Professor Emeritus of Presbyterian College, Montreal, requires a short explanation.

Teachers, colleagues and doctoral students of Professor McLelland met in Montreal for a symposium, May 11-14, 1992, sponsored jointly by Presbyterian College and the Faculty of Religious Studies, McGill University. Its purpose was twofold: first, to acknowledge the outstanding contribution of Professor McLelland, holder of the McConnell Chair of the Philosophy of Religion at McGill from 1964 to 1991 and a Professor at Presbyterian College from 1957 to 1993; secondly, to explore a topic at the heart of his academic interest, Theology and Religion and its three sub-themes: Religion and Philosophy, Reformation Studies and Theology, and Religious Pluralism.

Philosophy, theology, and world religions have been Professor McLelland's three main academic loves and intimate interaction among them has character-ized his teaching, research, and writing career. Of the three loves, philosophy, perhaps more by academic chance than by choice, has been his first love, followed closely by theology and finally by world religions. If his first has been philosophy, this has been closely connected with his second love, theology. In Professor McLelland's view, philosophy is and must always remain a close partner of theology. Positively, it serves as a valuable apologetic tool for theology and negatively, it is a useful critic of theology's pretensions. Not surprisingly, Professor McLelland has always had a keen interest in the philosophical theology of the Alexandrian theologians. Research into Philo, Clement and Origen, who wedded philosophy and theology, found expression in his monograph, *God the Anonymous: An Essay in Alexandrian Philosophical*

Theology. This interest was also reflected in his participation in Reformed-Orthodox Conversations and the publication along with an Orthodox theologian, John Meyendorff, of a collection of essays entitled *The New Man.*

At the same time, Professor McLelland's philosophical interests are not limited to the patristic period. He has pursued his interest in philosophy into the late medieval and the Renaissance and Reformation periods. The thought of Thomas Aquinas has been especially important and over the years Dr. McLelland has given seminars on Aquinas' philosophical theology. Yet it is principally the Renaissance and Reformation periods that have occupied his attention. He was co-founder of the Renaissance and Reformation Group at McGill University and he has written extensively on this period and on topics like "Calvin and Philosophy" and "Calvinism Perfecting Thomism." More recently, Professor McLelland has turned to the nineteenth and twentieth centuries and produced a book on the "irony" of atheism, *Prometheus Rebound.*

Professor McLelland's second, indeed his true love, is theology. From the outset of his career he has shown a deep interest in the Reformation of the sixteenth century. His doctoral dissertation, *The Visible Words of God,* was written on the eucharistic theology of Peter Martyr Vermigli, a "Calvinist Thomist." This keen fascination with the Italian Reformer has been maintained over the years. He has translated and edited along with G. E. Duffield, *The Life, Early Letters and Eucharistic Writings of Peter Martyr.* Earlier, he edited a collection of essays and wrote the introduction to *Peter Martyr Vermigli and Italian Reform.* As his retirement project he has become General Editor with John Patrick Donnelly, S.J., of the translation into English of the chief works of Peter Martyr Vermigli.

At the same time, Professor McLelland's theological interests have not been merely historical but also contemporary and practical. He has written on the Church, on the laity, on liturgy, on ethics, on the eucharist and Christology, on the Holy Spirit, on comedy and tragedy, and on suffering, to mention a few topics to be found in his diverse theological writings. He has served on the editorial boards of such theological journals as *Canadian Journal of Theology, Theology Today, Studies in Religion/Sciences Religieuses, Christian Outlook* and *The Presbyterian Record.*

As if these preoccupations with philosophy and theology were not sufficient, Dr. McLelland has also displayed a keen interest in world religions, a subject he taught for seven years at Presbyterian College when he first came to Montreal. In recent years he has addressed the theme of religious pluralism and has sought to construct a philosophical theology which he describes as "modal." By proposing a "modal" theology, Dr. McLelland aims to affirm religious pluralism without falling into the pitfall of relativism. Through the exploration of the different modalities of belief and unbelief from one religion to another and by discovering modal analogies in logic, physics and aesthetics, Dr. McLelland hopes to arrive at "universal" criteria for the truth claims of religion and for referential religious language.

This is an ambitious and exciting undertaking. Here his three loves—philosophy, theology and world religions—are brought together in a unique and creative way to develop an integrated philosophy of life with relevance to the Church, the world community, and the individual.

To honour Professor McLelland and to celebrate his significant achievement, his friends and colleagues and former students organized a symposium, the addresses from which are published in this *Festschrift*. The volume has three main sections: Philosophy of Religion, Reformation Studies and Theology, and World Religions in which the symposium speakers explore issues which have to do with his three loves. We are grateful to the contributors: Bruce Alton, Gregory Baum, Maurice Boutin, Richard Cooper, Donald Evans, Edward Furcha, Douglas Hall, Morny Joy, David Lochhead, Alister McGrath, Alastair McKinnon, Arvind Sharma and Wilfred Cantwell Smith. We also wish to thank the McGill Faculty of Religious Studies, the Senate of Presbyterian College and the McGill Faculty of Graduate Studies and Research for their financial support. Dr. George Harper has served as managing editor of the volume and we express our heartfelt thanks to him.

Robert C. Culley
William Klempa

July, 1994

A BIOGRAPHICAL NOTE
JOSEPH CUMMING MCLELLAND

Born in Port-Glasgow, Scotland in 1925, Joseph McLelland came to Canada at an early age. He attended elementary and secondary schools in Hamilton, then McMaster University from which he graduated B.A. in English literature in 1946. This was followed by graduate studies at the University of Toronto and theological studies at Knox College. In 1947 he married Audrey Mary Brunton of Hamilton. Upon graduation from Knox College and from the University of Toronto with M.A. in philosophy in 1949 he was ordained as a Presbyterian minister and served as Ordained Missionary in Val D'Or and Perron, Québec.

In 1951 he began doctoral studies at New College, Edinburgh, under Professor Thomas F. Torrance, serving at the same time as assistant at the Old Parish Church in Cupar-Fife. His thesis on the eucharistic theology of Peter Martyr Vermigli (1953) was published later as *The Visible Words of God*. On his return to Canada he became minister of the Bolton and Nashville congregations, Ontario. From 1954-57 he was also Secretary of the Board of Evangelism and Social Action. He studied with Gerald Phelan at the Pontifical Institute of Mediæval Studies, Toronto, 1955-56.

In 1957 the Presbyterian General Assembly appointed Dr. McLelland to the new Robert Chair of History and Philosophy of Religion and Christian Ethics at The Presbyterian College, Montreal. He also taught at McGill and in 1964 was named McConnell Professor of Philosophy of Religion at McGill University, a position which he held for twenty-eight years. He was Dean of the McGill Faculty of Religious Studies from 1975-85. He has served on the Faculty of Presbyterian College for over thirty-five years and in the fall of 1992 was Acting Principal of the College. In 1992 Dr. McLelland was named McConnell

Professor Emeritus, McGill University, and in 1993, Professor Emeritus of The Presbyterian College.

As a scholar Dr. McLelland has been prolific in publication. He is the author of fifteen books and more than one hundred articles in scholarly journals and magazines. He has served on the Editorial Board of *Theology Today*, as Associate Editor of the *Canadian Journal of Theology*, *Christian Outlook*, and *Studies in Religion/Sciences Religieuses* of which he was Editor 1973-77. Currently he is on the Editorial Board of *Humane Medicine*, a consulting editor for the *Blackwell Encyclopedia of Medieval, Renaissance and Reformation Thought*, and a contributing editor of *The Presbyterian Record*.

In addition to his busy scholarly life, Dr. McLelland has been an active churchman at Presbytery, Synod and General Assembly levels. He served as Moderator of the Presbytery of Montreal in 1970, and in 1985 was elected Moderator of the 111th General Assembly of The Presbyterian Church in Canada. His ecumenical involvements have also been numerous at local, national and international levels. These have included Catholic-Protestant, Lutheran-Reformed and Orthodox-Reformed consultations.

Dr. McLelland has received the Doctor of Divinity degree from Montreal Diocesan Theological College and from his alma mater, Knox College, Toronto. In May 1992, a Symposium was held in his honour sponsored by Presbyterian College and the McGill Faculty of Religious Studies. The Presbyterian College Graduate Society commissioned and presented a fine portrait of him to the College; the artist was Maria Gabankova of Toronto.

Dr. McLelland and his wife, Audrey, have four children and seven grandchildren. They continue to make their home in Pointe-Claire, Québec. Dr. McLelland is now devoting his energies to two projects. One is the editing of Peter Martyr's works, as general editor of *The Peter Martyr Library*. The other is a study of the subject "Pluralism without Relativism," using modal theories of explanation.

PUBLICATIONS
OF JOSEPH C. MCLELLAND

BOOKS

The Visible Words of God: The Sacramental Theology of Peter Martyr Vermigli. Edinburgh: Oliver and Boyd, 1957; Grand Rapids: Eerdmans, 1965.

The Other Six Days. Toronto: Burns and MacEachern, 1959; Richmond: John Knox, 1960; Japanese translation, 1968; Spanish translation, 1977.

The Reformation and its Significance Today. Philadelphia: Westminster, 1962.

Living for Christ. Richmond: John Knox, 1963.

New Look at Vocation. Toronto: Ryerson, 1964.

Toward a Radical Church. Toronto: Ryerson, 1967; Edinburgh: St. Andrew's, 1969.

The Clown and the Crocodile. Richmond: John Knox, 1970.

Edited with J. Meyendorff. *The New Man.* New Brunswick, N.J.: Standard, 1973.

God the Anonymous: An Essay in Alexandrian Philosophical Theology. Philadelphia Patristic Foundation. Cambridge, MA: Greeno, Hadden and Co., 1976.

Edited with introduction, *Peter Martyr Vermigli and Italian Reform*. Waterloo: Wilfred Laurier University Press, 1980.

Doxology: Perpetual Celebration, and *A Seder*. Toronto: Presbyterian Church Publications, 1982.

Celebration and Suffering. Toronto: Presbyterian Church Publications, 1983.

Prometheus Rebound: The Irony of Atheism. Waterloo: Wilfred Laurier University Press, 1988.

Translated and edited with G. Duffield. *Life, Early Letters and Eucharistic Writings of Peter Martyr*. Appleford: Courtenay Library of Reformation Classics, 1989.

"Ralph and Hugh and Robertson and Margaret: Canlit's View of Presbyterianism." In *The Burning Bush and a Few Acres of Snow: The Presbyterian Contribution to Canadian Life and Culture*, ed. William Klempa, 109-22. Ottawa: Carleton University Press, 1994.

Edited and translated with Introduction and Notes. *Early Writings*. Peter Martyr Library, Vol. 1. Kirksville, MO: Sixteenth Century Journal Publishers, 1994.

Translated. "Theses for Debate." In *Early Writings*. Peter Martyr Library, Vol. 1, 81-160. Kirksville, MO: Sixteenth Century Journal Publishers, 1994.

ARTICLES

"The Reformed Doctrine of Predestination (according to Peter Martyr)." *Scottish Journal of Theology* 8 (1955): 255-71.

"Covenant Theology—A Re-evaluation." *Canadian Journal of Theology* 3 (1957): 182-88.

"Mythology and Theological Language." *Scottish Journal of Theology* 11 (1958): 13-21.

"The MacDonnell Heresy Trial." *Canadian Journal of Theology* 4 (1958): 273-84.

"The Authority of the Canon." *Canadian Journal of Theology* 5 (1959): 35-43.

"Reformed and Lutheran Relations." *The Reformed and Presbyterian World* 26 (1960): 53-64.

"A Symposium on Life and Death: A Study of the Christian Hope." *Canadian Journal of Theology* 6 (1960): 9-11.

"La Tradition Protestante." *Cité Libre* 12 (1961): 3-5, 24.

"The Theology of the Preaching Office." *Canadian Journal of Theology* 7 (1961): 4-12.

"Three Challenges for the Christian: Liturgy (Time); Evangelism (Talent); Socialism (Treasure)." *Stewardship Explorations*, 109-41. Toronto: Ryerson, 1963.

"Come, Creator Spirit, for the Redemption of the World." *Frankfurt 1964*, ed. M. Pradervand, 189-200. Geneva: WARC, 1964.

"The Mundane Work of the Spirit." *Theology Today* 22 (1965): 205-17.

"Calvin and Philosophy." *Canadian Journal of Theology* 11 (1965): 42-53.

"Corporate Stewardship: The Congregation; The Denomination; The Nation." *Stewardship in Contemporary Life*, ed. T.K. Thompson, 89-144. New York: Association Press, 1965.

"Lutheran-Reformed Debate on the Eucharist and Christology." In *Marburg Revisited*, ed. P. C. Empie and J. I. McCord, 39-54. Minneapolis: Augsburg, 1966.

"Ethics and Ethos—A Reformed Viewpoint." In *Marburg Revisited*, ed. P. C. Empie & J. I. McCord, 153-64. Minneapolis: Augsburg Publishing House, 1966.

"Die Sakramentslehre Der Confessio Helvetica Posterior." In *Glauben und Bekennen*, ed. Joachim Staedtke, 368-91. Zurich: Zwingli Verlag, 1966.

"Comedy—Human and Divine." In *The Church in the Modern World*, ed. George Johnston and Wolfgang Roth, 273-87. Toronto: Ryerson, 1967.

"Symbol of Hope for 'Man and His World'." *The Christian Century* 84 (1967): 893-96.

"Religion in Canada: A Study in Polarities." *Theology Today* 24 (1967): 295-305.

"The Alexandrian Quest of the Non-Historical Christ." *Church History* 37 (1968): 355-64.

"Speaking About Faith—Doxology and Theology." In *What It Means to Confess the Christian Faith Today*, ed. William Klempa, 5-7. Toronto: The Presbyterian Church in Canada, 1972.

"The New McGill—A Place of Liberty?" In *Tripartite Commission Position Papers on University Government*, ed. J. C. McLelland, 1-8. Montreal: McGill University, 1969.

"Bullinger's Testament—The Sacraments According to Helvetic II." *Renaissance and Reformation* 8 (1971): 46-59.

"The Teacher of Religion: Professor or Guru?" *Studies in Religion/Sciences Religieuses* 3 (1972): 226-34.

"Arguments for the Existence of Philosophy of Religion: A Survey of Recent Writings." *Studies in Religion/Sciences Religieuses* 4 (1972): 361-69.

"The Meeting of East and West, A Report of Orthodox and Reformed Churches in Dialogue." *Reformed World* 32 (1972): 121-27.

"Sailing to Byzantium." In *The New Man*, ed. J. C. McLelland and J. Meyendorff, 10-25. New Brunswick, N.J.: Standard, 1973.

"Teacher or Guru? Approaches to Moral and Religious Instruction." *The Sentinel* (Montréal: Provincial Association of Protestant Teachers Monthly Journal) November 1974 to May 1975, 21pp.

"Doxology as Suspension of the Tragic." *Theology Today* 31 (1974): 114-20.

"Philosophy and Theology—A Family Affair (Karl and Heinrich Barth)." In *Footnotes to a Theology*, ed. H. Martin Rumscheidt, 30-52. Ottawa: The Corporation for the Publication of Academic Studies in Religion in Canada, 1974.

"Vermigli, Pietro Martire." *Encyclopedia Britannica*, 16th ed.

"Orthodox-Protestant Dialogue: A Matter of Opinion." In *The Orthodox Church and the Churches of the Reformation*. WCC: Faith and Order Paper 76. Geneva: WCC, 1975: 87-90.

"The Place of Worship in Bilateral Conversations." In *Confessions in Dialogue*, ed. N. Ehrenstrom, 224-26. Geneva: WCC, 1975.

"The Purpose of Purpose: Goals of a University Faculty of Religious Studies." *Theological Education* 14 (1978): 110-13.

"Calvinism Perfecting Thomism." *Scottish Journal of Theology* 31 (1978): 571-78.

"Peter Martyr Vermigli—Scholastic or Humanist?" In *Peter Martyr Vermigli and Italian Reform*, 141-51. Waterloo: Wilfred Laurier University Press, 1980.

"Walter Bryden—'By Circumstance and God'." In *Called to Witness: Profiles of Canadian Presbyterians*, Vol. 2, ed. W. S. Reid, 119-26. Toronto: The Presbyterian Church in Canada, 1980.

"Meta-Zwingli or Anti-Zwingli? Bullinger and Calvin in Eucharistic Concord." In *Huldrych Zwingli, 1484-1531: A Legacy of Radical Reform*, ed. E. J. Furcha, 179-95. Montreal: Faculty of Religious Studies, McGill University, 1985.

"Renaissance in Theology: Calvin's 1536 Institutio—Fresh Start or False?" In *Papers from the 1986 International Calvin Symposium*, ed. E. J. Furcha, 154-74. Montreal: Faculty of Religious Studies, McGill University, 1986.

"Philosophy of Religion in Transition." *Toronto Journal of Theology* 5 (1989): 47-53.

"A serious playfulness." *The Way* 31 (1991): 196-205.

"A Theory of Relativity for Religious Pluralism." *Journal of Religious Pluralism* 1 (1991): 1-20.

"Zeus Unbound—The Irony of Theism." *Toronto Journal of Theology* 7 (1991): 30-34.

"Vermigli, Peter Martyr." *Encyclopedia of the Reformed Faith*, ed. D. McKim. Louisville: Westminster/John Knox, 1992.

*   *   *   *   *

Book reviews: *Canadian Journal of Theology, Studies in Religion, Theology Today, Queen's Quarterly,* etc.

Editorials: *Studies in Religion/Sciences Religieuses*, 1974-78

Peter Martyr Newsletter (occasional). Editor.

Peter Martyr Library. General Editor: series of English translations. Kirksville, MO: Sixteenth Century Journal Publishers and Thomas Jefferson University Press, 1994-.

IN PRESS

- "Philosophy and Theology in Canada." In Festschrift for Douglas Jay, ed. G. Brown.

- "Aristotelianism." In *Blackwell Encyclopedia of Medieval, Renaissance and Reformation Christian Thought*.

POPULAR ARTICLES, ADDRESSES

'The Lord's Presence at the Lord's Table' Toronto: Church Worship Association, 1956.

"The Evils of 'Church Work'." *Christian Outlook* 15/10 (Oct., 1960): 3, 17-18.

"What Presbyterians Believe About Jesus Christ." *The Presbyterian Record* (Feb., 1956): 12-13.

"Setting the Earth on Fire." *Letter to the Laos* 2/3 (May-June, 1960): 1-2.

"Decision Tomorrow." *Letter to the Laos* 2/4 (July-August, 1960): 3-4.

"What is the Spirit Saying to the Church?" *Presbyterian News* (April 30, 1961): 1-5.

"A Cast for God's Drama." *The Presbyterian Record* (Dec. 1961): 4-5.

"Can Canada be a Pinch of Spice?" *Letter to the Laos* 3/1 (Jan.-Feb., 1962): 1-2.

"Dead and Living Faith." *The Presbyterian Record* (June, 1962): 5-7.

"Questions About the Vatican Council." *The Presbyterian Record* (Oct., 1962): 10-12.

"Hurry Up, Judas!" In *Preaching the Passion*, ed. A. M. Motter, 114-22. Philadelphia: Fortress Press, 1963.

"Dimensions of the Racial Crisis." *Christian Outlook* 19/2 (Nov., 1963): 3-6.

"Frankfurt Profile." *The Ecumenist* 3/1 (1964): 12-15.

"Sanctified by Faith." *The Presbyterian Record* (Nov., 1965): 14-15.

"The Silence of God in the Age of Film." *Christian Outlook* 20/5 (Feb., 1965): 6-10.

"Why our Pond is Lukewarm or Forty Years in the Wilderness." Two addresses to the Toronto-Kingston Synod at Sudbury, Ontario (Oct., 1965): 1-15.

"St. Paul on Campus." In *The Face of the Church*, ed. A. L. Farris, 21-26. Toronto: Presbyterian Publications, 1967.

"The Eighth Day—Expo's Christian Pavilion." *The Ecumenist* 5/4 (1967): 55-57.

"Remember the Future." *The Presbyterian Record* (Sept., 1967): 12-14.

"Blueprint for a New Model." *The Presbyterian Record* (Sept., 1967): 10-17.

"Man and His World: Theseus or Sorcerer's Apprentice?" *Ferment '67* (Sept., 1967): 295-305.

"Reformation, Revolution and Democracy." *The Presbyterian Record* (May, 1969): 8-9.

"Have we Really a Passion for Peace?" *The Presbyterian Record* (Nov., 1970): 13.

"East and West Together—An Orthodox and Reformed Dialogue." *The Presbyterian Record* (Jan., 1974): 6-7.

"A Future for Mission? From Apologetics to Transposition." *ARC* 11 (1984): 28-32.

The Presbyterian Record: monthly columnist 1985-6, quarterly 1986-91, contributing editor 1991-.

RESEARCH IN PROGRESS

Modal theology: pluralism without relativism. A constructive philosophical theology. With modal analogies in logic, physics and aesthetics, seeking properly "universal" criteria of religious truth-claims and referential language.

Peter Martyr's Philosophical Treatises. Translation, with introduction and notes, of selected treatises on knowledge, providence and free will. PM Library vol. 4.

Peter Martyr's 1549 Oxford Disputation and Treatise on the Eucharist. Translation, with introduction and notes. PM Library vol. 11.

CONCEIVING THE INVISIBLE
Joseph C. McLelland's Modal Approach
to Theological and Religious Pluralism

Maurice Boutin
McGill University

> . . . it took decades before astronomers could begin to "see" the planet Uranus, because their accepted paradigm could admit only star or comet. They were not truly seeing what they were looking at. Is it a similar case with our God-models? If so, then we need self-critical experimentation, in the cubist style, until we learn to see through the pictures to that which is deeper still. (McLelland 1969, 10)

Studying Joseph C. McLelland's writings provides amazement, and even greater enjoyment. Here, "the pleasure of the text"—an expression coined by the French literary critic Roland Barthes (Barthes, 1975)—makes reading a delightful activity because of a "bonheur de l'écriture" quite typical of the author of these writings. Using again one of Roland Barthes' favourite expressions one may say that McLelland is indeed "un écrivain heureux."

These two expressions I have just used are difficult to translate into English, or else they lose much of the rich ambiguity they have in French. Talking about a happy writer might mean his or her good or skilful style. Unfortunately, a *happy* writer is not always a happy *writer*; of course, this distinction fully applies in French as well. The ambiguity here consists in making use of the substantive 'bonheur'—'happiness'—and the adjective 'heureux' with reference not only to a person, but also to the work of this person.

To say that McLelland is a happy writer is not meant to inquire about the modality of the relation between these two possible meanings of 'happiness'. Let

1

us be content with the fact that McLelland is happy as a writer, leaving open the question of his 'happiness' as a person. If at all, the latter could be addressed only in a very implicit way which should leave no room whatever to curiosity, but rather to instruction, let alone edification. In other words: the rich ambiguity of the French 'bonheur' can in no way open up to some sort of psychological transposition of the satirical analyses of politics broadcast on Sundays under the label "Double Exposure," although such a radio program reminds us that "a geographer's dream" might well turn out to become "a politician's nightmare," as McLelland had the story in 1967 already (McLelland 1967, 295).

McLelland's happiness as a writer, I suggest, rests on the kind of irony to which he devotes himself with the earnestness and the equanimity proper to spiritual exercise. Irony, he says, "comes from ambiguity" and is called for by "the disproportion of our rationality, the humour of it all" (McLelland 1991, 232 and 230). Why is it so? Because, McLelland says, "there is much that does not meet the eye, something more for which clarity is inadequate" (McLelland 1991, 231). What does that mean for the philosophy of religion today? It means first of all the attempt to look "beyond the problematics of classical theism/atheism ('ontotheology') into a modality where categories may be transposed or sublated" (McLelland 1991, 233). This is what McLelland calls "my own position" (233).

Such a transposition, or even sublation, takes place within various types of logic in modern times. Even modal logicians cannot compete with the Creator, for modal logic cannot be elaborated out of nothing, apart from any specific topic or question, without historical markers of some sort. Philosophy of religion focuses quite significantly on the question of God's existence. Thereby, 'existence' undergoes a certain number of shifts always involving modal categories to some extent. This is the case at least within the following three types of logic: the logic of perfection, the logic of causation, and what could be called the logic of event-uality. Let us look how modal thinking is at work within each of these logics and what is thereby each time at issue.

1. The Logic of Perfection

Why look at modality for a possibly better insight into the question of God's existence? The answer is a kind of dissatisfaction concerning a decision made at the outset of modern times by Descartes with regard to this question: the decision to view existence as a predicate.

It would take too long to consider whether this decision has something to do with the rise of subjectivism for which Descartes is also held responsible. Suffice it to say that criticism of the Cartesian idea of existence as a predicate may eventually, though rather seldom, go along with the criticism of modern subjectivism. The latter, for sure, has not been initiated by the so-called 'postmodernism'—a word that functions as a very popular label going around these days in the cultural fabric of western societies. Criticism of modern subjectivism is indeed a central issue in works as different from one another as the works of Martin Heidegger, Claude Lévi-Strauss, Michel Foucault, Roland Barthes, or Jacques Derrida—among many others.

One thing, however, should be kept in mind about Descartes's view of existence as a predicate: the link between a particular type of argument called 'a priori'—that is, prior to, and apart from, experience as sense experience—and logical implications of the idea of perfection as related to God's reality. As the argument goes, it is more perfect for something to 'exist' both in human understanding and in reality, than it is for something to 'exist' only as an idea in someone's mind. Since God is the most perfect being, God must necessarily 'exist' not only in human understanding, but in reality as well. Therefore, existence is a necessary predicate of the most perfect being called God.

Descartes provides the "classical" type of argument for God's existence made possible through "The Logic of Perfection," as Charles Hartshorne calls it. Descartes's argument is called "classical" because it is based on, and part of, what Hartshorne considers as "a metaphysics of being, substance, absoluteness, and necessity as primary conceptions" (Hartshorne 1962, xiii). Hartshorne himself offers, under the same logic of perfection, what he calls a "neoclassical" argument which is no mere repetition of Descartes's, although Hartshorne also emphasizes the modal category of necessity in regard to God's existence. "Neoclassical metaphysics," as Hartshorne has it, is "the metaphysics of becoming or creativity," it is a metaphysics "of creative becoming, event, relativity, and possibility" (Hartshorne 1962, ix and xiii). Hartshorne's approach to God's existence shows a strongly modal side easily noticeable in his essay with the title: "Ten Ontological or Modal Proofs for God's Existence" (Hartshorne 1962, 28-117).

In the "neoclassical" approach a twofold set of logical decisions takes place. The first one is provided by 'classical' logic with its distinction between necessity and contingency, and also between potentiality and actuality. The second set of logical decisions is to view God's existence as necessary and to consider contingency with equal right, and even greater relevance, because it is an intrinsic aspect of God's actuality. Therefore, according to Hartshorne, God is not only necessarily existent; God is also and 'necessarily' actual, that is, contingent. Contingency is, as it were, taken up within God's reality. The modal category of necessity undergoes here a radical transformation thanks to the modal category of possibility. As Hartshorne says:

> God *merely* as necessary is less than any contingent thing whatever, even the meanest. To worship the necessary is but a subtle form of idolatry. [. . . God] is the individual that could not fail to be actualized in some contingent particular form. This implies an immeasurable superiority; but what actualizes the superiority is God-now, or God-then, not just God at any time or as eternal, which is a mere abstraction. The necessity that there be some contingent actualization is inherent in the unique abstractness of the identifying divine individuality or essence. (Hartshorne 1962, 102)

In this respect, the logic of perfection necessarily involves what Hartshorne calls "the logic of contingency" (Hartshorne 1962, 90). For if we may say that "Our intellects are at home in the abstract," it is by no means enough to make us ignore that "the concrete is an infinitely-receding goal" (Hartshorne 1962, 109).

2. Existence and Reality

Before looking briefly at the logic of causation and at the logic of eventuality, let us consider some aspects of the relation between existence and reality and some implications of this relation for modal thinking.

Descartes's view of existence as a necessary predicate for God is in tune with our usual understanding of the relation between existence and reality: to be real means to exist, and vice versa. There are at least two ways to challenge this common assumption. One may use the word 'existence' for human beings only, while recalling that such a decision means in no way that only human beings are—'really'. Thus, God does not exist; God is. This is the suggestion sketched by Heidegger. In order to meet critically the identification of existence and reality, one may also look back to medieval western philosophy, particularly the 14th century. This is about the time when, to use McLelland's words, "another Modernity was born" (McLelland 1991, 4). Let us follow this path in order to gain a slight idea of some issues modal thinking is confronted with today.

The historian and philosopher Anneliese Maier, who did seminal work on the philosophy of nature and its development from the 13th to the 18th centuries, has shed some light on the question we are tackling here. The monograph she published in 1930 on Kant's categories of quality (Maier 1968, 69-147) could, of course, not ignore that the first category of quality is called "reality," whereas "existence"—"Dasein"—is the second category of modality. As categories, reality and existence do belong to two different classes, and each of these two classes belong to a separate group: quality, to the "mathematical" group of categories together with class 1 (quantity); modality, to the "dynamical" group of categories together with class 3 (relation) (*KrV* B 110).

Kant's Table of Categories (*KrV* B 106)

1. *Of Quantity*
Unity
Plurality
Totality

2. *Of Quality*	3. *Of Relation*
Reality	Of Inherence and Subsistence
	(substantia et accidens)
Negation	Of Causality and Dependence
	(cause and effect)
Limitation	Of Community
	(reciprocity between agent and patient)

4. *Of Modality*
Possibility - Impossibility
Existence - Non-existence
(Dasein - Nichstein)
Necessity - Contingency

The sources analyzed by Maier to trace back the formation and meaning of 'realitas' indicate the following (Maier 1968, 71-80):

- The meaning of 'reality' is referred in scholasticism not to the adjective 'real' or even to the expression 'real being' (esse reale), but to the word 'res' as an 'abstractum' which expresses the essence of 'reality'. The same happens with words like 'entity' referred to 'ens' ('being'), or 'formalitas' referred to 'forma' ('form') (77, n. 14).

- 'Reality' is originally a diminutive of the word 'res' (77).

- 'Reality' has been forged by Scotist philosophers who drew the following distinction between 'reality' and 'res': the latter is that which can exist by itself, whereas 'realitas' is something smaller than 'res'. In one and the same 'res', therefore, there can be many 'realities', that is, smaller 'res' or parts of 'res' also called 'formalitates' such as—in regard to human beings for instance—the being of substance, life, animality, rationality (77).

- The tendency to identify 'reality' and 'existence' has probably developed within late-scholastic nominalism (77).

Concerning Kant's distinction in the table of categories Maier says:

It is perhaps a result of Kant's philosophy when for us today the word 'reality' exclusively expresses a modality. In Kant's system modality is indeed much more central and typical than the categories of quality. Therefore it is possible that the growing acceptance of Kant's thought made modality increasingly dominant over against quality. In any case, it is established that Kant's categories of quality very soon were no longer understood in their proper meaning, and were apprehended as categories of being and non-being. (80, n. 21)

In English philosophy of the seventeenth and eighteenth centuries—at least in Locke, Newton, Clarke, Berkeley and Hume—'reality' is either a synonym of 'existence', or means the 'degree of existence' of concepts and representations. It is so, for instance, in expressions like 'reality of ideas', 'reality of notions', 'reality of things', 'real existence', 'real being'. 'Reality' is used as a modal concept, whereas continental rational philosophy has a much more general, but also much more indeterminate concept of 'reality' (76).

Such an indeterminacy seems to prevail also and particularly at the beginning of Ludwig Wittgenstein's *Tractatus Logico-Philosophicus*. The "Tractatus" opens with a statement which seems to have the shape of a definition: "The world is all that is the case" (T, 1). In order for the definition to be meaningful, one has to inquire about the expression 'all that is the case'. Obviously, Wittgenstein operates here in a very peculiar manner: this time, and quite exceptionally, determination has to take place on the basis of indeterminacy proper. The operation of discarding indeterminacy fails, or it is at most puzzling.

A clarification of Wittgenstein's indeed strange expression leads to the proper place for modal thinking. The expression 'all that is the case', I suggest, is the exact translation of a basic word in western thought: the word 'res'.

One may recall here Thomas Aquinas's famous statement: "Actus autem credentis non terminatur ad enuntiabile, sed ad rem"—"The act of the believer ends not in a statement but in 'res'" (ST, 2a2ae, q.1 a.2 ad 2). This distinction provides a relativizing of language—at least as expression in the agency-process—in favour of that about which language talks and refers to, that is, that which is and remains outside language, the so-called extralinguistic reality. Aquinas's statement is strongly semantic in structure, and it does express a matter of fact: obviously it is more important to know and talk about something than to know and talk about our knowing and talking and categories of mind. This was so before Wittgenstein and it remains so up until today.

Yet there is also another way to refer to 'res' and to use it. The French historian and philosopher of law, Pierre Legendre, recalls this in the following words:

> We shouldn't believe that our notion of object is made more simple through the generic term *res*. In Roman culture 'res' is a grammatical category which varies greatly. Precisely in regard to what we call 'object', 'res' is a very efficient invention of Roman Law. It is capable of maneuvering equivocation by activating the relations between the classifications involved in this legality-system. Thus, *res publica* (the public thing which we call the State after having operated a whole set of transpositions); *res nullius* (the thing that does not belong to anybody, the good without owner or ruler); *res sancta* (the sacred thing referred to divine law, for instance the walls of a city or the markers of a field); *res judicata* (the thing that has been judged, that is, the final judgment in a court-process). All these are indeed categories that stay quite far from one another. *Res* provides the link between these categories and refers back to the logic of the whole, to the functioning of interpretations, to the science of the lawyers and of the professors. In other words: *res* refers back to all that which is implicit, particularly to that which is political in nature, to that which sustains the system. *Res* holds the place for all that which could be determined under particular circumstances. I want to add this: *res*—this is a way of talking which is tautological. If I were to suggest an acceptable translation of 'res', I would refer to the Greek paraphrase which is used sometimes as a definition of the Greek *pragma* which is one of the possible equivalents of *res*: *to peri ou o logos*—*what one talks about*. Thanks to this reference one can apprehend the semantic status of our term *object* insofar as it refers to the Latin *res*. On the various levels of its use an object is nothing else than *something that is the case*. Take for instance *res publica*; the most precise translation is the following: that which is the case when the question of the *publicum*, of that which is public, is raised or arises. (Legendre 1985, 25; Boutin 1990)

The link between 'res' and the Greek 'pragma' made by Legendre is also suggested by Heidegger in *Being and Time*. "Pragmata," Heidegger says, is "that which one has to do with in one's concernful dealings (praxis). But ontologically, the specifically 'pragmatic' character of the 'pragmata' is just what the Greeks left in obscurity; they thought of these 'proximally' as 'mere Things'" (Heidegger 1962, 96-97).

What Legendre says about 'res' is worth considering when 'world' is defined as 'all that is the case'. This expression and 'res' mean nothing in particular.

They are not univocal in meaning because they are pluralistic in structure. They provide language with the possibility of enjoying both indeterminacy and determination. Both are equally necessary. Even when language is taken as a subject matter (metalanguage) it cannot escape history (Koselleck 1985, 83-87).

Yet 'res' does mean something quite definite and precise each time it is used, provided that careful attention be given to the very context of its use. Using it makes language function, not because it would refer to something quite particular and specific, to an individual considered merely in terms of 'substance as such', and therefore without reference to any other aspect or dimension or context. Even when there is no explicit, univocal reference to any given individual, language may and does function because through the use of 'res' or equivalent expressions it refers to that which we call 'reality'. In such cases the particular linguistic context of its use brings the determination or specification.

Determination or specification cannot be had only in one and the same way, namely with reference to an individual as such, independently from anything else. Contextuality is here important; and it can provide the determination necessary for language to function meaningfully without ignoring the basic indeterminacy also necessary for its very functioning. Language has the constant possibility of having determination without being stripped of the indeterminacy which makes the factual determination each time possible when language is used.

What does this all mean with reference to modal thinking? It means that modal thinking stands at the threshold between semantics and pragmatics. It does not make us think of 'res' simply in terms of 'mere things' because it makes us think of language with reference to its users as well. Here, the following image finds full application. It was suggested by the young Karl Barth in 1922 to picture the common situation of theology at the beginning of the twenties, and it is typical of Barth's homeland: "schmaler Felsengrat"—"mountain ridge" (Barth 1922, 212). On a ridge, one can but keep moving, one cannot stay, or else one soon falls, either to the right or to the left, but for sure—falls, Barth says. One may add: on a ridge, one cannot stay, unless one has one leg shorter than the other.

For modal thinking the two legs are logic and ontology. To stay would then mean that either logic or ontology had been cut down. Now, this is precisely what modal thinking strives to avoid, this is the very source of its concern, and this is also why modal thinking appears to be like a burden. For the point here is not how to find a place to stay; it is not either how to find a place to go; it is how to realize that the place to be looked at is given nowhere than together with the very move from and toward it. Here, connection—nexus—becomes what it can only be: co-incidence. This is, I suspect, the secret of McLelland's fascination for 'unitary field laws' in modern physics. This is also the reason why, as Heidegger says, "provenance remains future"—just between dream and nightmare (Koselleck 1985, 213-230).

One of the most obvious results, perhaps, of such a co-incidence is that questions have the tendency to proliferate rather than disappear. In some way or the other, attempts to moderate the situation go along with the search for categories of the mind. The outcome of this enterprise, however, seems to generate discontent of some sort.

Take Kant, for instance. He finds that Descartes argues directly from the logical necessity to the real necessity of God's existence. By so doing, Descartes confuses a logical with a real predicate, that is, "with a predicate which determines a thing" (*KrV* B 626). According to Kant, God's existence is not analytically contained in the concept of God as the most perfect being; it is added to this concept synthetically (*KrV* B 627). Even when God is understood as the most perfect being, we must go, Kant says, "outside" this concept, "if we are to ascribe existence" to God (*KrV* B 629). In other words: 'Being' is "not a real predicate" (*KrV* B 626). "When, therefore, I think of a being as the supreme reality, without any defect, the question still remains whether it exists or not" (*KrV* B 628). As Kant has it, "we can no more extend our stock of insight by mere ideas, than a merchant can better his position by adding a few noughts to his cash account" (*KrV* B 630).

Kant is no less critical of Aristotle than he is of Descartes on the issue of categories. For sure, Kant picks up a word used by Aristotle to talk about categories, and he acknowledges that his "primary purpose is the same as" Aristotle's (*KrV* B 105). While contemplating his own achievements in this delicate matter Kant makes, however, quite clear in the paragraph which immediately follows his "table of categories" that his proposition is for sure far better. Kant finds that Aristotle, no doubt "an acute thinker," nevertheless went on searching for categories "on no principle" (*KrV* B 107). Aristotle, Kant also says, "merely picked them up as they came his way, and at first procured ten of them, which he called *categories* (predicaments). Afterwards he believed that he had discovered five others, which he added under the name of post-predicaments. But his table still remained defective" (*KrV* B 107).

As we all know, Kant's critical appreciation either of Descartes or of Aristotle cannot be considered as the final and last word on the issue of categories. Kant's own "table of categories" has been challenged, its structure and meaning have been questioned many times up until today. However, Kant's table has never been truly replaced so far. This is probably not quite accidental, for—as the linguist Emile Benveniste says—"modern epistemology does not try to set up a table of categories" (Benveniste 1971, 63). For Benveniste the reason for this is the following: "It is more productive to conceive of the mind as a virtuality than as a framework, as a dynamism than as a structure" (63).

Let us remind ourselves also that Kant's criticism of Aristotle in regard to categories echoes Aristotle's own view on those who preceded him "in the search for causes," as he calls it. Aristotle says about them in the first book of his *Metaphysics* (988 a 10) that they gave names to the first principles and debated also about them; unfortunately they did so in a confused way, without knowing what they were talking about even when they had found something right. And Aristotle compares them to inexperienced fighters capable of striking back, yet only now and then, in a haphazard way, and without *epistēmē*.

Categories stay in close connection to language, as Benveniste argued in 1958 by referring to Aristotle. In "Catégories de pensée et catégories de langue"—"Categories of Thought and Language" Benveniste shows convincingly that Aristotle did not find the categories he proposed in the things themselves, that is, through reflection on the process of predication; these categories rather correspond to, and do express, the classification provided by language as such—more precisely: by oral language. The French historian and philosopher Jean-Pierre Vernant, a specialist of ancient Greek culture, agreed with Benveniste on this point, and he suggested the following correction: according to Vernant one should speak here not of oral language, but of written language (Vernant 1980, 188). In any case, it might well be enough to say the following here: if—as Benveniste recalls—"to think is to manipulate the signs of language" (Benveniste 1971, 64), this capability has a close and constant connection to the relation between indeterminacy and determination to be found in language, either written or oral. As I have suggested above, this relation is the central concern of modal thinking today.

3. The Logic of Causation

Whereas the logic of perfection is called 'a priori'—that is, prior to experience—the logic of causation is called 'a posteriori' for it is taken from, or it has its source in, experience. Let us look briefly at the basic structure of the logic of causation in regard to the question of God's existence. If we do it with reference to Kant, it is simply because this may illustrate how Kant's "table of categories" is used in regard to this kind of argument.

Two remarks may serve as an introduction to our examination here. First, the whole setting-up of Kant's "table of categories" rests on a "common principle," the following: the faculty of judgment which, Kant says, "is the same as the faculty of thought" (*KrV* B 106). The second remark to be made pertains to the third and last category in each of the four classes: in each class this category has the same formal structure in regard to the first two categories respectively (*KrV* B 110). Totality is nothing else than plurality *considered as* unity; limitation is nothing else than reality *combined with* negation; community is the causality of substances *reciprocally determining* one another; and necessity is nothing else than existence which is *given through* possibility itself (*KrV* B 111). Like the first two categories in each class the third category should not be thought of as "merely derivative"; it should be thought of—like the first two categories—as a "primary" concept of "pure understanding." The reason is that each and every category demands "a separate act of the understanding" (*KrV* B 111).

With reference to "that which in its concept contains a therefore for every wherefore" (*KrV* B 613) and thus leaves "no room for any further question" (*KrV* B 612) the "natural procedure of human reason" (*KrV* B 614) is summarized by Kant in the following steps which describe the interplay of the various categories involved and the proper dynamic of the whole "procedure":

- First, human reason "persuades itself of the existence of *some* necessary being" that is "unconditioned" (*KrV* B 614).

- Second, human reason "looks around for the concept of that which is independent of any condition, and finds it in that which is itself the sufficient condition of all else, that is, in that which contains all reality" (*KrV* B 614-15).

- Third, "that which is all-containing and without limits is absolute unity, and involves the concept of a single being that is likewise the supreme being" (*KrV* B 615).

- Fourth, human reason concludes "that the supreme being, as primordial ground of all things, must exist by absolute necessity" (*KrV* B 615).

In each of these four steps reference is made to the following classes of categories and to the following categories:

1. class 4 (modality) - category 2 and 3 (existence and necessity);
2. class 2 (quality) - category 1 (reality);
3. class 1 (quantity) - category 1 (unity - with implicit reference to monotheism [*KrV* B 618]);
4. class 3 (relation) - category 2 (causality).

The first two steps show a close relationship between existence and reality. There is also a close relationship between steps 4 and 1: causality is the link between the modal categories of existence and necessity—a link which, Kant recalls, is a matter of 'self-conviction'.

Yet causality is also central to the process resulting in self-conviction as the goal to be achieved according to step 1. This is so because the third modal category involves not only necessity but also contingency. As such, "the contingent exists only under the condition of some other contingent existence as its cause, and from this again we must infer yet another cause, until we are brought to a cause which is not contingent, and which is therefore unconditionally necessary" (*KrV* B 612). Thus, the terms of the third modal category are related to one another through the second relational category, causality. As regards the question of God's existence, this relationship allows for a departure from the contingent. In this type of argument the contingent is left behind, and causality provides the adequate means for this.

Looking back to this first step—and particularly to the point of departure: contingency—Kant says that "it by no means follows that the concept of a limited being which does not have the highest reality is for that reason incompatible with absolute reality" (*KrV* B 616). 'Limitation' here does not refer to the third category of quality, but rather to finitude. Human finitude and contingency are mutually inclusive, and 'finitum' shows itself 'capax infiniti'. This 'capacity' belongs to the first modal category, possibility, and it cannot by itself pass into the second modal category, that is, actualize itself.

4. The Logic of Event-uality

Kant uses the word *Feld* (field) also with reference to the categories of modality (*KrV* B 278-81). The structure of such a field of modality unveils a whole range of relations that would be too long to analyze here because of the many issues to be dealt with. Besides, and more importantly, it is not at all clear whether Kant's reference to a field of modal categories has something to do with the question to be examined here: the possibility of relating the categories of modality and the categories of relation. Such a possibility is not only seen, it is also realized by Kant, for instance with reference to the third modal category whose correlate is: contingency.

When the "concept of the contingent" is being apprehended as containing the category of relation, it is apprehended "as something which can exist only as consequence of something else" (*KrV* B 290), that is, with reference to causality as the second category of the third class. The first category of the third class, namely "inherence and subsistence"—understood also as "substance and accident," reminds us that the categories of relation are to be thought of in regard to something "permanent" (*KrV* B 224, B 291), to a 'whatness' different from, and at the basis of, the 'thatness' of any kind of event to be apprehended. Should, however, the "concept of the contingent" be apprehended as containing the category of modality, then it is apprehended "as something the not-being of which can be *thought*" (*KrV* B 290), that is, with reference to the second category of modality, existence, whose correlate is: non-existence.

Each time, the "concept of the contingent" is apprehended in a different way as referring either to an effect, or to non-existence. The logic of event-uality to be looked at relies on a logic of relations of a different kind, whose task consists in the examination of the following statement: the 'content' ('whatness') of an 'event' ('thatness') is a 'mode' of being ('howness'). Or—to quote from Hartshorne: "Events, not things or individuals, are the final subjects of predicates" (Hartshorne 1962, 66). To give just an example which is probably to be found in a reflection on religion and religious experiences: how is it possible to speak of an event as a salvation-event? When we are told for instance that the New Testament writings do not provide any kind of definition of what salvation is about, can this issue be simply dismissed by saying that the early Christians did not really have the time—let alone the intellectual skill—to ponder on this and similar matters, or by saying that when 'salvation' seems to apply to religious matters it is always so radically basic that it escapes human apprehension?

In the end of the sixties already, McLelland speaks of "the depth in human being" in terms of a "field of relations" (McLelland 1969, 9). At that time, there was indeed little to be heard about relationality or relational thinking. The paper from which this expression is quoted has remained unpublished for reasons that are unknown to this writer. This is regrettable because "Ideas of God as Analogue Models"—so the title of the paper—is still very relevant. Perhaps it was not quite timely when McLelland wrote it and delivered it; perhaps it was too much ahead of its time. Be that as it may—this paper reads like an agenda for present and future research in philosophy and theology. A rather heavily loaded and daring agenda, indeed, but an agenda that clearly shows a capacity to tackle the present situation which can only rest on a vision made possible on no other ground than what has to be—simply—called: generosity. This is the requirement if one is willing to enter the darkness of the present. By this, I absolutely do not mean that the present situation for philosophy and theology over the last twenty-five years or so is gloomy altogether. I mean rather the fact that every present—not only our's—is dark when it begins to be seen. As the proverb has it: "No weaver knows what he or she weaves." Another proverb clothes the same idea in these words: "There is no light at the foot of the lighthouse" (Bloch 1986, 295). The darkest place is underneath the lamp.

For Kant, the categories of modality have the following "peculiarity" as to the concept to which they are attached as predicates: they only express the relation of the concept to the faculty of knowledge; they do not in the least enlarge the concept insofar as it determines an object (*KrV* B 266, 286-87).

Before Kant, Robert Boyle (1627-1691) and his 'corpuscular philosophy' did acknowledge that modes referring to physical objects do entail relations. These relations do not alter the determinations of these objects; they are rather aspects of the concepts of these objects. A lock for instance is nothing else than a piece of iron with a peculiar form, and the same obtains for keys. It belongs, however, to the very concept of a lock that a lock can be unlocked or locked, to the very concept of a key that a key can close or open, and all this does not change anything to the two pieces of iron thereby referred to (Maier, 1968, 62-63).

What is at issue here pertains to the 'equipmentality'—"Zeughaftigkeit"— as analyzed by Heidegger in *Being and Time* (§§ 15-18). It also has to do with an issue giving rise to considerable debate in Kant's First Critique and ever since until today: the question about the reality of the real and of the possible as compared with each other. This question can be addressed otherwise when the relation at stake here is understood as the relation between use and non-use of objects, for instance locks and keys. For these objects are not changed and do not begin or cease to exist simply because they are used or not used. Such a case points to the relation within the second modal category: existence. This relation can now be viewed as a relation of event-uality, thus making it possible to think of this relation in terms of event. All this, however, offers but a remote picture of what has to be thought of as event under the 'unitary field laws' of modern physics—an issue which has captured McLelland's attention for more than twenty years now because, McLelland is convinced, this issue can hold what it promises: a fresh look at the connection between logic and ontology. Here, however, McLelland's stand needs correction. In his paper presented in 1991 to the Canadian Theological Society's annual meeting at Queen's University, McLelland said: "Such connection between logic and ontology . . . is the burden of my story" (8). It is rather, I suggest, the burden of *our* story.

Conclusion

Attention to the use of modal categories in the question of God's existence helps to know more about language and its functioning. It helps to better understand ourselves in the first place. Therefore, such an enterprise does remain inchoative in character. Concern about modality faces the difficult and delicate task of dealing with the question whether and how it is possible to think otherwise. This is what problematic is all about.

What is called 'problematic' may provide appropriate understanding of what it means to be humble—intellectually. Humility—almost by definition—cannot be had, or else it is simply lost. The same occurs with problematic: it can only be had under the very negation of it, a negation usually called 'dogmatism'. Like love, or even—amazingly enough—reading, humility cannot be dealt with in the imperative mood: be humble! Such an obligation would express one's own refusal of humility.

Modality makes one more cautious about the business of referring to arrogance to qualify others and their works. Often enough, what may seem so at first sight shows to be endeavours—albeit more or less questionable—to avoid being caught up within one's own cultural habits of thinking. Exploration and experimentation of possible or event-ual new ways of thinking is a necessary task in a pluralistic situation like today's. We should not let humility be practiced only by so-called postmodernists; we probably have enough humour to share with them the common task of looking for resources—even un-known—awaiting closer examination, as the Italian philosopher of religion, Enrico Castelli, the founder of the International Conferences on Hermeneutics, used to say. As McLelland recalled in 1991, there is room—even in theology, and of course in philosophy of religion as well—for what he calls a "via postmoderna" in terms of modal thinking.

No doubt, there is much to be asked for here. The reason is that modal thinking is in about the same situation as philosophy in general, or science. As we all know, Heidegger refers to that situation in the next to the last paragraph of his *Letter on Humanism* published in 1947. He writes: "It is about time to break the habit of overestimating, and thus asking too much to, philosophy." On the question of how to avoid plunging science into a normative role alien to it and which science itself does not covet, Legendre suggests that the bent towards "stopgap-answers," as he calls it, is not becoming more popular today than it was in the past. It prevents us, though, from realizing that those issues addressed by stopgap-answers—here, Legendre has in mind bioethics in particular—should be acknowledged in their fully aporetical character (Legendre 1985, 374).

This state of affairs means something Aristotle knew very well, as can be seen for instance in the first chapter of book 'B' of his *Metaphysics*: aporetical issues cannot be avoided; therefore, they ought to be gone through—not around. In such cases intensifying our expectations—and questions—goes along with an increase in the awareness needed to recognize not only stopgap-answers, but also our very longing for them. This, of course, cannot go without a certain amount of irony, McLelland would probably say. The proper insight into all this in regard to philosophy of religion, and to the question of God's existence in particular, is expressed by Hartshorne in the following:

> The basic significance of the divine existence is not to tell us something particular about the world, but rather to tell us what it means to be particular, and why anything in particular matters. (Hartshorne 1962, 110)

Modal thinking does not answer questions. It does not simply add questions to those we might already have. It helps situate the questions we have and the answers being offered. Modal thinking is heuristic thinking. As such, it is not content with inquiries about presuppositions, consequences, influences, internal cogency of questions and answers, as useful and needed such inquiries may be. Modal thinking is also—at least in a negative way—basically pluralistic: it does neither exclude nor include, because belief or knowledge has not to be kept safe and immune over against history. "Neither 'identity' nor 'quality' has any recognizable reference where all diversity is denied" (Hartshorne 1962, 120). Modal thinking is in tune with the basic task of philosophy of religion: the task of warning the philosophical enterprise not to turn into a religion and so rule out any religious claim or trend, and also the task of reminding us that religious experience is in constant need of self-knowledge in order to stay alive.

To understand the task of philosophy of religion today one must appreciate what time it is. McLelland puts modal thinking high on today's agenda for philosophy of religion and theology—an agenda which has a timetable of its own, probably as peculiar and paradoxical as the title of an article published by McLelland in the journal *Arc* in 1975: "Quebec: Year Seventeen." This article quotes also from the play "Les beaux dimanches" by the great Québécois playwright Marcel Dubé who said recently in an interview: "Je ne cherche pas la voie la plus étroite; je cherche l'issue la plus sûre vers la clarté"—"I do not look for the gloomiest path; I do look, instead, for the most promising road toward light."

BIBLIOGRAPHY

Barth, Karl. "Das Wort Gottes als Aufgabe der Theologie." *Die Christliche Welt* 36 (1922), cols. 858-73. Reprinted in *Anfänge der dialektischen Theologie*, vol. 1. 2d ed., ed. Jürgen Moltmann, 197-218 [Theologische Bücherei 17/1]. Munich: Chr. Kaiser, 1966.

Barthes, Roland. *The Pleasure of the Text*. New York: Hill and Wang, 1975.

Benveniste, Emile. "Categories of Thought and Language" (1958). In E. Benveniste, *Problems in General Linguistics*, 55-64. Coral Gables, FL: University of Miami Press, 1971.

Bloch, Ernst. *The Principle of Hope*, vol. 1. Cambridge, MA: MIT Press, 1986.

Boutin, Maurice. "Méprises du langage, énigme du monde: A propos d'une expression étrange du *Tractatus* de Wittgenstein." *Religiologiques* 1 (1990): 37-49.

Hartshorne, Charles. *The Logic of Perfection and Other Essays in Neoclassical Metaphysics*. Lasalle, IL: Open Court, 1962.

Heidegger, Martin. *Being and Time*. New York: Harper and Row, 1962.

Kant, Immanuel. *Kritik der reinen Vernunft*. Philosophische Bibliothek, 37a. Hamburg: Felix Meiner Publ., 1971; *Critique of Pure Reason*. London: Macmillan, 1961 (Abbreviation: *KrV*).

Koselleck, Reinhart. *Futures Past: On the Semantics of Historical Time*. Cambridge, MA: MIT Press, 1985.

Legendre, Pierre. *L'inestimable objet de la transmission: Etude sur le principe généalogique en Occident*. Paris: Fayard, 1985.

Maier, Anneliese. *Zwei Untersuchungen zur nachscholastischen Philosophie*. 2d ed. *Die Mechanisierung des Weltbilds im 17. Jahrhundert* (1938): 11-67 and *Kants Qualitätskategorien* (1930): 69-147. [Storia e Letteratura 112] Rome: Edizioni di Storia e Letteratura, 1968.

McLelland, Joseph C. "Religion in Canada: A Study in Polarities." *Theology Today* 24 (1967): 295-305.

---. "Ideas of God as Analogue Models." 1969, 11 pp., unpublished.

---. "Quebec: Year Seventeen." *Arc* 2 (Summer 1975, No. 4): 1, 3-7.

---. "Zeus Unbound: The Irony of Theism." *Toronto Journal of Theology* 7 (1991): 230-34.

---. "Via Postmoderna: Toward Modal Theology." 1991, 14 pp., unpublished.

Thomas Aquinas, *Summa Theologiae* 2a 2ae. Ottawa: Commissio Piana Publ., 1953 (Abbreviation: *ST*).

Vernant, Jean-Pierre. "The Reason of Myth." In J.-P. Vernant, *Myth and Society in Ancient Greece*, 186-242. [European Philosophy and the Human Sciences, 57] Brighton: Harvester Press; Atlantic Highlands, NJ: Humanities Press, 1980.

PART I

PHILOSOPHY

INCOMPLETE RATIONALITY AND RELIGIOUS FAITH

Bruce Alton
University of Toronto

1. The Irony of Agnosticism

Is religious faith acquired on practical (commonly called "prudential") grounds possible, reasonable and proper? Philosophers generally have rejected "practical theism" (and less often, with a curious inconsistency, practical atheism) on the straight-forward assumption that evidence-based reason must always take precedence over prudential preferences, and that hence agnosticism is the only "reasonable" position on matters religious. It is my claim that Pascal and other so-called prudential theists have not been given proper credit for their sophisticated grasp of the complexity of human *judgement* as distinct from (narrowly understood) belief. My argument draws on some recent philosophical studies in decision theory rather than a detailed re-examination of classical prudentialism, however. At its core is my conviction that philosophers of religion need to pay more attention to an emerging consensus on the "openness" or "incompleteness" of human rationality; hence the title "Incomplete Rationality and Religious Faith."

I might well have subtitled the paper "The Irony of Agnosticism," and not merely out of deference to Joseph C. McLelland's authoritative study of Promethean anti-theism.[1] Part of my claim is that the modern agnostic's cognitive stance is incoherent: that—in the context in which religious judgement must be exercised—agnosticism *may* avoid both a Promethean "postulatory atheism" and an absolutist theism, but at a cost which is ironically self-defeating. In large part this is due to an uncritical adoption of scientific determinism and a naive form of post-modernism which opens the agnostic to another set of unbreachable absolutes. D. C. Muecke, for example, in his classic study, *Irony and the Ironic*, refers to much of modern literature as

> reducible to one great incongruity, the appearance of self-valued and subjectively free but temporally finite egos in a universe that seems to be *utterly* alien, *utterly* purposeless, *completely* deterministic, and *incomprehensibly* vast.[2]

The result can be, and often is, a curious new form of enslavement—to the self, to a new narcissism—as Christopher Lasch has explained; it is an enslavement which might explain mindless returns to past obediences, to simpler-minded tyrants, however maniacal or tyrannical:

> Men used to rail against the irony of fate; now they prefer it to the irony of unceasing self-consciousness. Whereas earlier ages sought to substitute reason for arbitrary dictation both from without and within, the twentieth century finds reason, in the debased contemporary form of ironic self-consciousness, a harsh master; it seeks to revive earlier forms of enslavement. The prison life of the past looks in our own time like liberation itself.[3]

What is "ironic" about tragi-comic self-awareness is that hope is defeated along with despair, theism along with atheism, self-transformation along with "cosmic" meaning. In levelling ourselves to the probable, the humanly possible becomes super-humanly unlikely. There is no Promethean spirit in postmodern agnosticism, just a dull bureaucracy and a tasteless distrust of those who seem—but only seem—to rise above it. Ours is an era and a mood of radically ironic expectation without aspiration and of faithful dedication to the absurdity of faith.

The irony of modern, or rather postmodern, agnosticism is that in its celebration of human finitude it exercises closure on an unfinished reality and, in doing so, achieves its end (its *telos*) without purpose. It is ironically self-destructive. Worse, it declares *complete* (or nearly so, since some admit a very modest role to narrowly limited "bootstrapping" activities) that which—in all the world studied by modern science—is demonstrably *incomplete*. Hence it rests on an inexcusable error, a failure of the so-called humane disciplines to dialogue with the so-called "inhumane" sciences.

2. Faith and Judgement

Joseph McLelland's recent study begins with the assertion that "the central subject of philosophy of religion is belief and unbelief."[4] That the task of philosophy of religion entails a close examination of unbelief as well as belief has not been evident to all philosophers of religion, though it should have been. To become a person of faith or to renew or strengthen one's faith is, I maintain, to make a judgement (i.e. to form an opinion with implications for action) *against* unbelief.

It is important to try to clarify what I mean when I speak of human decision-making as judgement—as "forming an opinion as the basis for action." Broadly and informally I mean what is intended by the catch-phrase "an all-things-considered better decision." Such decisions are by no means limited to religious matters, although for a very simple reason religious judgement is paradigmatic, since it takes place under conditions of radical uncertainty arising from incomplete knowledge. Religious judgement is also paradigmatic in its seriousness and personal relevance; in William James's memorable phrase, some decisions are "of the forced, living, and momentous kind."[5] I will not belabour the point, but simply say that when I speak of a person "forming an opinion" or "making a judgement" I mean, at a minimum, that the person doing so understands the matter to be *relevant* to her or his life and *non-trivial*. Further, I mean that for such a person the judgement carries implications for action and therefore marries belief with feelings, attitudes and intents.

Yet to repeat: I do *not* mean by such judgements, any more than did James, *only* religious faith-decisions. Anthony Flew, in discussing John Wisdom's parable of the invisible gardener, refers to Wisdom's "haunting and revelatory article 'Gods'"[6] from which it is drawn. That article haunts and reveals still, I think, not only for its sensitivity to the nature of religious belief but for its perspicacity in pointing to important aspects of life in which, daily, we humans judge or decide without benefit of a calculus of choice or a "vertical deduction." In courts of law, affairs of the heart, appreciation of beauty, allocations of our energy, trust of friends, to name but a few kinds of situations, we *must* decide without benefit of more study in order "to release us from human bondage into human freedom."[7] Wisdom argues that, concerning judgement, "we must not forthwith assume that there is no right or wrong about it, no rationality or irrationality, no appropriateness or inappropriateness, no procedure which tends to settle it, nor even that this procedure is in no sense a discovery of new facts."[8]

The study of human judgement—that immensely complicated interplay between our preferences, desires, will, beliefs, cultural conditioning, interpersonal commitments, ideology, self-consciousness, and so on—to say nothing of their attendant pathologies—remains a vast and daunting frontier of knowledge even after centuries of theory construction and testing, and decades of intensive empirical research. We humans go about our task of deciding and acting on our decisions all the same, not quite sure how we do it but convinced that it is of the essence of our humanness to do so. It is judgement to which the rearing and education of our young is dedicated: that they not slavishly imitate or mindlessly adopt the way of their elders (however wise and good) but consciously decide for themselves, and with proper respect for others, what is true and good. Such exercise of sound judgement, we rightly think, is more important than warranted belief or knowledge; for it displays that refined blending of fact and value—of the "is" and the "ought"—that is our species' distinctive achievement.

What it is to exercise sound judgement is elusive, and its logic is far more complex than can be captured in any algorithm yet known. Training in "good judgement," we have learned, is more a matter of tutoring or mentoring than teaching, more a matter of wisdom than knowledge, more a matter of maturity than mere intelligence. For this reason we train lawyers by having them study cases of good and poor judicial reasoning, train art critics by sending them to art galleries, train pastors and psychiatrists "on the job" as much as in seminary and the Institute. But what are these observers of good judgement looking for? When an expert "judging faculty" is formed, what is the shape of it? What "inner logic," what "reasonableness," in-forms it?

The sceptic or cynic might say, and with some justification, that such "formation" is often little more than an exercise in socialization into the norms and values of the training "class." But this will not explain those remarkable judgements which we recognize to go beyond or above the limitations of the socialization experience. Nor will it explain the experience we have of our own new insights and fresh ideas as we advance in our judging of the world. There is no doubt a qualitative dimension to good judgement, a quality we recognize and name "reasonable"; though we cannot explain it adequately, we are also certain that it is not an arbitrary label nor a quality we simply intuit. For philosophers, who have with some justification been described categorically as "obsessed with rationality," the nature of good judgement is particularly problematic. Why this is so is not hard to isolate and explain, since it is rooted in the ways judgement must deal with conflicting evidence.

3. The Myth of Ideally Rational Agents

Imagine a typical case calling for judgement: whether to continue to trust a friend when there is evidence that she has betrayed you, and of course strong evidence that on many other occasions she has not. "Trust me," she says, "I can't explain why it only seems that I've betrayed you when I haven't; I doubt if I ever can explain; our friendship surely goes deep enough for you to trust me on this without explanation." It takes little, I think, to make of this case that the decision to trust or not is pressing, lively and momentous. And suppose you do genuinely reaffirm your trust in her? What shall we say of your dealing with the apparently conflicting evidence? There are many possibilities, ranging from a kind of forced forgetfulness, through suspension of disbelief, to self-deception, all of which must be considered problematic from the point of view of evidence-centred rationality. For the problem is this: *qualified* trust—faith which cannot overcome counterevidence, or has special difficulties doing so—we recognize to be less than adequate to the demands of love or friendship or spiritual wholeness.

Evidence-centred rationality might be considered itself the problem, though this I think is unfair to the tradition. The general concern of "evidence-based rationality" is simply this: we *abandon* evidence-centred rationality at the enormous cost of loosening the foundations of all scientific knowledge. We must therefore see and label such decisions, if they manipulate the evidence in any *inappropriate* way, as irrational, non-rational, pseudo-rational, imperfectly rational, incompletely rational, etc. It is perhaps tempting to say that such a view of human nature is "rationalistic" rather than rational. But philosophers did not invent the position or the argument; they have simply given it particular shapes and forms. It is the conviction of our scientific culture, and the growing conviction of others, that we have more to lose than to gain by playing carelessly with evidences that contradict our wishes. But what is not widely recognized is that much of modern philosophy of mind is dedicated to exploring the *limitations* of human rationality in such a way as to find a full and proper place for the "logic of the emotions."[9] What has gone by the way is precisely the old rationalistic model of the human person as an "ideally rational agent." Two long-known and well-studied "garden variety" forms of human irrationality—*akrasia* (weakness of the will, incontinent action) and self-deception—pose such enormous theoretical problems that they alone form the basis for most of the theoretical and empirical studies.

4. Incompletely Rational Situations

The demise of the model of the "ideally rational agent" does not mean that philosophy of mind or the sciences of human choice are licensed to retreat from the goal of scientific *explanation*. But among philosophers of mind and social scientists there is a growing recognition that *human* rationality is characterized by the ability to relate to the future rather than merely to adapt biologically at the individual level and functionally at the social level. This means, for one thing, that we are an *incompletely* rational species in the following sense: we can and do decide (and consequently act, though not without some "misfires") precisely in order to achieve an end or ends which we have *some* reason(s) to think our choice will help us achieve but about which there is some degree of uncertainty. In one sense this says little more than the familiar phrase "humans have reasons to act as well as causes"; but I hope to show that there is more fruit to be plucked here than simply the insight that we learn from experience.

In the history of Western logic, Kurt Gödel's 1931 incompleteness theorem established proof of a limitation embedded in all but the most trivial linguistic structures. Gödel proved that—for any consistent system with formal rules for manipulation of its symbols—there are propositions which can be expressed in the system that are true but cannot be proven true in that system. Simply put, if we create a logically consistent set of beliefs it will be (provably) incomplete. What are the implications of Gödel's incompleteness theorem for a science of *judgement*? Michael Polanyi argued that

> Gödel reveals both that any formal system (of sufficient richness) is necessarily incomplete and that our personal judgment can reliably add new axioms to it. It offers a model of conceptual innovation in the deductive sciences, which illustrates in principle the inexhaustibility of mathematical heuristics and also the personal and irreversible character of the acts which continue to draw upon these possibilities.[10]

In 1936, Tarski proved that this amounts to saying that there is no complete language—either in the sciences or in any existing or possible "natural language." Tarski's proof essentially consists in showing that, as soon as you not only assert a proposition but add that the statement "is true," you run the risk of landing in contradictions which can be resolved only by moving to a more comprehensive language. And this is true of *all* languages: there is no ideally rational language or logical system. The paradoxes, in fact, arise because of the *self-referential* property of truth-claims and meaning-claims. Jacob Bronowski comments:

> The notion that you really cannot get rid of the paradoxes of self-reference from what seemed to be the ordinary descriptive sentences of science is very strange. The point is that these paradoxes enter into the language of science because we not only want to write sentences in science, we want to say about them that they are true or false.[11]

> It is of the nature of human language that among the things that it talks about is itself. It is of the nature of human beings that among the things they talk about are themselves.[12]

The provable incompleteness of judgement is a condition rooted in the self-referential properties of those who make such judgement: human beings. This does not mean that to desire or to will something to be the case is necessarily to engage in paradox and contradiction. It does mean, however, and not metaphorically, that if you *want* something to be the case, to *become* true, and act on that desire willfully, only a different system will be able to show whether you have succeeded or not. The "reasons of the heart" may very well contradict those of the mind; but that does not mean they are contradictory in every possible language system.

5. Instability Situations

More can be said, if recent studies in self-referential language and *self-transformation processes* are to be trusted. It appears that certain beliefs (and attendant attitudes, dispositions and values) which are *necessary* for the correct "firing" of the will into desired action are *invariably inconsistent* with empirical evidence. And, conversely, it appears that certain beliefs (and attendant attitudes, dispositions and values) which are *invariably consistent* with empirical evidence must be spurned because they *cannot* lead to desired action.

We can dub these, respectively,

- "self-fulfilling beliefs" (beliefs which, in the formation of good judgement, *must be believed* despite their apparent falsity), and
- "self-defeating beliefs" (beliefs which, in the formation of good judgement, *must not be believed* despite their evidential truth).

Both of these "self-transforming beliefs" arise in what has come to be called in the study of choice "instability situations." They are best explicated by example. Rather than use a religious example to begin with, let me illustrate an instability situation with a quotation from that astute observer of the socio-econ-

omic scene, the darling of neo-conservative "free market" philosophy, Friedrich
von Hayek:

> It certainly is important in the market order (or free enterprise society, misleadingly
> called 'capitalism') that the individuals believe that their well-being depends
> primarily on their own efforts and decisions. Indeed, few circumstances will do
> more to make a person energetic and efficient than the belief that it depends chiefly
> on him whether he will reach the goals he has set himself. For this reason this belief
> is often encouraged by education and governing opinion—it seems to me, generally
> much to the benefit of most of the members of the society in which it prevails, who
> will owe many important material and moral improvements to persons guided by
> it. But it leads no doubt also to an exaggerated confidence in the truth of this
> generalization which to those who regard themselves (and perhaps are) equally able
> but have failed must appear as a bitter irony and severe provocation. . . .

> It is therefore a real dilemma to what extent we ought to encourage in the young
> the belief that when they really try they will succeed, or should rather emphasize
> that inevitably some unworthy will succeed and some worthy fail.[13]

I cite this passage not to promote von Hayek's argument that belief in social
justice, while an illusion, *might* be justified in the service of capitalism, but as
illustrative of the notion of *necessary* (if statistically false) beliefs serving a
prudential choice. To this example from economic theory, let me add brief
reference to "the voter's illusion" and the theory of "diagnostic choice"
developed by Quattrone and Tversky:

> Political scientists have long noted the paradoxical nature of an individual's voting
> in large national elections. A single vote is highly unlikely to be decisive, and the
> time and effort required to register and vote can be considerable. . . . To the rational
> *causal* consequences of voting, we suggest adding a less rational *diagnostic* aspect.
> People may reason that, within the electorate, there are citizens whose political
> orientation is similar to theirs. . . . That is, an individual may regard his or her
> *single* vote as diagnostic of *millions* of votes, and hence as a sign that the preferred
> candidates will emerge victorious.[14]

Now clearly such a belief in "signs" is not, in the language of individual
voter choice, warranted; the authors call it "diagnostic" because such a belief
will *become* true if and only if a large number of people believe it. Their study
of voter reasoning, in fact, showed this to be the case: the belief was sociologi-
cally self-fulfilling. Conversely, the more evidential belief—that one's vote
counts for nothing, really—when held by many, is self-defeating for the
democratic process.

I draw the term "instability situation" from a philosopher of mind, Roy A.
Sorensen, in his study of rational choice, and I cannot resist an interesting

religious example in his discussion of the "paradox of Dives and Lazarus."[15] In this familiar parable, a rich man, Dives, and a beggar, Lazarus, both die. Lazarus enters heaven; the rich man is condemned to hell. To the latter it is explained "you in your lifetime received good things, and likewise Lazarus evil things: but now he is comforted and you are tormented." Having given up hope for himself, the rich man asks that Lazarus be sent to warn his rich friends of what lies in store for them should they not change their ways. But the request is denied. Why?

Sorensen locates the problem of Dives and Lazarus in a nest of puzzles which can be called "instability situations" because their actual outcome depends on a belief contrary to present available evidence. In this case, Lazarus's request is denied because it would *yield* an instability situation: the living rich would be forced to accept the evidence from beyond the grave and be perversely sad about their present good fortune, and the poor would be required to accept their poverty and unhappiness as their lot yet be oddly happy in their knowledge that they will eventually be happy. Put another way, some knowledge about the outcome of our choices *cannot* be contained within our present judgement, for if it were the outcome could not occur as the result of our decision. Genuine choice must in some sense be blind to the future.

Nor can one solve the problem by declaring oneself a non- or anti-expert, says Sorensen. This, of course, is often the claim of the agnostic, which I have challenged as incoherent. To the extent that one recognizes the force of an instability situation—that acceptance of the counter-evidence to one's belief system will require acceptance of inconsistent presuppositions, i.e. that it will require irrationality—agents are properly rational and cannot be faulted for, or excuse themselves as, inexpert. In this sense "full-fledged instability situations (those requiring awareness of one's anti-expertise) are impossible,"[16] though in thought-experiments, so to speak, they may function in the service of rational agents. Summing up, an *instability situation* is one in which, out of practical necessity and with due regard for the formation of judgement, one *must* be—apparently unaccountably—insensitive to the evidence. But also, evidence from the domain of discourse about the *results* of our actions—evidence which is intrinsically closed to us by the incompleteness of our present situation—can only be found in a language yet to be formulated. Real choice must entail risk.

6. The Rationality of the Emotions

William James, it is said, argued for the rationality of prudential over against evidential options under conditions of forced, living, and momentous choice-situations. It seems to me more accurate to speak of James's "will to believe"—the prudential decision as against the evidential—as simply arising from an agent's judgement of the necessity, relevance and non-triviality of one option over against the other(s). That is to say, the "will to believe" is an "all-things-considered better judgement"; and among the things considered are the agent's emotions. Ronald de Sousa[17] and others have argued, to my mind persuasively, that emotions are rooted in an axiology, that their logic is understandable though as yet (and indeed if ever!) far from perfectly so, and that their function is precisely to aid humans in making decisions where reason alone is inconclusive and might lead to self-debilitating indecision. Without embracing every part of that argument, I will adopt as a working hypothesis that what has been called "practical reasoning" by Aristotle, and what I have referred to as "all-things-considered better judgement," is the attempt of an agent to bring intellect and will into proper alignment with one's over-all value system in those instances when the emotions identify a choice as (in James's language) "forced, living, and momentous" in the context of that value system. I will claim that such decisions are not "irrational" or "arational" or "non-rational" but, on the contrary, emotionally rational. I am, indeed, prepared to argue this, but the argument would go far beyond the scope of this paper. For our purposes here it is sufficient to point to the *cleverness* of the emotions.

The philosopher/economic theorist Jon Elster has similarly argued persuasively that human beings are, in his terminology, "imperfectly rational" but that this is, in fact, our evolutionary advantage. His argument can be summed up as follows. Natural selection in all species operates by chance and necessity; in humans, by means of self-consciousness, *we* take the chances and *we* exploit the laws of causal connections. Intelligence in non-human species, even a fair degree of intelligence, does not capture the risk-taking, "globally maximizing" nature of human judgement:

> The crucial features of the locally maximizing machine refer to what it *cannot* do. In particular the machine is incapable of *waiting* and of using *indirect strategies*. These notions are defined as follows. The machine is capable of waiting if it can say No to a favourable mutation in order to be able to say Yes to an even more favourable one later on. . . . The machine is capable of indirect strategies if it can say Yes to an unfavourable mutation in order to be able later on to say Yes to a very favourable one. . . . Waiting and the use of indirect strategies are crucial

features of human choice. I suggest that man may indeed be seen as a globally maximizing machine, a characterization that goes back to Leibniz.[18]

Elster's use of "machine" language should not be taken as mechanistic reductionism, though he certainly is reductionistic in this sense: ultimately, we must try to explain our "*general* capacity for rational problem solving"[19] by the workings of natural selection—by the way in which it has, and perhaps continues to have, selective advantage for our continuation as a species. What is more important to understand is that it is the *generalized* capacity for global maximization, our ability to apply waiting and indirect strategies to qualitatively new situations, which marks human choice: we employ these strategies "to the future and the merely possible."[20] It is our *failures* to so act which need explaining; we should act on the presumption that human choice *normally* is indirect and in search of maximal advantage, and train our young with that in mind:

> We may say that in creating man natural selection has transcended itself. This leap implies a transition from the non-intentional adaptation, be it local or globally accidental, to intentional and deliberate adaptation. . . . With this generalized capacity *mind* enters the evolutionary arena. . . . Man . . . can choose between unactualized possibles.[21]

Elster's notion of global maximization is nicely and anciently illustrated by the behaviour of Homer's Ulysses who, to overcome the overpowering attraction of the Sirens, instructs his crew to bind him fast to the mast of the ship and, his demands and protestations not withstanding, to bind him even tighter should he order them to release him before they have passed the region of the sirens. Elster comments:

> Ulysses was not fully rational, for a rational creature would not have to resort to this device; nor was he simply the passive and irrational vehicle for his changing wants and desires, for he was capable of achieving by indirect means the same end as a rational person could have achieved in a direct manner. His predicament—being weak and knowing it—points to the need for a theory of *imperfect rationality* that has been all but neglected by philosophers and social scientists.[22]

Elster's claim is that Ulysses' "binding" is a case of indirect rationality; the other major alternative for Ulysses would be "a rearrangement of the inner space," the existentialist option. "I would not deny that some degree of self-control can be achieved simply by pulling yourself up by the bootstraps, but . . . more durable results are achieved by acting on the environment."[23] Clearly, human beings do not *always* act or choose to act *for* a reason, and some of us often (too often) act or choose against our better judgement. But we are much closer, I submit, to understanding the notion of "all-things-considered better judgements"—their logic, their distinctively human qualities—on these and similar accounts.

7. The Ethics of Faith

The question inevitably arises about "prudential," "emotional," or "indirect" means to self-fulfillment: Yes, but is it moral? The question is more complex than it appears on the surface. Modern would-be theists face a philosophical conundrum scarcely known to classical Protheans. The conundrum arises out of the nature of self-consciousness, which is both a blessing and a curse, and takes the shape of a crisis of conscience usually associated, in philosophical literature, with the phrase "ethics of belief." But here the term "ethical" is misleading, for the issue is one of rationality more than—if not instead of—morality. The rational "purist" is well illustrated by William Clifford, who in 1886 denounced the human tendency to overlook or dismiss contradictory evidence in these ringing words: "To sum up: it is wrong always, everywhere, and for any one, to believe anything upon insufficient evidence."[24]

At the other end of the spectrum from the rational purists we find what has come to be called recently the "vital lie" tradition. In the early years of this century, the British Pragmatist F.C.S. Schiller and the American Pragmatist William James both argued for a less rationalistic view of human nature, for a place for "prudential" reasons even against the evidence, and for the priority of such "non-cognitive values" as goodness, beauty and pleasure when, as they sometime must, they fly in the face of "mere truth." The truth—evidential truth—according to many, is sometimes destructive of health and life. Consider this passage from Otto Rank:

> With the truth, one cannot live. To be able to live one needs illusions. . . . This constantly effective process of self-deceiving, pretending and blundering, is no psychopathological mechanism, but the essence of reality.[25]

Recent psychological literature supports a cautious affirmation of this position. Recent clinical studies[26] have confirmed a long-held suspicion that "self-examination" and the reduction of self-deception may lead to lowered self-esteem, indecision, and a debilitating atrophy of judgement. Other studies suggest that illusions, even delusions, despite their careless handling of evidence, may be adaptive behaviour. But often, those who offer such a view distinguish between short-term gains to be achieved by such means as against its long-term dysfunctionality. Others suggest that "prudential reasoning" is a strategy of preference only where other options are not present or visible, and only in selective (usually non-life-threatening) situations. Still others suggest that where self-esteem is low, and threatening to deteriorate radically, any form of "vital lie" is functional if it conforms with psychoanalytic views on the etiology and therapy of "necessary defense mechanisms."

In a similar vein, Amelie Rorty has argued, on the basis of a case such as that of a dying doctor who deceives himself about his illness and thereby prevents himself from collapsing into despair, that "individual instances of self-deception can be beneficial and perhaps in some sense rational, or at least canny."[27] The basis of such a position *philosophically* is that an obsession with truth is, after all, an obsession, and it can inhibit that spontaneous emotional repertoire upon which human personality, interpersonal relations, and social cohesion are built.

Most moderns, I would argue, lie somewhere between the extremes of Clifford and James, though occasionally dipping their big toes in each of these murky waters when crisis arises. The tension between evidence-centred and will-centred choice is the stuff of good literature; the tension between evidential and prudential reasons is the stuff of ethical dilemmas; and the tension between evidence-based rationality and will/desire centred judgement is said to be the stuff of the conflict between science and religion. But, I have argued, studies in philosophy of mind suggest that these polarities are naive. The basic question *is* a moral one, but it is not *simply* whether contra-indicated beliefs are moral or immoral, but whether a particular contra-indicated belief is self-(and other-)fulfilling or is inherently self-defeating.

8. Faith and Self-Transformation

Self-transforming judgement ("bootstrapping") is not as rare as Elster and de Sousa claim. It can occur in many forms, but all seem puzzling because they are expressed in oddly self-referential language. Can one *really* "be one's own best friend"? Would one have to send oneself roses? Take oneself to the movies occasionally? Write (and of course answer) letters to oneself? T. S. Champlin has argued[28] that self-reflexive language of this sort is unduly mystifying; upon careful analysis, we realize that indeed we *can* do such things self-fulfillingly; bootstrapping is far more common than philosophers think, though almost always complicatingly *indirect*. Champlin presents a number of oddly puzzling notions, quite commonly enough expressed in ordinary English, which appear similarly paradoxical or at least foolish:

- teaching oneself something
- reminding oneself of something
- enjoying one's own company
- promising oneself a reward
- appointing oneself a task
- surprising oneself about something

His point is that these activities are neither irrational nor paradoxical; nor are we mistaken in reading them in a *literal* rather than a *literary* way. They are short-form expressions for immensely complicated "global" strategies of the self-transformative kind. All of these activities are possible, and indeed understandable, so long as we do not commit the "fallacy of isolationism"—assuming the absence of appropriate "props" and "context." To teach oneself something, for example, does not, as Socrates thought, mean already knowing it. Nor does it entail a bifurcated brain or mind: a teacher part and a learner part. It means that an agent wants to know, and then finds the means to that end—sometimes a complicated process involving libraries, laboratories, other people, etc. And it means being, at some point(s) in the process, neither what we were nor what we will be (an unsettling experience: not without values so much as between values, a pretender).

The fact that one can pretend and be in some sense a hypocrite does not entail that you cannot *in another sense* succeed in being what you are not. If you succeed, it proves to be no pretense. Pretending and hypocrisy can have self-fulfilling goals: *if* they succeed, you are no longer faking or a hypocrite. The notion of "success" in self-transformation calls for a new level of truth-analysis. Hypocrisy and faking, "not being yourself," etc., are self-transforming projects in this sense: if they succeed, the self is transformed into the not-yet-self. These activities are self-defeating only if they cannot or, unfortunately, do not succeed. Amelie Rorty similarly identifies various strategies for self-manipulation in situations of indeterminacy—"bootstrap" operations which allow us

> to act energetically and loyally beyond our standard emotional means, in ways we might not be able to do if we were careful to avoid manipulative shadow-falsification in the service of making it all come true. Marriages, work, devotion to children, friendships and causes do not of course absolutely require such self-manipulation. Nevertheless, they involve risks we would find difficult to accept with absolutely clear and open eyes.[29]

There is a parallel insight in that master of self-reflection Blaise Pascal. Recall that Pascal argues that *if* his "wager argument" is in any way persuasive it must eventuate in changed behaviour, and this by indirect means. Of this part of Pascal's argument Brian McLaughlin writes:

> Tom, a non-believer, studies Pascal's Wager and becomes convinced by it that it is in his best interest to believe that God exists. So, taking Pascal's advice, he embarks on a program for inducing belief: he takes holy water, has masses said, associates with believers and avoids nonbelievers, and so on. When he embarks on his belief-fixing strategy, he views it as one by which he will mislead himself into falsely believing that God exists: he views himself as embarking on an attempt to carry out an elaborate deceitful stratagem. However, it may be possible for the program to succeed without Tom's ever having forgotten his stratagem. If, after a period of vacillation and confusion, Tom becomes a believer, he will view the program from a changed perspective. From the new perspective, the stratagem will reflect the desperate attempt of a lost soul with the *hubris* to think he could manufacture belief, when all that was required was that he open his eyes to see how God makes his presence known. From Tom's new perspective, he once was lost but now is found, once was blind but now can see.[30]

Let me conclude with one more curious case of religious self-transformation through practical reasoning. It is cited by Quattrone and Tversky in their study of diagnostic belief, and might be of interest to theologians as well as philosophers of religion. It concerns an odd inversion of outcomes in the belief systems of strict predestinationalist Calvinists and those of causal-salvationist Roman Catholics:

> Both believe that one's conduct on earth (virtuous or sinful) is correlated with one's post-mortal fate (paradise or hell). But the Catholic subscribes to a causal theory in which the location of one's soul after death is a direct consequence of how one leads one's life on earth. In contrast, the Calvinist champions a diagnostic theory in which earthly conduct and post-mortal fate are both consequences of the deity's prior decision. [But] Calvinists may be even more motivated than Catholics to select the virtuous acts correlated with paradise. To the Calvinist, even a single sinful deed is evidence enough that he or she is not among the chosen. To the Catholic, it is more a matter of one's total good and bad deeds that determine heaven or hell. And besides, there's always confession.[31]

It is of course a matter of some complexity (and not without controversy) to decide which beliefs—religious or otherwise—are self-fulfilling and by what global strategies. I have done little more than open a few windows onto the nature of necessary though contra-evidential faith. Still, it seems to me that the predestinationalists and Pascal and James were onto something which in our day is becoming clearer, if still uncannily canny, about human judgement. The agnostic option appears less and less coherent with every new study on human decision-making. Only if people believe can the "god-option" be a possibility; if they do not, the "god-option" will die and, with it, the future of certain types of transformed humanity if not all. Not to decide is to decide not, with perhaps more serious consequences than even Pascal imagined.

Many, reading Pascal and James, have wondered if it would not be a very tolerant and uncritical God who bestowed grace on someone whose faith was acquired by self-trickery. My claim is that Pascal intuited better than he could explain the rationality of the emotions and the will—a rationality which is becoming more open for philosophers to see (and which has never been hidden to poets, novelists and playwrights). As for theology I cannot speak. But my hunch is that those who have imagined the gods frowning upon human self-cleverness should re-examine the stories of their traditions. Jews and Christians, for example, might start with Abraham's bold, daring, risky "binding" of his son Isaac. If they still think Luther and Kierkegaard were right in interpreting this story, they will certainly disagree with most of what I have said above.

NOTES

1.   Joseph C. McLelland, *Prometheus Rebound: The Irony of Atheism* (Waterloo, ON: Wilfred Laurier University Press, 1988).

2.   D. C. Muecke, *Irony and the Ironic*, 2d ed. (London: Methuen, 1982), 67-68, my italics.

3.   Christopher Lasch, *The Culture of Narcissism* (New York: Norton, 1978), 99.

4.   McLelland, *Prometheus Rebound*, xv.

5.   William James, "The will to believe," in *Essays on Faith and Morals* (New York: World Publishing Company, 1962), 34.

6.   Anthony Flew, "Theology and falsification," in *New Essays in Philosophical Theology* (London: S.C.M., 1955), 96. Wisdom's article was originally published in the *Proceedings of the Aristotelian Society*, 1944; it is more readily accessible in his *Philosophy and Psychoanalysis* (Oxford: Blackwell, 1969).

7.   John Wisdom, "Gods," in *Philosophy and Psychoanalysis*, 168. See note 6.

8.   "Gods," 159.

9.   The following are representative of the type of studies I have in mind: Ronald de Sousa, *The Rationality of Emotion* (Cambridge: MIT Press, 1987); Jon Elster, *Ulysses and the Sirens: Studies*

in Rationality and Irrationality (Cambridge: Cambridge University Press, 1979, revised 1984), *Sour Grapes: Studies in the Subversion of Rationality* (Cambridge: Cambridge University Press, 1983), (ed.) *The Multiple Self* (Cambridge: Cambridge University Press, 1985); Alfred Mele, *Irrationality* (Oxford: Oxford University Press, 1987); David Pears, *Motivated Irrationality* (Oxford: Oxford University Press, 1984).

10. Michael Polanyi, *Personal Knowledge: Towards a Post-Critical Philosophy* (Chicago: University of Chicago Press, 1958), 259. My italics.

11. Jacob Bronowski, *The Origins of Knowledge and Imagination* (New Haven, Yale University Press, 1979), 84.

12. Bronowski, *Origins*, 83.

13. Friedrich von Hayek, *The Mirage of Social Justice* (Chicago: University of Chicago Press, 1976), 74.

14. George A. Quattrone and Amos Tversky, "Self-deception and the voter's illusion," in *The Multiple Self*, ed. Jon Elster (Cambridge: Cambridge University Press, 1985), 49-50.

15. Sorensen, Roy A., "Anti-expertise, instability, and rational choice," *Australasian Journal of Philosophy* 65 (1987), 301-15.

16. Sorensen, "Anti-expertise," 315.

17. de Sousa, *The Rationality of Emotion*. See note 9.

18. Elster, *Ulysses and the Sirens*, 9-10. My italics. See note 9.

19. *Ulysses and the Sirens*, 3.

20. *Ulysses and the Sirens*, 16.

21. *Ulysses and the Sirens*, 16-17.

22. *Ulysses and the Sirens*, 36.

23. *Ulysses and the Sirens*, 37. Elster's claim about bootstrapping is challenged in section 8, below.

24. William Kingdon Clifford, "The ethics of belief," in *Lectures and Essays*, 2d ed. (London: Macmillan, 1886), 346.

25. Cited in Mike W. Martin, *Self-Deception and Morality* (Lawrence, KS: University of Kansas Press, 1986), 109. Chapter 6 gives a thorough discussion of the vital lie tradition.

26. E.g., Richard J. Lettieri, "Consciousness, self-deception and psychotherapy: an analogue study," *Imagination, Cognition and Personality* 3 (1983-84), 83-97.

27. Amelie Rorty, "Belief and self-deception," *Inquiry* 15 (1972), 387-410, 402. See also her "Adaptivity and self-Knowledge," *Inquiry* 18 (1975), 1-22.

28. T. S. Champlin, *Reflexive Paradoxes* (London: Routledge, 1988).

29.   Amelie Rorty, "Self-deception, *akrasia* and irrationality," in *The Multiple Self*, ed. Jon Elster (Cambridge: Cambridge University Press, 1985), 126.

30.   Brian P. McLaughlin, "Exploring the possibility of self-deception in belief," in *Perspectives on Self-deception*, ed. B. P. McLaughlin and A. Rorty (Berkeley: University of California Press, 1988), 32-33.

31.   Quattrone and Tversky, "Self-deception and the voter's illusion," 57.

KIERKEGAARD'S UNFOLDING OF FAITH:
The Initiation of "My Reader"

Alastair McKinnon
McGill University

The title of this paper is intended to alert the reader to the difficulties in writing about Kierkegaard and faith in a way he would have approved. He did not provide any single, definitive account of faith, intended his works primarily for "my reader," assumed that this reader had read and assimilated all the earlier works, was not primarily concerned with what the tradition calls its essence or nature and would have rejected any summary of his "concept of faith" as totally misleading. In fact his authorship contains a series of unfolding presentations of faith intended to initiate his reader into his own ever deepening experience and understanding of faith and to encourage him to embark upon the life of faith as thus far presented. This paper attempts to respect that aim by identifying changes between his most important presentations and tracing the process by which he initiates his reader into that understanding. Indeed, it aims to create for its reader a counterpart of the experience Kierkegaard intended and achieved for his own. Briefly, it does this by the apparently simple process of identifying and describing changes in his "faith vocabulary," i.e. in those words which he uses with exceptional frequency in these presentations.

The first part of this study uses a statistical model of the life cycle of various words to determine when they become and cease to be part of Kierkegaard's faith vocabulary while the second explores their roles and relations at five of the most important points in these presentations. Both parts presuppose results produced by our aberrant frequency word program which has already been discussed at length elsewhere[1] and which we here describe only briefly and as used in this study.

Kierkegaard's authorship contains 16 books in which the principal forms of "faith" (*Tro, Troen* and *Troens*) together show a relative frequency of 4.00 or more.[2] These books, T, FB, BA, PS, AE, OTA, KG, TSA, CT, SD, IC, FV, TAF, EOT, TS and DS[3] are shown with all others in the relevant chronological order in table 1 thus allowing the reader to see them in their original context. After identifying these books we extracted from each all sentences containing one or more of these forms, did a complete count of all words in each of the resulting 16 files and used our ABFREQ program to compare the frequency of every word in each file with that of the same word in a selected sub-set of the corpus,[4] this with the minimum Z-score[5] set at 7.00 and the minimum absolute frequency at 4. Note that this Z-score is extremely high and means that there is less than one chance in several million that any of the words discussed in the rest of this study could have occurred in these "faith" sentences with their present or some higher frequency simply by chance. Indeed, this and all of the many other much higher scores represent such radical departures from Kierkegaard's normal rates that they can be explained only on the assumption that their frequency was required by what he wished to say about faith in the work in question. It follows therefore that these words can and should be taken as wholly reliable indices of his meaning and intentions. I find it helpful to think of Kierkegaard as more or less deliberately adding these words to his "faith vocabulary," as putting them "on stream" or "into place"[6] between himself and his "reader" and, of course, thereby notifying his "reader" of this fact. Indeed, I am convinced that we should think of these words as the chief means by which Kierkegaard initiates his reader into his own understanding of faith and of his faithful reader as capable of recognizing them as such. For example, it is inconceivable that Regine, the first and primary "my reader," could have read FB without sensing that Abraham was central to its presentation of faith and that she was to be sacrificed. However I do not insist upon this terminology and am concerned only to find a method which does justice to the fact that each of Kierkegaard's presentations clearly has its own distinctive vocabulary which plainly reflects its central emphasis.

The reader may find it helpful to glance briefly at the slightly modified version of the aberrant frequency list for the faith sentences in FB shown in table 2. Its first line shows that "the faith" (*Troen*) occurs 109 times in these sentences and that this frequency represents an astounding Z-score of 78.46. Perhaps more surprisingly, its third line shows that "knight" (*Ridder*) occurs 38 times and has a Z-score of 56.52. He may also wish to note that these lists vary greatly in size, that that for FV contains no such words (and hence does not exist), that for EOT one, that for TAF two, that for DS three but that for FB 23, that for IC 31 and that for AE 43. Not surprisingly, these numbers correspond roughly to the number of faith sentences in these books. For example, FV contains only two such sentences, EOT only three and TAF only four while FB contains 159, IC 86 and AE 226.

The very brief account of our aberrant frequency word program given above assumes that each book is treated separately but the aim of the first part of this study is to provide a dynamic model of the words present in Kierkegaard's faith vocabulary up to and including various points in his authorship and available to his reader as such. In this part of our study we therefore identified the aberrant frequency words in the first book taken separately and thereafter in these books treated cumulatively, i.e. in the first plus the second, in the first plus the second and third, etc. Counting that for T, this yielded 16 such "cumulative lists" which we henceforth identify as T, +FB, +BA, etc. Note that these lists are similar in form to that already shown for FB but, with the exception of that for T, differ somewhat from their non-cumulative counterparts. For example, that for +FB shows Z-scores of 18.17 for "Abraham" and 43.34 for "knight" and 29 aberrant frequency words rather than the 23 in the original FB. By contrast, that for +DS shows 95 such words as compared with three for DS taken by itself. In fact these lists together show a total of 201 different words the variety of which is indicated by the fact that, excluding our three search forms, only 8 or 8.70% of the 95 words in that for +DS also appear in that for T. These lists are very rich and informative, would doubtlessly repay the closest study and are available upon request but it is plainly impossible to consider all these words in the present study and we have therefore selected the 40 we judged most interesting and important and shown these in table 3 together with their respective Z-scores in each of our "cumulative lists" except those for +FV, +TAF and +EOT, this because these contribute relatively little to our understanding of Kierkegaard's developing faith vocabulary and, particularly, to keep it narrow enough for reading and display. Note that the column heads represent successive points in the history of the authorship and that Z-scores less than 7.00 have been omitted to make it more readily intelligible. Of course this table assumes that Kierkegaard presupposes his own earlier works and that his faithul "reader" has assimilated their vocabulary and insights.

Before considering these results the reader may wish to note that the Z-scores shown for these words are a function of the relation of the number of occurrences of the word to the length of the cumulative text in question. Thus, to choose a very simple example, "glory" (*Herlighed*) shows a Z-score of 10.78

in T because it occurs five times in the 3,629 tokens of the faith sentences in this work, falls below our cut-off point in all of the next nine cumulative texts because its six occurrences in three of these works fail to keep pace with the expanding text, shows a score of 10.63 at +IC because its six new occurrences in IC compensate for the fact that the total number of tokens has now risen to 36,483 and declines steadily thereafter because there are no further occurrences of this word though the size of the cumulative text of course continues to rise.

The advantage of this tabular display is that one can see at a glance the entire life cycle of each of these 40 important words as a part of Kierkegaard's faith vocabulary. For example, "expectation," (*Forventning*), "expect" (*forventer*) and "victory" (*Seier*) all appear in T but steadily decline in importance across these 13 points in the authorship. "Courage" (*Mod*) also comes "on stream" in T, becomes more important with both +FB and +BA, disappears at +OTA and reappears at +SD. "[H]umanly" (*menneskeligt*), as in "humanly speaking," is prominent in T, disappears at +PS, is reinforced or refreshed at both +OTA and +TSA and survives until the end of the authorship. "Abraham" (*Abraham*) appears at +FB, gradually fades and finally disappears at +IC while "knight" (*Ridder*), by contrast, survives until the end. Some supposedly important terms obviously have a very brief life span. "[M]ovement" (*Bevægelse*) appears only at +FB and +BA, "(the) condition" (*Betingelsen*) only at +PS, "of inwardness" (*Inderlighedens*) only from +AE to +SD and "passion" (*Lidenskab*) only in +AE and, residually, +OTA. Perhaps more strikingly, "Christ" (*Christus*), "God" (*Gud*) and "the God-Man" (*Gud-Mennesket*) do not even appear until +IC. "[O]f offense" (*Forargelsens*) appears in +SD but rockets into prominence in +IC as part of the expression "the possibility of offense." The word "(the) doubt" (*Tvivlen*) is present in T and from +PS until the end but "unbelief" (*Vantroen*) does not appear until +TSA. All the verb forms of "believe" (*troe*) are relatively late with the infinitive first appearing as an aberrant frequency word in +AE, the present tense in +OTA, the past tense in +CT and the present passive in +TS. Of course, not everything is this simple. "[G]lory" (*Herlighed*) appears in T as part of the expression "the glory of faith" but in +IC in connection with faith that Christ will return in glory. However there are very few such changes and it is obvious that this table provides a clear, memorable and substantially accurate picture of the life cycle of these words as parts of Kierkegaard's faith vocabulary.[7]

Of course the 16 individual aberrant frequency lists from which this table has been derived contain a great deal of further important information. "Renunciation" (*Afkald*), "universal" (*Almene*), "the individual" (*Enkelte*), "is acquired" (*erhverves*), "received" (*modtog*) and "humility" (*Ydmyghed*) all appear for the first time at +FB. So, too, "fact" (*Faktum*), "the Historical" (*Historiske*), "contemporary" (*Samtidig*) and "immediate" (*umiddelbart*) at +PS; "spiritual trial" (*Anfægtelse*), "interest" (*Interesserethed*), "martyrdom" (*Martyrium*), "almost" (*næstendeels*), "objective" (*objektive*), "the paradox" (*Paradoxet*) and "probable" (*sandsynlig*) at +AE; "the yoke" (*Aaget*), "to confess" (*bekjende*), "confessors" (*Bekjendere*), "abolish" (*forskaffer*), "Providence" (*Forsyn*), "openness" (*Frimodigheden*), "profitable" (*gavnlig*), "obedience" (*Lydigheden*) and "heavy" (*tunge*) at +OTA; "the command" (*Budet*), "wonder" (*Forundring*), "secret" (*Hemmelighed*), "to promise" (*love*), "promise" (v.) (*lover*), "to test" (*prøve*) and "sincere" (*uskrømtet*) at +KG; "to comprehend" (*begribe*) and "greater perfection/more perfect" (*Fuldkomnere*) at +TSA; "forsook" (*forlod*), "fortress" (*Fæstning*), hope (*Haab*), "indifference" (*Ligegyldige*) and "carefree" (*Sorgløshed*) at +CT; "Christ" (accus.) (*Christum*), "consequences" (of Christ's life) (*Følgerne*) and sign (*Tegn*) at +IC; "to disprove" (*modbevise*) and "the test" (*Prøven*) at +FV; "the works" (*Gjerningerne*) at +TS and, finally, "Luther" (*Luther*) at +DS. This list of "first appearances" should give anyone familiar with Kierkegaard's authorship and language a much clearer and more precise picture of the development of his presentations of faith than he could gain simply from reading these texts. More importantly, it should enable him to read these texts with preconceptions actually generated from the texts themselves. As I have thought for a long time, no one should ever read a good book for the first time.

The data generated in the second part of this study could actually be used to produce a holographic display of all of the three dimensional plots of Kierkegaard's presentations of faith already noted, a display in which you could actually see the named dimensions of one plot change and merge into those of the next and which has considerable promise. However that technology is not yet available for scholars in the humanities and 16 separate discrete displays would simply boggle the mind. Accordingly we here present and discuss plots or "still life" pictures of faith in T and all of our works up to and including AE, CT, IC and DS or the end of the authorship. These have been generated by a correspondence analysis of the relevant matrices but before explaining these terms I must first attempt to explain the nature and convince you of the importance of dimensions. I do so with two stories the first of which some of you may already know.

In 1968 Professor Myron Wish of the University of Wisconsin asked 18 of his students to rank 12 countries of the world in terms of their "overall perceived similarity," this without any guidance for making these judgements since one of his aims was to discover the basis which they actually used. After averaging their scores and analyzing the result with the KYST multi-dimensional scaling program, he noted that the pro-Western and pro-Communist countries were in one set of diagonally opposite quadrants, that the developed and under-developed ones were in the other and that these two dimensions together "explained" almost all of the variation in the original data matrix. Given these facts he concluded that these dimensions should be called "political alignment" and "economic development" and that his students had rated these countries primarily in light of these features or dimensions. Details aside, I believe that Wish was entirely right, that this simple exercise provides a radical insight into his students' collective perception of the relation of these countries and that understanding in terms of dimensions is one of the most radical and fundamental of which the mind is capable. For example, knowing these dimensions permits any informed person to understand the position of any of these countries in this simple two-dimensional array, to explain why a particular country is here rather than there and even to predict where these students would place, say, the next five countries within this same space.

My second story is shorter and builds upon the first. Some years ago I told the Wish story to a friend and colleague who is also one of Montreal's outstanding psychiatrists. His face became radiant with understanding and he declared that he had never been able to help any patient until he had first succeeded in identifying the fundamental dimensions of their thought.

Correspondence analysis is an exploratory data technique which represents the information contained in any data matrix in a graphic display of lower dimensionality and hence more readily intelligible form. In the present case it compares the "profile"[8] of each word with that of every other word and that of each chapter or book with that of every other chapter or book and finds the optimal array of these two sets of points in two separate true multi-dimensional spaces on the basis of the similarity of their profiles. For example, it places the two clouds of points with the most dissimilar profiles at either end of the first dimension, the two with the next most dissimilar profiles at either end of the second, etc. It then merges these two spaces into a new single true multi-dimensional space, aligns the dimensions of this array with the geometical axes of its plot and, crucial for the present study, reports the percentage contribution of every point to the inertia of every dimension thus enabling the user who knows the text to name them. This means that dimensions are objective features of a space but that their names are provided by the user and are in that sense subjective.

Since this sense of the word may be unfamiliar to many readers I pause to note that the name of a dimension ordinarily represents what is common to its two opposing poles. For example, in an earlier study I discovered or, rather, was forced to see that the negative pole of the fifth dimension of FB represents Abraham proceeding as an unbeliever and the positive pole his doing so as a believer and I therefore named this dimension "Abraham." Note, however, that, for reasons to be discussed later, few of the poles of the dimensions in this study appear to have any such obviously common feature and I have therefore had to content myself with naming these dimensions in terms of their opposing poles, e.g. DIVINE vs. HUMAN. I know that this type of name is more direct and informative but I have been spoiled and would welcome any suggestions helping me to identify the feature common with which I could name each of my dimensions.

The faith sentences in T occur in only 13 of its 18 discourses and together show only 21 aberrant frequency words. The matrix for this work therefore consists of 21 rows and 13 columns and, of course, the frequencies of these words in these discourses. This matrix is shown as an example in table 4 and its correspondence analysis plot in figure 1. Note that the latter's dimensions or axes are shown as dashed lines, that its true point of origin is represented by the small ball near the middle of its third dimension and which of course represents the true point of origin of this space, that it shows the locations of all 13 discourses, the three different forms of "faith" and most of the chief word contributors to each of these dimensions.

The chief contributors to the positive pole of the first dimension are the first discourse and the word "You" (nom.) and "expectation" and to the negative pole the eighteenth and seventh discourse and the words "humanly," "speaking" and "(the) doubt" and, using my knowledge of these discourses and words, I have therefore named this dimension the DIVINE vs. the HUMAN. Those to the positive pole of the second dimension are the second and seventeenth discourses and the words "courage" and "faith" (*Tro*) and to the negative pole the first discourse and the words "the faith" (*Troen*), "expectation," "the Good" and "victory" and I have therefore named it COURAGE vs. EXPECTATION. Those to the positive pole of the third dimension are the second discourse and the words "courage," "You" (nom.) and "the faith" (*Troen*) and to the negative pole the eighth and thirteenth discourses and the words "soul," "man," "(the) doubt" and "of faith" (*Troens*) and I have therefore named it ENJOINING COURAGE vs. CARE OF THE SOUL. Thus, if these names are correct, the first or strongest opposition or contrast within T's presentation is that between faith seen from the divine and from the human perspective, the second that between faith's relation to courage on one hand and to expectation on the other and the third that between enjoining courage and urging the care of the soul as specific and more general paths to faith.

Our second "still life" depicts faith in all the works up to and including AE. Hence the column heads of its matrix are no longer discourses or chapters of a book but rather the books T, FB, BA, PS and AE or, more precisely, the faith sentences therein. Further, its row heads are not the aberrant frequency faith words in these books treated cumulatively, as in the first part of this study, but rather those words in these books treated separately, this in order to assure that those peculiar to a particular book are kept and allowed due influence in shaping the whole. Of course there are some duplicates in addition to the three forms of "faith" and this matrix is therefore only 105 words or rows by 5 books or columns. Its correspondence analysis plot is shown as figure 2 and includes all books, most of the chief "word" contributors, the names we have given the poles of its dimensions and, again, the three principal forms of "faith." Note, however, that it does not show the other 90 words all of which have played a role in defining its space.

The chief contributors to the positive pole of the first dimension are FB, T, "had" and "courage" and to the negative pole PS, "fact," "immediate," "the Historical," "object" and "condition" and, recalling the emphases of these books and their use of these words, I have named the former COURAGE and the latter "THE GOD AS OBJECT AND CONDITION." The chief contributors to the positive pole of the second dimension are FB, AE, "paradox," "movement," and "passion" and to the negative pole T, "You" (nom.), "expectation," "You" (dep.) and "victory" and I have therefore named the former PASSION and the latter EXPECTATION. Finally, the chief contributors to the positive pole of the third dimension are AE, "objective" "faith," "inwardness" and "of inwardness" and to the negative pole FB, "knight" and "Abraham," and I have therefore named the former ANALOGY TO THE SOCRATIC and the latter BEYOND THE HUMAN. The first reflects the contrast between the emphasis upon courage as a requirement of faith in FB and T and that upon the God as the necessary object and condition of faith in PS. The second reflects the emphasis upon faith as a passion in FB and AE and faith as expectation in T. The last, of course, underscores the contrast between AE's emphasis upon the analogies between faith and Socratic inwardness and FB's insistence that it is completely beyond any human capacity.

As a matter of general interest we note that, for example, the main contributors to the positive pole of the second dimension have "split" and become the chief contributors to the postive and negative poles of the third, that such "splits" and "joins" are characteristic of correspondence analysis results and that this is no doubt one of the reasons it seems so well suited to map and analyze even the most sophisticated work of the human mind whose operations are perhaps essentially dialectical.

Our next portrait shows faith in all the works up to and including CT, the ninth of our 16 books. The column heads of the relevant matrix therefore include all the books from T to CT and the row heads the 160 different aberrant frequency words in these books taken separately. The correspondence analysis plot is shown in figure 3 and, to avoid crowding, shows only the chief book and word contributors and, of course, the names we have given the poles of its dimensions.

The chief contributors to the positive pole of the first dimension are KG, T, CT, OTA, "You" (nom.), "You" (dep.), "the Good," "hope," "glory" and "love" and to its negative pole PS, to a much lesser extent AE, "fact," "immediate," "the Historical," "object" and "condition" and, remembering these books and the role of these words, I have named the former ENJOINING PRACTICE and the latter THE GOD AS OBJECT AND CONDITION. The chief contributors to the positive pole of the second dimension are FB, "knight" and "Abraham" and to the negative pole PS, KG, "believes," "secret" and "the Historical" and I have therefore named the former ABRAHAM AS KNIGHT OF FAITH and the latter, perhaps obscurely, FOR FAITH ONLY. Finally, the chief contributors to the positive pole of the third dimension are AE, "inwardness," "objective," "passion," "of inwardness," "doctrine" and "certainty" and to its negative pole PS, T, "then" (or "when") and "doubt" and I have therefore named these FAITH AS THE HIGHEST and CONFUSIONS OF DOUBT. The first shows that the most fundamental contrast in the presentations to date is that between the injunction to practice the life of faith and the quite different emphasis upon the God as its object and condition. The second shows that the next most important contrast is that between Abraham as the knight or model of faith and the claim that faith is a secret which must be held as such and its substance available only to faith. The third shows that the next contrast is that between AE's repeated declaration that faith is the highest good and the careful and minute exposures of the confusions of doubt in PS, T and, to a lesser extent, FB and OTA which, incidentally, make repeated use of *da*, sometimes as "then" and sometimes as "when," but almost always as part of a rigorous analysis of basic concepts. Note that the only pole surviving from either of our previous plots is the negative one of the first dimension and that all others are clearly new and different.

Our next plot shows faith in all the works up to and including IC, the eleventh of our 16 books. Its input matrix therefore has as column heads all our books from T to IC and as row heads the 188 aberrant frequency words in these books treated separately. The correspondence analysis plot in figure 4 shows only the chief book and word contributors[9] and the names we have given the poles of its dimensions.

The chief contributors to the positive pole of the first dimension are FB, "Abraham," "knight" and "paradox" and to its negative pole IC, "the God-Man," "of offense" and "possibility" and I have therefore named the former ABRAHAM AS KNIGHT OF FAITH and the latter THE GOD-MAN AS POSSIBILITY OF OFFENSE. The chief contributors to the positive pole of the second dimension are KG, T, CT, OTA, "You" (nom.), "You" (dep.) and "love" and those to its negative pole PS, "fact," "immediate," "the Historical," "the God" and "condition" and I have therefore named the former ENJOINING PRACTICE and the latter THE GOD AS CONDITION. Finally, the chief contributors to the positive pole of the third dimension are FB, IC, "knight," "Abraham," "of offense," "the God-Man," "paradox" and "possibility" and to its negative pole PS, KG, "fact," "believe," "the Historical," "You" (dep.) and "love" (n.) and I have therefore named these MODEL AND OBJECT and FAITH, HOPE AND LOVE. The first of these pairs shows that the most fundamental contrast in this plot is that between Abraham as the knight of faith and the God-Man as the possibility of offense. The second shows that the next most important contrast is that between the injunction to practice faith and the God as the condition of faith. The third shows that the next is that between FB's model and IC's object of faith on the one hand and the joining of faith, hope and love on the other. Note that in this case the chief contributors to the two poles of the first dimension have joined forces to become the chief contributors to the positive pole of the third and that this is shown clearly in this plot.

The reader will have no difficulty recognizing important differences between this plot and, for example, the previous one. ENJOINING PRACTICE and ABRAHAM AS KNIGHT OF FAITH have switched positions, THE GOD AS OBJECT AND CONDITION has been replaced by THE GOD-MAN AS THE POSSIBILITY OF OFFENSE and the former expression has now become THE GOD AS CONDITION and its object role transferred to the God-Man. Model and object have been brought together albeit on the third dimension and hope has been joined, though weakly, with faith and love.

Our last "still-life" shows faith in all our books up to and including DS and is based on a matrix of 16 columns or books and 201 rows or words. The correspondence analysis plot of this data matrix is shown in figure 5 and shows only the chief book and word contributors and the names we have given the poles of its dimensions.

The names of both poles of the first two dimensions of this plot are the same and those of the third dimension (CLARIFICATION OF CONCEPT and EXISTENTIAL EXPRESSION) essentially more generalized forms of their counterparts in the previous plot, the latter small change due mainly to the influence of the four new books, particularly TS. In short, the plot for all the books up to and including DS is essentially similar to that for all books up to and including IC. Put another way, Kierkegaard's presentations of faith appear to have reached some kind of climax in IC, a conclusion which will surprise no one familiar with either this work or the identity and status of its author.

Earlier in this study I suggested that understanding in terms of dimensions was a radical kind enabling one to explain the position of points and even to predict that of new ones. In fact it is easy to predict the location of many points not used in the naming of any of our dimensions[10] but we can hardly expect the reader to believe that we did not once peak at our own results and so will instead explain the position of some points in our last plot. This would be too easy for words with high co-ordinates so we focus upon those with lower ones.

"Absurde" (*Absurde*) has co-ordinates of 0.847, -0.714 and 0.547, the first reflecting its tie with Abraham in FB, the second its tie with "object," "knowledge," "the Historical," etc. in PS and the third its tie with Abraham in FB and the tie with God-Man in IC. "Reason" (*Forstanden*) has co-ordinates of 0.115, -0.507 and -0.326 because a slightly larger percentage of its occurrences are in the books with positive co-ordinates on this dimension, because 8.9% of all its occurrences in our faith sentences are in PS and because it does not occur in any of those in FB or IC. "Profit" (*Gavnligheden*) lies at 0.013, 0.777 and -0.423 because it is not associated with either pole of the first dimension, because it plays an important though indirect role in enjoining the practice of faith and is something the secret of which one learns in actual practice. "Courage" (*Mod*) lies at 0.711, 0.105 and 0.552 because it was shown by Abraham, celebrated in T as a condition of faith and is more closely tied to the expression than to the concept. Etc., etc.

In fact, one can even explain the position of the different forms of "faith." "Faith" (*Tro*) lies as 0.048, 0.232 and -0.145 because by this time it has become slightly more closely tied to the God-Man than to Abraham, because it is the form appropriate to an injunction to practice and because it too is tied more closely to the expression than the concept. "The faith" (*Troen*) lies at 0.068, -0.072 and -0.024 because it is slightly more frequent in FB than IC, in PS than in the religious discourses and, at least at this point in the authorship, apparently more strongly connected with the expression of faith than with the concept. Finally, "of faith" (*Troens*) lies at 0.157, -0.199 and 0.234 because it is still characteristic of the language of FB (as in "the knight of faith"), is frequent in PS and, naturally, occurs in connection with the clarification of the concept. In fact one could also explain the location of each of these forms in all of our earlier plots but argument must end sometime. Instead, we simply note that, though perhaps obscure to most English speaking readers, these differences reflect the extremely precise definition of our space and will certainly repay much closer study. Indeed, the above explanations are relatively superficial and, given time, could certainly be supplemented by other deeper and more revealing ones.[11]

I trust that at least some may have seen the promise of and perhaps even other uses for this method and conclude by noting some ways in which it might be improved. Of course I do so with the great benefit of hindsight.

My own chief disappointment with this study is that I have not succeeded in identifying factors common to the poles of its dimensions but have had to be content with naming them simply in terms of the opposition between their poles. This may be due to a lack of insight or imagination on my part but I believe that the explanation is rather the great variety and diversity of views concerning faith expressed in these books, particularly in the pseudonymous as distinct from the acknowledged ones.[12] For example, there is nothing obviously common to the courage emphasised by the acknowledged T and the God as object and condition of faith stressed in the pseudonymous PS which together represent the poles of the first dimension of our second plot. More generally, the opposition expressed in at least seven of the 11 remaining dimensions of our last four plots appears to be due primarily to differences between these two kinds of works.[13] Despite these difficulties it is clear that both belong and must be kept in this study.

This study was based upon all works in which the principal forms of "faith" showed a relative frequency of 4.00 or more but the use of this simple criterion resulted in the inclusion of three small books each containing only two to four "faith" sentences. It should therefore perhaps be supplemented or even replaced by another requiring that books show at least 10 or more occurrences of the key word in question.

We used as our control corpus the 20 "non-religious" works in Kierkegaard's authorship because it was obviously necessary to exclude his religious ones and because no other corpus of nineteenth century Danish is available. It is clear however that his entire corpus would be a better control for a less specifically religious subject and that the control for any such study should be as large and broadly based as possible.

We chose a Z-score of 7.00 as our cut-off point but now suspect we may have done so at least partly in order to keep the number of aberrant frequency words within what humanists would regard as manageable limits. In any event this value now seems very high and it would perhaps have been better to choose a lower one, consider a much larger number of aberrant frequency words and make the study more completely statistical. This would have helped fill in the detail in the various presentations of faith and would probably have yielded a wider variety of chief contributors thus facilitating the often difficult task of naming the poles.

One further point in this connection. Our model seems to be correct in showing in table 3 that "Abraham" ceases to be part of Kierkegaard's faith vocabulary at +IC but perhaps leaves too many words as part of this vocabulary for too long. In fact I believe that this is simply a problem with our model which can be remedied with a little more fine-tuning.

The question whether to derive aberrant frequency lists from "cumulative texts" or simply to add individual lists to one another (as in the second part of this study) is a difficult one with no easy answer. It could be argued that the latter is a perfectly adequate way of incorporating new texts into the sequence of works to date, that it has the advantage of preserving words peculiar to particular works and that it avoids a great deal of additional computer work. We chose the former for the first part of this study because it seemed more faithful to Kierkegaard's habit of presupposing earlier works and more consistent with his assumption that his reader had read and remembered them but note that this might not be so important for other authors.

In this study I have attempted to provide a detailed and accurate description of changes in Kierkegaard's faith vocabulary and the structure of his main presentations of faith across his authorship, to use these same results to represent the experience of his faithful reader who has followed and understood his works and, so far as possible, even to provide my own reader with a counterpart of the experience Kierkegaard intended and achieved for his own. This study is now complete and, like Kierkegaard's bird, I send it forth into the world not knowing how it may fare or who or what it may teach. No doubt some will see it as a strange and puzzling but perhaps possible alternative to the heavy task of reading the original text and if it helps the non-specialist to understand these presentations of faith I perhaps should not object. However the primary and underlying aim of this paper has been to send the reader back to Kierkegaard's own works better equipped to read and understand them on their own terms. This is the proper aim of all serious Kierkegaard scholarship and certainly the only one which he would approve.

NOTES

1.   Alastair McKinnon, "Aberrant Frequency Words: Their Identification and Uses," *Glottometrika* 2 (1980), 108-24.

2.   The relative frequency of a word or, in this case, of these three words is the sum of their absolute frequencies divided by the number of word-tokens in the book in question, itself divided by 10,000. Thus the 293 occurrences of these three forms in the 214,163 tokens of AE have a relative frequency of 13.68.

3.   These and all other title codes of Kierkegaard's works are explained in the Appendix.

4.   This sub-set consists of the following works: LP, BI, EE1, EE2, FB, G, F, PS, BA, SV, AE, LA, KK, SFV, FV, DS, B21, DSS, O and BFF.

5.   Briefly, the Z-score of a word is a measure of the extent to which its relative frequency in some smaller text exceeds its relative frequency in an appropriate control corpus.

6.   One would normally express the precise meaning I want to convey with the phrase "into the public domain" but this neglects the primacy of the "reader" and could be taken to mean that Kierkegaard imagined one could help "the public."

7.   The reader should be warned that one cannot similarly scan the columns of this table in order to determine the relative importance of these words, this because all the scores shown for each word are strongly dependent upon its frequency in our control corpus. For example, "expect," "of offense" and "the God-Man" occur there 3, 8 and 5 times, respectively, while "courage" and "Christ" occur 217 and 171 times. Of course this problem does not arise when comparing Z-scores across rows.

8.   Briefly, the profile of a word is, literally, a profile showing the percentages of all its occurrences in each book and that of a book one showing the percentages of all occurrences of each word in that book. For a fuller account and illustration see, for example, Alastair McKinnon, "Mapping the Dimensions of a Literary Corpus," *Literary and Linguistic Computing* 4 (1989), 73-84.

9.   Note that the form "of faith" makes a significant contribution to the positive pole of the third dimension and has been included as such. This contribution appears to be due mainly to its mass rather than its position on this dimension.

10.   For example, "Abraham's" (*Abraham*), "absurd" (*Absurde*), "analogy" (*Analogie*), "spiritual trial" (*Anfægtelse*), etc.

11.   For example, one can explain the positions of "rode," "the mother," "expectation" and "The Lord" on the fifth dimension of the book FB by showing the role of the first two in the account of Abraham proceeding to his deed as an unbeliver (chapter 2) and that of the last two in the account of his doing so as a believer (chapter 3). Kierkegaard clearly supports this interpretation of the difference between these chapters and, hence, of this dimension. In a journal entry from 1843 he notes that Abraham sacrifices Isaac in both cases but that in the former "he does it, but not in faith." See *Papirer*, IV B 73. The quotation is from *Fear and Trembling/Repetition*, ed. and trs. by Howard V. Hong and Edna H. Hong (Princeton: Princeton University Press, 1983), 249.

12. This insight was not in this paper as first presented and is due ultimately to a question posed by J. C. McLelland to whom I am most grateful.

13. Hence, of course, this study is further evidence of the deep differences between these two kinds of works.

TABLE 1.
Relative frequencies of *Tro*, etc. in authorship

LP	0.62	AE	13.68	FV	6.58
BI	0.84	BFF	2.67	YTS	3.16
EE1	1.81	LA	1.11	TAF	7.46
EE2	2.41	OTA	10.51	EOT	7.46
T	7.60	KK	1.27	GU	2.03
G	2.47	KG	7.44	TS	19.53
FB	48.90	TSA	6.91	DS	4.15
BA	6.20	CT	11.43	B21	4.16
PS	27.23	SD	10.08	DSS	0.00
F	1.36	IC	13.05	O	1.70
SV	2.54	SFV	1.23	HCD	0.00
TTL	0.00	LF	1.31		

TABLE 2.
Aberrant frequency word list of FB

Word	Trs./Use	Z-sc.	F.
Troen	the faith	78.46	109
Troens	of faith	77.94	76
Ridder	knight	56.52	38
Abraham	Abraham	24.20	26
Paradox	paradox	20.86	16
Almene	universal	18.55	20
Tro	faith	16.20	15
staaende	staying	15.74	12
Absurde	absurd	15.53	10
Isaak	Isaac	14.71	11
Enkelte	the individual	14.27	24
Resignation	resignation	12.90	7
Bevægelser	movements	12.06	7
Abrahams	Abraham's	11.26	5
Resignationens	of resignation	11.18	4
Bevægelse	movement	11.06	16
Afkald	renunciation	10.23	5
Mod	courage	9.18	10
Forventning	expectation	8.38	4
videre	further	8.17	14
tragiske	tragic	8.04	6
Fader	father	7.33	7
Helt	hero	7.17	8

TABLE 3.
The life cycle of 40 "faith" words

word/time	T	+FB	+BA	+PS	+AE	+OTA	+KG	+TSA	+CT	+SD	+IC	+TS	+DS
expectation	69.55	50.60	48.58	42.46	33.35	30.42	28.56	28.41	26.96	26.43	25.12	24.52	24.35
expect	52.56	33.26	31.95	27.99	21.40	19.58	18.43	18.34	17.44	17.11	16.31	15.94	15.84
victory	25.70	15.88	15.20	13.14	10.53	11.10	10.32	10.26	9.64	9.42	8.86	9.27	9.20
courage	7.86	12.08	13.02	11.08	8.21	7.65				8.20	7.59	7.31	7.24
humanly	14.58	10.18	9.72	8.33		10.10	9.38	10.08	9.47	9.25	9.37	9.10	9.03
(the) doubt	7.46			10.77	7.77	11.41	10.60	11.24	11.23	10.98	10.33	10.65	10.57
you	10.58								7.30	7.02	7.33	9.75	9.56
glory	10.78										10.63	10.33	10.25
wish	7.57	8.51	8.09										
Abraham		18.17	17.36	14.86	10.57	9.34	8.53	8.47	7.83	7.60	7.01		
knight		43.34	41.58	36.24	30.31	27.56	25.80	25.67	24.29	23.79	22.55	21.99	21.83
movement		7.87	7.43										
absurd		11.68	11.16	10.62	16.54	14.95	13.93	13.85	13.05	12.76	12.04	11.70	11.61
paradox		15.74	15.05	12.94	12.04	10.78	9.97	9.90	9.26	9.03	8.45	8.18	8.10
object				7.39	13.00	12.57	12.22	12.81	12.25	11.91	18.40	18.16	18.01
(the) condition				7.26									
risk					10.03	9.10	8.50	8.46	7.99	7.82	7.40	7.20	7.15
(the) reason					10.21	10.15	9.87	9.80	9.14	8.90	8.30	8.02	7.95
certainty					17.00	15.99	16.73	17.24	16.26	16.47	17.19	16.73	16.61
uncertainty					11.51	10.38	9.66	9.61	9.04	8.84	8.32	8.08	8.02
of inwardness					8.52	8.28	8.29	8.23	7.69	7.49			
passion					8.30	7.05							
(the) suffering						13.02	12.11	12.03	11.32	11.06	11.01	10.69	10.61
sufferer						16.30	15.27	15.18	15.39	15.08	14.30	13.94	13.84
(the) profit						16.47	15.49	15.41	14.64	14.36	13.67	13.35	13.26
(the) love						10.00	26.52	26.39	27.41	26.90	25.63	27.18	27.01
Providence						12.58	11.80	11.74	11.13	10.91	10.39	10.12	10.05
to confess						17.79	16.73	16.64	15.81	15.51	14.76	14.42	14.33
to comprehend									11.44	12.30	12.70	12.28	12.30
shrewdness									8.26	8.09	7.65	7.46	7.40
Christ											10.92	11.02	10.92
God											7.08	7.32	7.18
the God-Man											48.49	47.42	47.13
of offense										8.06	68.66	67.14	66.73
the proofs											12.47	12.19	12.11
unbelief								12.58	11.95	11.72	19.79	19.34	19.22
to believe					8.66	10.43	15.02	16.30	16.55	17.42	18.17	17.63	17.48
believe						7.04	11.85	11.76	15.10	14.69	14.65	14.89	14.75
believed									12.04	11.77	11.90	11.58	11.50
was believed												10.90	10.83

TABLE 4.
Matrix of "faith" words in T

word/discourse		1	2	5	6	7	8	9	10	12	13	16	17	18
da	then, when	31	7	3	0	3	1	0	0	0	1	5	0	2
Din	Your	11	2	0	0	0	0	0	0	0	1	0	0	0
Du	You (nom.)	33	9	0	0	2	0	0	0	0	0	0	1	0
forventer	expect	5	0	0	0	0	0	0	0	0	0	0	0	0
Forventning	expectation	26	0	0	0	0	0	0	0	0	0	0	0	0
Gode	the Good	7	0	0	0	0	0	0	0	1	0	0	0	0
havde	had	16	1	2	0	1	0	0	0	0	0	5	0	1
hellere	rather	5	0	0	0	0	0	0	0	0	0	0	0	0
Herlighed	glory	4	0	0	0	0	0	0	0	0	1	0	0	0
Menneske	man	17	0	2	0	2	2	0	0	0	1	0	0	0
menneskeligt	humanly	0	0	0	0	2	0	0	0	0	0	0	0	5
Mod	courage	0	5	1	0	0	0	0	0	0	0	0	1	0
Seier	victory	11	0	0	0	0	0	0	0	0	0	1	0	0
Sjel	soul	1	0	1	1	1	1	0	0	0	1	0	0	0
talt	speaking	0	0	0	0	2	0	0	0	0	0	0	0	5
Tilkommende	the future	4	0	0	0	0	0	0	1	0	0	0	0	0
Tro	faith	9	5	2	2	0	1	1	0	0	1	0	1	1
Troen	the faith	31	0	0	1	0	0	0	0	2	0	7	0	4
Troens	of faith	19	0	2	0	4	1	0	1	0	0	1	0	1
Tvivlen	(the) doubt	1	0	0	0	3	0	0	0	0	0	0	0	0
Ønske	wish	4	2	0	0	0	0	0	0	0	0	0	0	0

FIGURE 1.
Plot of "faith" in T

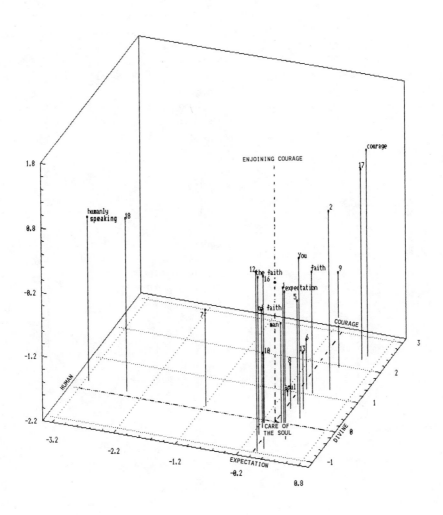

FIGURE 2.
Plot of "faith" in T . . . AE

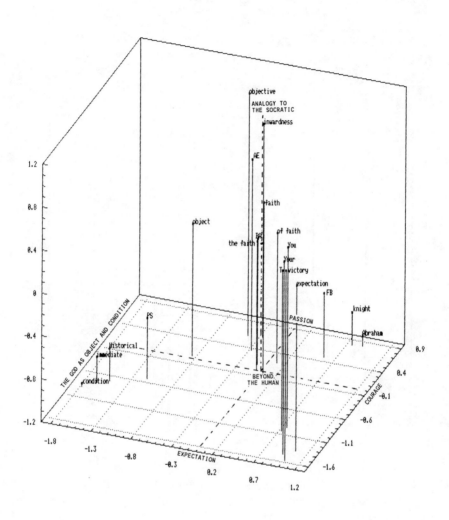

FIGURE 3.
Plot of "faith" in T . . . CT

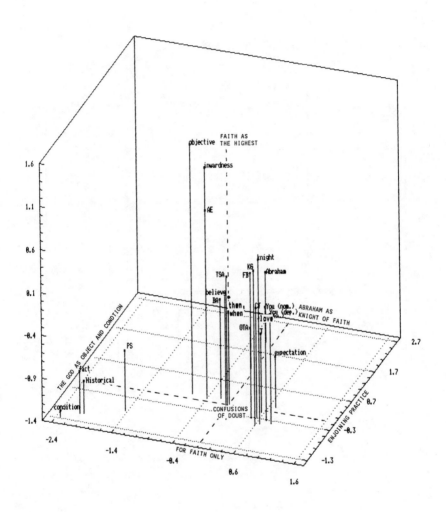

FIGURE 4.
Plot of "faith" in T . . . IC

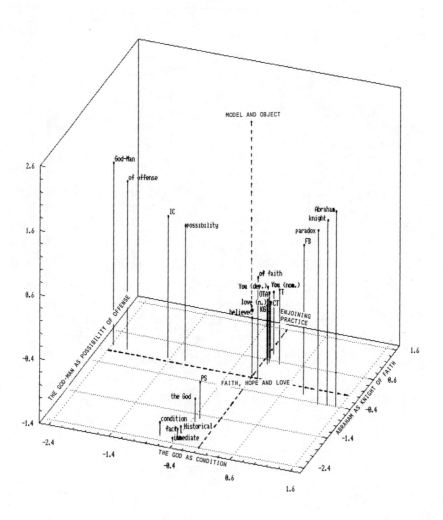

FIGURE 5.
Plot of "faith" in T … DS

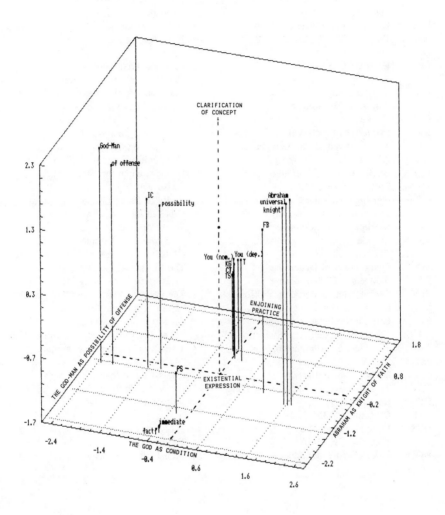

APPENDIX

LP	Af en endnu Levendes Papirer	[From the Papers of One ...]
BI	Om Begrebet Ironi	The Concept of Irony
EE1	Enten - Eller. Første halvbind	Either/Or, vol. 1
EE2	Enten - Eller. Andet halvbind	Either/Or, vol. 2
G	Gjentagelsen	Repetition
FB	Frygt og Bæven	Fear and Trembling
T	Atten opbyggelige Taler	Eighteen Edifying Discourses
BA	Begrebet Angest	The Concept of Dread
PS	Philosophiske Smuler	Philosophical Fragments
F	Forord	[Prefaces]
SV	Stadier paa Livets Vei	Stages on Life's Way
TTL	Tre Taler ved tænkte Leiligheder	Thoughts on Crucial Situations ...
AE	Afsluttende ... Efterskrift	Concluding Unscientific Postscript
BFF	Bladartikler, ... "Forfatterskabet"	[Articles about the Authorship]
LA	En literair Anmeldelse	Two Ages
OTA	Opbyggelige Taler ... Aand	Purity of Heart, Gospel of Suffering
KK	Krisen og en Krise ... Liv	Crisis in the Life of an Actress
KG	Kjerlighedens Gjerninger	Works of Love
TSA	Tvende ... Smaa-Afhandlinger	Two Minor ... Discourses
CT	Christelige Taler	Christian Discourses
SD	Sygdommen til Døden	The Sickness Unto Death
IC	Indøvelse i Christendom	Training in Christianity
SFV	Synspunktet ... Forfatter-Virksomhed	The Point of View ... an Author
LF	Lilien paa Marken og Fuglen ...	"The Lilies of the Field and ... "
FV	Om min Forfatter-Virksomed	On My Work as an Author
YTS	"Ypperstepræsten" ... "Synderinden"	"'The High Priest' ... ' ... Sinner'"
TAF	To Taler ved Altergangen ...	Two Discourses at the Communion ...
EOT	En opbyggelig Taler	"An Edifying Discourse"
GU	Guds Uforanderlighed	God's Unchangeableness
TS	Til Selvprøvelse, Samtiden anbefalet	For Self-Examination
DS	Dømmer selv!	Judge for Yourselves!
B21	Bladartikler 1854-55 I-XXI	Newspaper articles, 1854-5
DSS	Dette skal siges; ...	"This must be said ..."
O	Øieblikket, nr. 1-10	The Instant, nos. 1-10
HCD	Hvad Christus dømmer ...	"What Christ thinks ..."

HAPPY FALLS:
A Philosophical Account of Evil

Donald Evans
Victoria College, University of Toronto

In this essay I will be assuming that evil in human beings is best understood in terms of *narcissism*. This was my central thesis in *Spirituality and Human Nature*,[1] and my arguments in support of the thesis still seem sound to me. In one important respect, however, my view of narcissism has changed. Throughout most of the book I claimed that it both can and should be eliminated, but by the end of the book I was veering toward the view that narcissism can not be eliminated without our ceasing to be human. Further explorations of various origins of narcissism have moved me even more strongly in this direction. Indeed, it now seems clear to me that various elements in narcissism originate within forms of communality and of individuation which are essential to our human nature. It also seems clear that these forms can be transformed, and that they should be.

A tendency toward narcissism was and is the price of our emergence as human beings from pre-human states and from primitive human states. Our fall from animal innocence to primitive narcissism was a "happy fall," for it made possible the eventual emergence of something new and better, a distinctively human good. What Adam and Eve should be seen as representing is not a perfect humanity but a pre-humanity. Their fall was part of their becoming human. Adam and Eve can also be seen as representing very early humanity in contrast with the intensified narcissism of later human beings: more individuated but caught up in heroic hubris. Each advance in the evolution of humankind involves a deepening of human evil. It also involves a deepening of possible human good, provided that we do not abandon our pre-human and early-human origins.

Although my use of the expression "happy fall"[2] indicates that this essay has important implications for theology, the essay itself is predominantly philosophical. That is, I am not appealing to the authority of Christian scripture or tradition to back my claims. Also, I will only be considering narcissism as a human motivation, not as a theologically-understood "sin." In *Spirituality and Human Nature* I also considered narcissism as a resistance to loving spiritual presences and as a self-separation from God, for these religious dimensions seem to me very important. Here, however, I will describe narcissism and its origins in a purely "secular" way, though various spiritual remedies for narcissism will be considered.

As a pattern of motivation, narcissism has three features. First, there is a tendency to swing between extremes of self-inflation (being like a god) and self-deflation (being utterly unlike a god). Second, these two poles are foils for each other because there is a preoccupation with possessions, power and prestige involving comparisons: "Where do I (or we) rate in comparison with others?" Third, the self, or the group from which the person has a sense of identity, is not merely distinguished from others but is actively separated from others in ways which are self-preoccupied, self-centred, self-enclosing and self-preferential.

Since narcissism as a basic motivation works mostly unconsciously, uncovering it involves uncovering a great deal of self-deception. We conceal our individual and group egoism by means of many convincing rationalizations and ideologies. Much that *seems* altruistic is not, though sometimes we do break free, or are liberated, from our bondage to narcissism. Then genuine love is at work, perhaps even as our main motivation. Indeed, diverse thinkers[3] have presented what seem to me to be strong reasons in support of the view that human beings have an inherent capacity and inclination towards motivation by love. But that is not my topic in this essay. Instead, we ask why, in spite of such an alleged inherent tendency towards love, human beings have such a strong tendency towards the narcissism which prevents love.

In my exploration of various origins of narcissism I will be drawing on a wide range of sources: Paul Ricoeur's conceptual analysis of distinctively human society and the selfish desires which arise in it; Dorothy Dinnerstein's depth-psychological and evolutionary account of the origin of the desire to be god in our distinctively human infancy; Soren Kierkegaard's existentialist account of the origin of self-idolatry in a clinging to oneself against the dizziness of freedom and the dread of death; and David Toolan's portrayal of the "heroic," self-conscious individual, separating himself from quasi-animal fusion with tribe and nature. I will devote more time to Ricoeur than to the others, for his approach is more widely accessible than those of depth-psychology, existentialism and mysticism, which appeal to experiences that some people have and others do not.

In *Fallible Man*[4] Ricoeur claims that the very concept of "human being" involves some awareness of, and desire for, possessions, power and prestige. Concerning possessions he says, "I cannot imagine the I without the mine or man without having;"[5] it is part of the essence of the human. He contrasts a desire for an object, e.g. a fruit which one sees and wants to eat, and a desire for an "economic" object, an object set aside as something for me (or for us). "Insofar as the thing is 'available' it creates the whole cycle of feelings relative to acquisition, appropriation, possession and preservation. . . . I experience both my *control* over the having of which I can avail myself and my *dependence* . . . on it as a thing which can escape from me, degenerate, be lost or be taken away; the possibility of no-longer-having is inherent in the tendency to avail oneself of."[6] And insofar as the economic object is mine or ours, it is not yours.

Ricoeur's claim that to be human is to desire to own is supported by Martin Buber's analysis of how human beings set aside some objects as *tools*. Buber notes how human beings set aside objects which for the moment have become tools "in order to use them the next day in a similar fashion." And we may also devise or create tools to set aside in this way. The tool continues to exist, "ready for a function;" "it is at one's disposal."[7] A tool, like the other economic objects to which Ricoeur refers, is owned by someone or by some group of people. Ricoeur points out that one's sense of owning things is transferred to one's own body and even to one's own thoughts, accentuating our sense of being separate and preferred.[8]

Ricoeur's second allegedly-inherent human awareness and desire pertains to power over other human beings. Just as the desire to possess arises from the objective practice of setting things aside to be at human disposal, so the desire for power arises in relation to objective, institutionalized arrangements in society: technological, economic and political. As human beings try to master nature they organize themselves so as to carry out diverse functions. These organizational structures always involve some subordination of functions. Moreover, the subordination of technological functions becomes a subordination of *persons* to the extent to which persons come to be identified, by themselves and others, with their functions. Like tools, persons become means of production, and whoever owns or controls tools and/or producers tends to dominate (in varying degrees) the others. Ricoeur is interested in worker-ownership and worker-management as attempts to reduce the domination of some people over others, but he sees no clear way to eliminate all power-differences. And beyond the economic organization of society, intimately related to it, there is also the political-legal authority, which typically has a monopoly on legitimate physical compulsion. Ricoeur claims that institutionalized power is inherent, essential, in human society, and that some awareness of, and desire for, such power is part of human nature.

Ricoeur's third allegedly-inherent human awareness and desire has to do with prestige (or honour or status or rank). Prestige is a superiority which others recognize; we depend on them for it. As I see it (here I am presenting my own account rather than Ricoeur's),[9] the starting-point for understanding prestige is in the objective social world: if you have more possessions and/or more power than others this brings more status, for the desires of the others for possessions and/or power have been thwarted or less fulfilled. These desires may be smothered by an ideology encouraging resignation, but the fulfilled desires of the rich and powerful do signal higher status. Possessions and power do provide clear bases for being recognized as superior by one's fellow human beings. And other bases also emerge, mostly in various roles which a society values, e.g. the seer, the entertainer, the military leader, etc. Sociological and anthropological studies shed much light on the intricacies of such matters and the differences between primitive societies and our own.

I am not convinced, however, that various kinds of social analysis adequately explain our human preoccupation with comparative status. Underlying it is a concern which does not itself have anything to do with ranking, though it is often expressed in concerns about ranking. The concern arises from an insecure sense of our own reality and an insecure hold on our own existence. Our human birth and early infancy involves separation from a mother on whom we depend for the fundamental self-acceptance and self-esteem which provides a sense of our own reality. And our awareness of freedom separates us from the security provided by brute facts, while our awareness that "I might not have been at all" and "At any moment I might cease to be" makes existence feel strange and precarious. As you will notice, I am here briefly alluding to depth-psychological and existential considerations which are remote from what I have been presenting in Ricoeur. These further considerations will be explored in the paper later on.

If, as Ricoeur claims, desires for possessions, power and prestige are an essential part of being human so that a total absence of these social desires would involve the absence of humanity, it is important to ask whether there can be an *innocent* version of any of these social desires. Ricoeur acknowledges no innocent versions in recorded human history. These desires have been evil, both in their self-centredness and in the injustice which they often cause when acted upon. He insists, nevertheless, that we would not be able to see that our versions of these desires are *evil* if we could not *imagine* a contrasting innocent version of them, nor would we be *responsible* for them if no alternative were *possible*. So he invites us to imagine a primitive paradise or a future utopia where innocent versions of the desires could occur. They could occur because the objective communal arrangements would make them possible. For example, he says, one would possess only what one "cultivates" or "creates"[10] oneself, and any political authority would "educate the individual to freedom" and would be "a power without violence."[11] Ricoeur implies that such arrangements would not involve the *abolition* of possessions and power and of the desire for these. Rather there would be, in some future utopia, a *return* to an innocent Golden-Age society.

Ricoeur does not claim that there ever was such a society, but it seems to me plausible to hold that probably something like it existed at very early stages of our human history, stages where we still had some of the innocence of our animal ancestors although distinctively human social arrangements and desires were beginning to emerge. We have fallen from innocence into narcissism and part of us longs to return to a pre-fall state; but that state would also be pre-human. So our actual human task is somehow to *include in a revised* way what we have lost in our origins as we have become human. This is the theme of this paper.

One way of trying to do this, which Ricoeur does not even mention, is an ascetic path within a great religious tradition where one tries to eliminate all the social desires for possessions, power and prestige by embracing poverty, obedience and self-abnegation. Perhaps Ricoeur ignores this route because it involves human beings trying to become non-human, which is either an impossible task or an inappropriate one. My own view is that such a path when practiced by a minority can provide a valuable critique of our social desires and our social frameworks. The ascetic path, however, has a crucial flaw, for typically it has involved a withdrawal from the social framework. Such withdrawal is an abdication of one's responsibility to revise that framework so as to reduce injustice and thereby also to reduce the degree of temptation of strongly self-centred social desires. A different, more "worldly" asceticism is needed, one which involves, as it were, not having one's cake and yet eating it. One does not *have* one's cake in the sense that one has it *lightly*, without attachment. That is, in general, one does not cling to possessions, power or prestige which one has acquired, and one does not cling to the desires for what one has not acquired. One nevertheless actively involves oneself in society, partly motivated by the social desires, but in a subordinated, revised way.

Such a worldly asceticism is not possible unless one lets go of not only one's attachments but also one's longing for total innocence. Such a worldly asceticism involves realizing that being human intrinsically involves a loss of innocence. Then what one can long for is not innocence but a *transformation* of our human desires and human social arrangements. Such transformation would include more of our pre-human innocence, but in a human mode. Insofar as such transformation paradoxically involves both non-clinging and involvement, both detachment and commitment, it is *better* than pre-human innocence, yet it includes much of the freshness, spontaneity and simplicity of innocence.

The quest for innocence through renunciation of worldly social desires has an additional drawback. It tends to be distorted into a self-humiliating path that disparages healthy self-love. One aims at eliminating narcissistic social desires with their implicit ranking in relation to images of self which are self-inflating or self-deflating. In practice, however, one plumps for self-deflation. What one actually needs is not self-deflation, but a good dose of healthy self-love, which would reduce the preoccupation with ranking and thereby reduce the intensity of the social desires. What I mean by "healthy self-love" as contrasted with narcissism can only be sketched here.[12] Roughly it is whatever ways of loving are appropriate and required towards *others*, where something *like* these ways of loving are directed towards *oneself*, e.g. caring, affection, confirmation, commitment, respect, patience, and so on. Healthy self-love also can be seen as the individuated transformation of pre-human *joie de vivre*: the unselfconscious enjoyment of being alive which remains accessible to us insofar as we are in touch with the pre-human, animal mode of existence which is still part of us.[13]

Before I conclude my consideration of the social desires I should consider an important objection to what I have proposed. Our culture receives with bewilderment and antagonism any suggestion that desires for possessions, power or prestige are always self-centred and therefore evil. If we ask the common sense of our culture what is evil the answer is that only the excessive and harm-producing instances of these desires are evil. I must concede that this common sense view is true in one respect, namely that people do vary greatly in the extent to which narcissistic avarice, ambition and vanity motivates them. And another variable is the amount of harm that the desires, whether weak or strong, cause when acted upon. Some instances are obviously far worse than others, and by comparison the small-scale instances seem quite innocent. But if they are innocent, at what point do they cease being innocent and suddenly become evil? And if there is a continuum, is not this continuum for most of us a slippery slope? Once we've begun to slide a little, counsels of moderation do not tend to influence us much. On the other hand, an obsessive scrupulosity which aims at complete innocence is usually counter-productive. What is needed is a shift into a new stance which includes our social desires while transcending and transforming them. I have suggested three elements in this new stance: We let go of our *clinging* to the social desires without trying to eliminate them; we cultivate a healthy *self-love* which complements our love for others; and we are *socially active* in revising our social arrangements so as to reduce injustice and thereby also reduce the intensity of the temptation to be dominated by social desires.

I have devoted most of this paper to reflections in response to Ricoeur's phenomenological-conceptual exploration of the social arrangements and correlative social desires which are part of what constitutes us as human beings prone to narcissism. I now turn to consider other accounts much more briefly, though I do not see them as less important. Although Ricoeur did not speculate concerning the historical process in which animals became humans, I applied his account in that way, considering the early evolution of distinctively human social arrangements and social desires. The next account which we will consider also looks back to that evolutionary period, but differs in that it focuses on the emergence, not of human society, but of the human *infant*. Another difference is that the discipline brought to the exploration is not the conceptual analysis of philosophical phenomenology. Instead, evolutionary anthropology and depth psychotherapy are brought together to illuminate human infancy.

In *The Mermaid and the Minotaur*,[14] Dorothy Dinnerstein focuses on our animal ancestry. Three changes took place together: Adaptation to bipedal, upright locomotion *decreased the size of the birth canal* at roughly the same time that *brain-size was increasing* by natural selection because the best tool-users survived and they had bigger brains, and at roughly the same time the bipedal locomotion *freed up the mother's hands* to hold her infant, who did not have to be sufficiently mature to *cling* to her. Thus the problem created by bigger brain and therefore bigger head proceeding down a narrower birth-canal was solved by *premature birth*, which in turn was feasible because the mother could hold the premature infant.

Dinnerstein draws the conclusion from this that from our earliest history as human beings we have been birthed into the world as premature infants who, as compared with other infant animals, are more *dependent* on mother and, because of the large brain, more *aware* of that dependency. Thus far her thesis is checkable by behavioural and evolutionary-anthropological evidence. Dinnerstein's brilliance, however, is in linking such evidence with what is largely testimonial evidence from experiences of regression to infancy during psychotherapy. These reports fill in the *contents* of the experience of dependency.

What is reported is complex and varied, but one common theme emerges: an awareness of a process of *reluctant separation*. On the one hand the sense of almost undifferentiated union with mother in the womb has been partly shattered by the experience of birth; one longs to return there, but one also can become fascinated with the new mode of existence, which involves a vague self-world distinction—mother being the world—where intimacy is both enjoyed and needed. Mother is the centre not only of bodily comfort and pleasure but also of emotional well-being and of confirmation of one's existence. As mother satisfies these needs one's dependency on her is experienced blissfully, for it also reminds one of the oceanic feeling in the womb. But insofar as our needs are not met immediately as we become aware of them, we become acutely aware of our own powerlessness in relation to the all-powerful provider, who is experienced as a depriver and controller. This gives rise to the desire to separate ourselves from the all-powerful being, a desire which includes fear of being overwhelmed and anger at being limited. One would like to be an all-powerful being comparable to the being on whom one is so dependent. Yet there is also fear and anger concerning the possibility of abandonment; fear that one would thereby become nothing and anger that one lacks the power to prevent it. Also there is an intense longing to return from self-separation to an earlier dependent intimacy and even to undifferentiated union.

As human beings we are caught between an elemental desire to return to our origins in the womb or early infancy and a desire to separate from our human source, to distinguish ourselves from her, to individuate. We have been expelled from our garden of innocence, and we long to return; yet we expel ourselves, for this is necessary if we are to become human beings. Becoming a human being, however, involves us in a tendency towards narcissism, caught up in alternation between fantasies of being god-like and fantasies of being utterly helpless. But the split between original innocence and fallen self-separating narcissism can be healed to some extent if we return to our pre-natal state, our birth and our early infancy to re-experience them, and if we then integrate these original states with our present individuated state.

I am convinced that something like this is true for all *men*, but probably only a revised version of it may apply to women. One of Dinnerstein's themes is the difference in the typical experience of baby boys and baby girls. The female infant soon has a sense that she will eventually have access to a similar power to that of her mother, who is also female. If this is true, then a description of an inherent (narcissistic) tendency to evil in men may well have to be revised before it is applicable to women. More generally, I suspect that not only psychological but other accounts of narcissism will need to be revised as the testimony from women concerning their experience is given more and more of a hearing.

Similar considerations obviously also apply to the historical-symbolic account of the origins of narcissism to which we now turn: the emergence of heroic consciousness in various human communities. David Toolan, in his book *Facing West from California's Shores*,[15] combines impressions of village life in contemporary India with anthropological accounts of early-aboriginal life in his picture of an "oral" stage in human communities where language, unlike a Victorian child, is never seen and always *heard*. Here consciousness is only minimally *self*-consciousness. There is little awareness of an individual mind mediating and storing an experience of a self which is capable of free, individual initiatives. Rather, everything seems to participate in everything else and "the mind, insofar as one could call it one's own at all, was felt to be the precipitate of cosmic mind, like rain condensing from air."[16] Even the expression "cosmic mind" may be misleading, for what is experienced is a pervasive, numinous energy which is vaguely conscious. One's participation in this energy is diffuse; one merges with it. Such an intimacy with community and cosmos provides a dreamlike but assured meaningfulness in life, and the blurred sense of personal individuation facilitates equanimity in the face of death. One feels at home in the universe, minimally alienated in spite of all the dangers to life and limb. The price, however, is minimal self-differentiation, and minimal freedom and responsibility for shaping one's own individual life. For humans living in the oral stage the price of organic affinity with everything was and is a passive rootedness in Mother Earth with restricted awareness of alternative possibilities.

A radical break with this stage is signalled for Toolan by the rise of heroic consciousness in the tales of the Iliad, Norse saga, Beowulf, the Gilgamesh epic, and the story of Abraham's trek from Ur. The hero separates himself from home and community and Mother Earth to engage in distinctively masculine ventures, conscious of creating or responding to his own individual projects. But as the hero begins to disconnect himself from Mother Earth's spiritual-energy nourishment he tends to blame her for the broken bonding and he flails out at goddesses. As Toolan says, "Ariadne is abandoned, Cassandra ravaged, the altar of Athena defiled."[17] New rituals emerge to deal with the fear of death and the hope of individual survival which the new inner sense of selfhood evoked. Also, the hero experiences gods more and more as individuals with wills like his own. Indeed, a concept of a supreme (and masculine) deity eventually arises as a projection of the heroic illusion that one might somehow be one's own self-cause, vulnerable to none of the imperfections of a passive, dark or feminine side. The heroic illusion is the pretension that one is like a patriarchal god, defying the limitations of Mother Earth from whom one has emerged and to whom one will return, breaking dependency-connections with community and cosmos, trying to justify and immortalize oneself by slaying enemies and dragons. The response to this inflated ego in various parts of the world several thousand years ago was the invention of interior contemplative disciplines for transforming hubris into something else. These disciplines were not simply ways of regressing to the state of merging with everything and everyone that characterized oral consciousness. On the contrary, the disciplines relied on the newly-discovered inner self as a "containing vessel"[18] which had replaced the oral-primitive's "leaky sieve."[19]

Various modern mystics have noted that one has to have developed an ego already if one is to let go of it. They are not merely noting the truism that, in general, one has to have X if one is to let go of X. In the case of an ego, having it involves having access to that which can *enable* one to let go of it, for one has become capable of making a free, conscious decision to stop clinging to anyone or anything. So the "fall" from oral into heroic consciousness, though it gave rise to hubris, also makes possible a third, contemplative stage which is better than the first. Unfortunately, the third stage often confused contemplative detachment with the heroic dis-connection for which it was supposedly the remedy. The hero initially disconnects from the feminine and the earthly and the "dark" by repressing them, along with his associated fear and anger, into his unconscious. Sometimes however, he proceeds further with an interior journey which can also be part of a contemplative path, and in this journey he ventures down into the underworld where he faces his repressed feminine dimensions. For example, he may meet a female dragon and instead of killing it he identifies with it and experiences it transforming into its positive "flip-side," which he then integrates into himself. Emerging from the underworld is like being born again, and this time one emerges as a mature self who experiences Mother Earth in a new way. As Toolan puts it, Mother Earth "nurtures while she lets go."[20] Thus heroic hubris is replaced by an integration of oral consciousness and individuated consciousness. The fall from oral consciousness can eventually make possible something far better, and distinctively human.

Unfortunately few men have pursued the heroic journey to such a happy ending, and the price of male hubris has been terrible. In recent decades we have become acutely aware of its frequent outcome in rape of the earth and rape of women. And whereas in the past the repercussions from the heroic duels sought out by adolescent men were perhaps tolerable, the situation changes when the war-toys become nuclear. Now, the heroic-macho fixations of our leaders have become too dangerous for humankind and for all life on the planet. It is imperative that more men return to our human origins—in this case, to oral consciousness—so as to integrate this in a transforming way with the individuated consciousness of the hero. It is also important that more *women* undergo a similar, though different process. Women's experience of oral consciousness and of individuation through separation has not yet been adequately explored and heard. Perhaps the heroic process was *pioneered* mainly by men. Certainly it has been *dominated* by men, so that the distinctively feminine version has been largely suppressed, and even repressed. In recent times, however, many women have renewed their access to what Toolan called "oral consciousness" and although some have become fascinated and largely fixated there, others have begun the relatively-unchartered journey of integrating this with their own sense of self as a woman. This involves discovering and creating their own "containing vessel," to use Toolan's expression. The pattern of integration which they are pioneering is something from which not only other women but also men can and must learn.

Thus far I have presented three accounts of the origin of an inherent human tendency towards narcissism. The first, responding to Ricoeur, notes a "fall" from an innocent, pre-human state into social arrangements linked with social desires which are intrinsically narcissistic. This new evil could be remedied in either or both of two ways: first, a contemplative stance of non-clinging, and second, a return to the pre-human state so as to somehow integrate it with the fallen human state, thereby transforming it. The second account, responding to Dinnerstein, followed a similar pattern, though here the "fall" occurs with birth, whether in earliest humans or us. The third account, responding to Toolan, differs in that the "fall" is not from a pre-human state, but from a primitive stage in human evolution into a heroic consciousness tending towards hubris. This change is viewed by some people as an unambiguous advance rather than a fall, for primitive consciousness should be despised. For other people the change is viewed as an unmitigated disaster, for heroic consciousness is a fall into evil. In contrast with both these views, Toolan and I see heroic consciousness as both an advance and a fall, and we see our task as human beings as an attempt to make the fall a "happy fall," that is, to make the ambiguous advance a genuine one. This task involves returning as *non*-primitive human beings to primitive consciousness and then coming back, having integrated this consciousness with a heroic consciousness which is thereby transformed. Such a proposal is based partly on a realistic sense that we *can* not simply revert to primitive consciousness and stay there, but partly on a conviction that we *ought* not to do so even if we could. We ought not to because something both worse and *better* emerged with heroic consciousness, and something much better can emerge if heroic consciousness is transformed by integration with primitive consciousness. Human nature is still evolving, not in a pattern of inevitable progress, but in the emergence of new human forms of consciousness which increase the possibilities for both worse evil and greater good. And one crucial way to shift towards greater good is to integrate our origins and our past with our present.

The fourth account of the origins of human narcissism claims to be universal in scope, applying to all human beings since the dawn of history, but it seems to me that it applies most plausibly to Western Christian (indeed Protestant) individuals in recent times. It has some continuity with the heroic individualism which emerged several millenia before, but there is a more radical self-separation and self-isolation. As you may have guessed, I am referring to Kierkegaardian existentialism.[21] By including it I am implicitly recommending that the kind of individuation which it reports and proposes is not to be simply discarded because of obvious inadequacies, but on the contrary should be somehow integrated with all the perspectives mentioned thus far in this essay, including the communal interdependence which Ricoeur stresses. An existentialist account of our original tendency towards evil emphasizes the unlimited scope of our imaginings concerning what *might* be or what *might* have been. On the one hand this involves a sense of individual freedom which is so unboundaried that we both feel like gods and yet anxiously, idolatrously cling to ourselves (that is, to whatever we find ourselves to be at the moment). On the other hand, the awareness that "I *might* not have been at all" combined with the awareness that "I *might* cease to be," moves us to endless preoccupation with being confirmed as powerful and important in our own eyes and in the eyes of others.

Note how my description of human consciousness in this existentialist account involved a repetition of a subjunctive word, "might." As George Steiner points out in his remarkable work, *Real Presences,*[22] the unbounded character of human language is most distinctively and essentially human when we "beget and speak counter-factuals,"[23] talking about what might have happened and what might happen and what we might have done or might do. Perhaps early post-primitive awareness of contingency and mortality and freedom required the development of subjunctive language. In a 20th-century existentialist, however, such awareness has intensified far beyond that of early human beings. It has become a radically self-isolating sense of limitless insecurity and foundationless freedom.

Today only a few card-carrying, zealous Sartreans claim to see this as a simple advance in human consciousness. For most of us it involves a fall from an existence which was less disconnected, less lonely and less anxious. Indeed, it involves a tendency towards the most extreme form of narcissism, where one is consciously and completely caught up in alternating between a megalomanic fantasy of being a god and a masochistic resentment that one is not. This is the picture[24] which both Kierkegaard and Sartre present. Perhaps, however, the fall is a necessary condition for a greater advance. Perhaps, as Kierkegaard implies in *The Sickness unto Death*, the realization of such narcissism is necessary if one is to move beyond it to become authentically human. Perhaps even here—indeed, especially here—the "fall" into a state of tending towards evil (narcissism) can make possible a far better human state. Perhaps Sartrean existentialism is a potentially happy fall.[25]

What remedy is there for the extreme narcissism of the existential individualist? Here my two-fold approach is similar to what I have proposed earlier. On the one hand, the individualist, with his or her acutely self-conscious and self-differentiating ego, must somehow return to experience a primitive sense of interconnection with everything and everyone and then come back, having integrated this in a transforming way. That is, what Toolan calls the ego as "containing vessel" must allow itself to become a "leaky sieve" for a time and then come back transformed, including what it can from primitive consciousness. On the other hand, I propose a mystical discipline of non-clinging. In this case the contemporary self's extreme sense of individual uniqueness and responsibility can provide both the most formidable human *obstacle* to a mystical surrender into the divine Source and part of the best human *basis* for a worldly or humanistic mysticism after one has surrendered. That is, there can be a mysticism in which, having returned to unity with one's origin in the Source by surrendering the whole individuated self into that Source, one then returns to the world as this particular individual who incarnates the Source. Ultimately our origin is not our mother's womb, but the divine Source which is, as it were, the womb beyond all wombs. If we are to be truly born again, we must return not only to our mother's womb and to the metaphorical pre-infancy of the human race in primitive consciousness but also, and primarily, to our divine origin. And the purpose of the return to origins is, in each instance, not to stay there but to be born again, this time as this individuated human being consciously connected with one's origins.

NOTES

1.   Donald Evans, *Spirituality and Human Nature* (Albany, NY: State University of New York Press, 1992).

2.   The expression "happy fall" summarizes the meaning of an ancient passage in the Roman Missal, the Exsultet for Easter Saturday: "O certe necessarium Adae peccatum, quod Christi

morte deletum est! O *felix culpa*, quae talem ac tantum meruit habere redemptorem!" (O truly needful sin of Adam, which was blotted out by the death of Christ! O *happy fault*, which merited such and so great a redeemer!). Adam's fault, which brought about the fall of Adam and thereby the fall of humankind, was "happy" in that it necessitated the coming of Christ as redeemer. Cardinal Charles Journet, in a work on theodicy, explained that God permitted the fall to occur so as to make possible a greater good: "Our loss was a gain for us, since human nature has in effect received more graces by the redemption of its Saviour than it would ever have received by the innocence of Adam, should it have persevered in this"; see *The Meaning of Evil* (London: Geoffrey Chapman, 1963), 258; see also p. 259. In contrast with Journet, I find it implausible to hold that any of our human progenitors were ever completely innocent, for becoming human involved acquiring various tendencies towards narcissism, though they and we have some measure of freedom in choosing the extent to which these tendencies dominate over our tendencies to love. My proposal is formally similar to his, however, in that I see the fall (understood in a secular way) as making possible a distinctively human good. As a Christian I also agree with Journet that our human destiny in Christ is far better than any state known to our human ancestors.

3.   Erik Erikson's developmental psychology sees in human beings a succession of tendencies to relate to other human beings mutually and creatively through various stages which culminate in adult love and caring; see *Childhood and Society*, 2d ed., (New York: Norton, 1963) chs. 2, 7. Martin Buber holds that we are all born with an inclination and a capacity to enter what he calls "I-Thou" relations with other people, with nature and with God; see *I and Thou* (New York: Scribner's, 1970), Part II. Wilhelm Reich sees in people an inherent predisposition towards participation in creative life-energies which are present in people and nature and which are most intensely focused in profound sexual love; see *The Murder of Christ* (New York: Noonday, 1970), ch. 3.

4.   Paul Ricoeur, *Fallible Man* (Chicago: Henry Regnery, 1967).

5.   *Fallible Man*, 176.

6.   *Fallible Man*, 174.

7.   Martin Buber, *The Knowledge of Man* (Atlantic Highlands, NJ: Humanities Press, 1991), 55.

8.   Ricoeur, *Fallible Man*, 175.

9.   Ricoeur links the social desires for possession and power to objective institutionalized arrangements in society, but when he considers the social desire for prestige he mistakenly sets aside all institutionalized arrangements, even though possessions and power have much to do with prestige, and other social roles do as well. And as the distinctive "objectivity" of esteem he refers to formal notions in Kant's ethics, which calls on us to recognize all persons as ends in themselves, having intrinsic existence-worth. (See Ricoeur, *Fallible Man*, 186-7) Such a shift from phenomenological description to ethics is absent in his account of the desires for possession and for power, and it does not explain why our desire for prestige is not usually *felt* as a desire to have our existence-worth recognized. Usually it is felt as a desire to rate high in the opinions of others.

10.   Ricoeur, *Fallible Man*, 176.

11. *Fallible Man*, 182.

12. For a further exploration see *Spirituality and Human Nature*, chapter 2.

13. What I am trying to convey here is similar to what Gabriel Marcel calls an "exclamatory awareness" of self or of existence, though he focuses on the *child* within us rather than the animal. See *The Mystery of Being*, Vol. I, (Chicago: Henry Regnery, 1950), 111-12, 137.

14. Dorothy Dinnerstein, *The Mermaid and the Minotaur* (New York: Harper, 1976).

15. David Toolan, *Facing West from California's Shores: A Jesuit's Journey into New Age Consciousness* (New York: Crossroad, 1987).

16. *Facing West*, 111.

17. *Facing West*, 133.

18. *Facing West*, 157.

19. *Facing West*, 159.

20. *Facing West*, 168.

21. The main background for my account of existentialist narcissism comes from Soren Kierkegaard's *The Concept of Anxiety* (Princeton, NJ: Princeton University Press, 1980) and *The Sickness unto Death* (Garden City, NY: Doubleday, 1954). Kierkegaard was not an "existentialist" in the sense that Sartre was, for Kierkegaard saw our radical freedom and contingency as a self constituted in that way by God. But Sartre can be seen as having borrowed Kierkegaard's self while rejecting Kierkegaard's God, and although this move changes the notion of self in important ways, there are important similarities (see note 24).

22. George Steiner, *Real Presences* (Chicago: University of Chicago Press, 1989).

23. Steiner, *Real Presences*, 56.

24. Kierkegaard calls the syndrome of megalomania and masochism *despair*. See *The Sickness Unto Death*, Part I, section B(b)(2), 200-207. Jean-Paul Sartre says, "The best way to conceive of the fundamental project of human reality is to say that man is the being whose project is to be God"; see *Being and Nothingness* (New York: Washington Square Press, 1966), 724, cf. 713-34. Sartre's feeling of revulsion in his consciousness of objective-factual existence and his feeling of shame in his consciousness of being objectivized by another free locus of consciousness are both ways of realizing that I am *not* God. Concerning revulsion see *Being and Nothingness*, 765-84 and *Nausea* (New York: New Directions, 1964). Concerning shame see *Being and Nothingness*, 340-406.

25. In this essay I have focused on heroic and existentialist falls into narcissism. Another important fall is the rise of modern science. It is arguable that all the *new* human evils in the twentieth century have arisen from either an exclusively scientific mind-set which reduces human beings to physical objects or from applications of new technologies devised by science. Yet it is also clear not only that science has brought many benefits but that the emergence of scientific (wo)man can be an advance in human evolution if integrated with earlier dimensions of our human nature.

REFLECTIONS ON RICOEUR'S
Soi-même comme un autre

Morny Joy
University of Calgary

Ricoeur's hermeneutic interventions are sustained by an optimism that generates energy in proportion to the difficulty of the task at hand. Ricoeur's latest enquiry into the problematic of identity in *Soi-même comme un autre*[1] dramatically illustrates this propensity. It is a daunting task, in which Ricoeur both refines and amplifies earlier positions, while confronting new questions. His time-honoured dialectical procedure provides the strategy for both conceptual and practical movements, as Ricoeur attempts to portray identity as the nexus of forces of continuity and creativity.

In this paper, I shall concentrate not on Ricoeur's encounter with analytic philosophy and his effort to establish the practical and ethical grounds of identity (which consists of one half of the book) but with the thematic of narrative which Ricoeur develops from his preliminary explorations in *Time and Narrative* to provide the basis of a poetics of identity. Within this topic I will focus particularly on the question of identity—a topic of debate in our present postmodern climate—and the way in which Ricoeur's work has stimulated my own thinking. Though my conclusions are somewhat provisional and eclectic, and are indicative of a work in progress, they mirror the diversity of inquiries Ricoeur's work animates, as, in my case, I examine the relevance of questions of personal identity from a woman's perspective.

In the concluding section of *Time and Narrative*, Vol. 3, Ricoeur ventured the model of *narrative identity* as a solution to the antinomies of self-depiction that he diagnosed in the contemporary philosophical repertoire.

> Without the recourse to narration, the problem of personal identity would in fact be condemned to an antinomy with no solution. Either we must posit a subject identical with itself through the diversity of its different states, or, following Hume and Nietzsche, we must hold that this identical subject is nothing more than a substantialist illusion whose elimination merely brings to light a pure manifold of cognitions, emotions and volitions.[2]

In this context, Ricoeur's model of *narrative identity* appeared as a mediation, resulting from the interrelation of fictional and historical modalities that succumbs neither to timeless ontological essences of self, nor to interminably displaced notions of the subject according to the strategy of deconstruction. It is a hermeneutically based hypothesis which concedes that, though all self-knowledge is interpretation, heuristic insights can be gleaned about one's identity by narrative formulations. This negotiated form of identity can be seen as a development of Ricoeur's earlier model of a hermeneutics of "I am" that was presented in two essays on the Cartesian *Cogito* and Heidegger's *Dasein* respectively, in a collection of essays, *The Conflict of Interpretations*.[3] In these works, Ricoeur criticized the apodeictic pretensions of the *Cogito*, and the hypostatization of difference, which resulted from a semiotic or structuralist frame of reference. In place of these reductions Ricoeur sought a more encompassing purview of existence as being-in-the-world. In this sense it can be argued that the problem of personal identity and its definition has been a continued preoccupation of Ricoeur. In time Ricoeur modified this Husserlian and Heideggerian orientation with regard to understanding and interpreting the human predicament. This was marked by the introduction of his own formulation of a hermeneutic phenomenology. Such a qualification led in turn to the articulation of a hermeneutics of "I am." At this time, in the late sixties and early seventies, such a postulate of identity provided an itinerary that was neither solipsistic nor relativistic, but appealed to the cultural formalities of symbolic structures. It was a creative acceptance of the vicissitudes of existence, which nonetheless provided grounds for a qualified form of self-definition.

In his more recent three volume work, *Time and Narrative*,[4] however, Ricoeur confronted the enigmas of time. These variations shattered any easy visions Ricoeur had of an adaptation of a self-definition, even of a hermeneutic variety, to a sequential time-scale. Such an accommodation would merely give a linear and homogeneous portrait of a self, one at odds with the aporias of time and the interfaces of present, past, and future that Ricoeur discovered in his scrutiny of temporal incongruities. Ricoeur later became aware, after he completed *Time and Narrative*, that the concept of *narrative identity* that he had presented therein was a somewhat simplistic postulate that needed further study.

And this he has endeavored to do in *Soi-même comme un autre*. For what is at issue here is the very nature of identity itself within a time-bound scenario.

The dilemma of locating identity in time, proposed by Ricoeur as *narrative identity*, brings into stark relief an ambiguity in the meaning of the term *identity*. On the one hand *identity* can mean *sameness* (Latin *idem*; German *gleich)* or, on the other, *self* (Latin *ipse*; German *selbst).*[5] There is much overlap in the common usage of these two terms, but it is the failure to distinguish between these two that has, on Ricoeur's account, led to many misunderstandings in contemporary discussions of the nature of identity. But this is not to say that such a clarification on the part of Ricoeur will lead to an immediate resolution of the problem, for it is not as simple as that. Ricoeur will argue that though these meanings are indeed discrete, and need to be so acknowledged, it is in fact their very interplay that constitutes the notion of "identity." And so it is this very affinity, yet separation of the two meanings, against the backdrop of a "timescape," i.e., the confluence in experience of present, past and future, that generates the dynamics that provide the construct of *narrative identity*.

To begin his explorations on the topic Ricoeur distinguishes four different senses of the term *idem* as sameness. These are:

Sense 1. *Numerical identity in the context of* (re-)identification, i.e. this is the same thing again (identified at a later time), not merely something qualitatively similar. The opposite of this is *plurality*.

Sense 2. *Extreme resemblance* in the sense that the one may be substituted for the other—e.g., two dresses. (Can be used as an indirect criterion for Sense 1, e.g. John Demjanyuk looks like Ivan the Terrible; therefore, he might actually *be* the man. The opposite of extreme resemblance is *difference*. Ressemblance might also be a criterion of numerical identity.

Sense 3. *Uninterrupted continuity in development.* Again, a criterion of numerical identity; however, in this case, the thing may have changed radically over time, e.g. an acorn to an oak. This is quite different from Sense 2. The opposite of continuity is *discontinuity*.

Sense 4. *Permanence over time* (or substance as immutable substrate). It differs from Sense 1 in that the *temporal* element is essential to sense 4. Its opposite is diversity.[6]

It is this latter instance of the idea of permanence in time that provides the exemplary situation for the confusion of *idem* as sameness with *ipse* as self. For it is precisely with regard to the issue of temporal continuity that the two meanings do in fact intersect. Yet, on Ricoeur's reading, they cannot be identified. Ricoeur carefully delineates the subtle difference between *idem* with its objective correlates of description and the existential dimension associated with *ipse*. *Idem* is a response to the question of What?, while *ipse* is a response to the question of Who?[7]

Though it is the dialectic interplay of these two terms that establishes the basis for the formation of any *narrative identity*, Ricoeur will qualify the modality of their interchanges by many subtle modifications. For, in relating this process, Ricoeur introduces an intricate system of checks and balances between the two terms *idem* and *ipse*: one where *idem* and *ipse* coincide and constitute the dimension of *character*; the other where *idem* and *ipse* are utterly separated and which distinguishes the existential nature of the *who* that tends to be subsumed by the *what* of *idem*. It is the process of overlap and separation of these two dimensions, specifically in relation to the idea of "permanence in time," along a spectrum of possibilities of positions, that crystallizes the issue of identity. This entire exploration by Ricoeur is, as can be expected, intricate, for it is the mark of his own idiosyncratic dialectical process to explore all conceivable variations in the interactions of the terms under examination, before arriving at his own mediations of a conciliatory nature. Yet it is in depicting these very combinations and permutations of permanence/change, and relating them to the various modes, that narrative seeks to convey the multifaceted construct of *narrative identity*. *Narrative identity* can then be seen as a form of negotiation between contrary inclinations in the movements of self-portrayal.

To be more precise, by the dimension of *character*, and the coincidence of *idem* and *ipse*, Ricoeur seeks to convey the inclination towards a uniform element of permanence in time. Character is thus composed of habits and identifications that are constantly engaged in that struggle between sedimentation and innovation which, for Ricoeur, is indicative of cultural growth. In this notion of character as acquired dispositions, however, the tendency toward sedimentation seems traditionally to overwhelm the innovative aspect. So character, as an amalgamation of dispositions, usually emphasizes sameness and aligns identity with impersonal facts that can be categorized. Here Ricoeur would say that *ipse* has been equated with *idem*, and identity is regarded merely as an accumulation of psychological or physical characteristics. Many of the debates in analytic philosophy are concerned with this particular dynamic to the exclusion of the existential situation and its reverberations.

It is with reference to the understanding of character that Ricoeur admits his own appreciation has undergone a change from his earlier descriptions in *The Voluntary and the Involuntary*.[8] There, Ricoeur had also placed much more weight on the view of character as an invariant, as the part of our finite make-up which we could not change, but to which we must consent. He also saw it as the sole constituent of identity. In *Fallible Man*,[9] published in the same period, Ricoeur expanded this limited status of character by measuring it against an infinite possibility of human flourishing. Against this ideal of infinite possibility, our finite condition is always deficient. Nevertheless, in these contexts, character definitely had the quality of an object, a given, for Ricoeur. In this instance, not just stability, but even resignation was required. Ricoeur acknowledges that today, rather than designating character in such an absolutist fashion, as the fixed and finite pole of human existence, he would describe it as one element within the problematic of a dynamics of identity.

As a result in this present work, character has become a moment in a dialectic transaction, where the emphasis has changed from stasis to that of a lived reality. The resultant graphic fluidity between states of permanence and change discourages any facile designation of character, in the manner of Ricoeur's earlier descriptions, as an abstract or atemporal category.

Yet, all these qualifications are, nonetheless, limited in effect. For though in *Soi-même comme un autre* Ricoeur acknowledges that change in time can have a disruptive influence on any perception of character as invariable, he still concedes today that the momentum of forces involved tends to favour the "changeless" component. So it is that even with his modifications regarding the volatility of time and the vagaries of existence, Ricoeur admits a tendency to want to categorize the coincidence of *idem* and *ipse* with regard to character by some form of transcendental or foundational entity. Mutability would thus be displaced by an immutable substrate, which abides when all else changes.

Ultimately Ricoeur remains somewhat evasive as to his own stance on this issue, but whatever status he grants to the dimension of character, it can no longer monopolize the notion of identity. For character, as the form of identity where *idem* and *ipse* concur, must enter into an exchange with the form of identity as self-constancy where *idem* and *ipse* are discontinuous. This disruption can be observed most tellingly in current novels where it could appear that the qualifications constituted by *idem* are no longer relevant. Many a contemporary protagonist describes him/herself as rootless, absent or a void, i.e., without any definite or positive attributes. But, as Ricoeur notes, to state that one is nothing, or one has no identifying marks as prescribed by *idem*, does not eliminate or deny the existential dimension of the person (*ipse*) making the assertion, no matter how sceptical the pronouncement.[10]

Ricoeur will also emphasize an affinity of this position of *ipse* with that of *Dasein* (Heidegger) in that it can interrogate itself about its specific modality of being. Here, he makes a comparison of *ipse* with *Selbstheit*, as one of the *existentialia* which designate the being of *Dasein* (along with others such as of being-in-the-world, care, etc.).[11] In this sense, a comparison of Ricoeur's distinction between *ipse* and *idem* can also be drawn with the Heideggerian dichotomy between *Dasein* and *Vorhanden/Zuhanden*. For Heidegger *Dasein* alone has the implication of being mine or more pointedly being a self, and thus has connotations of steadfastness (*ipse*), whereas *das Vorhanden/das Zuhanden*, in their capacity as objects, either given or manipulated, elicit implications of determinate criteria.[12]

It is this Heideggerian analogy that then permits Ricoeur to amend his earlier notions of a hermeneutics of existence or, as Ricoeur then called it, the hermeneutics of "I am." In the work under discussion Ricoeur further elaborates this basic Heideggerian model of hermeneutics so as to accommodate the more nuanced demands of a narrative orientation. The hermeneutics of "I am" refined by the intricate interplays of *idem* and *ipse* can now be indicated by the notion of *narrative identity*. For to what end has Ricoeur engaged in these convolutions of *idem* and *ipse*, if not to bring to our attention the fact that identity, as portrayed by narrative, is the one form that can incorporate at once the discrepancies and fluctuations as well as the stagnations and fixations that distinguish our temporal situation. To be in time is to be subject to the disjunctions of time. To tell our stories is to try to extract a form of coherence from this manifold. The urge to impose a pattern thus works both at odds and in tandem with the creative impulse to depict this predicament in ever new ways. This propensity to innovation at the instigation of imagination has been a preoccupation of Ricoeur's work since *The Rule of Metaphor*,[13] where metaphor was the agency of creative change. As always, imaginative divergences challenge structural and theoretical restraints. It is Ricoeur's own vision of imagination and its kaleidoscopic spectrum of possibilities that has sustained all his investigations.

In this instance, he focuses on the possible variations one can ring from the theme of identity within narrative. In the case of *narrative identity*, the imaginative variations converge around the notion of plot (*mythos*). Plot, like metaphor, can contain the disparate and discordant components of existence that defy the laws of contradiction. Life, of itself, is not always harmonious. Dissimilar if not dissonant emotions punctuate our lives. Ricoeur postulates that a person's life, and thus the interpreted self, is, as it were, a distillation of all the works of art, literature and culture that a person has read and experienced. Any self, any form of subjectivity, is thus an act of transmuting experience into meaningful patterns by means of an imaginative dialogue with the received "plotted" possibilities that circumscribe our world. But Ricoeur does not leave this self in a rarefied theoretical vacuum. Theory is always in conversation with the concrete conditions of life. In his own conflation of Aristotelian terms, *poiesis* merges with *praxis* as *poiesis* reflects, yet refines, the disparate moments of existence. In their turn, plots serve as paradigms for the incorporation of the values and ideals that we seek to implement in our lives. This process is not without its critical phase of suspicion, so there is never a simplistic adoption of traditional formulas.[14] In addition, for Ricoeur, this creative procedure is always grounded in our life-world and the built-in critique is thoroughly grounded in the circumstances that impress our lives and that, in turn, we seek to understand and even transform. The *poiesis/praxis* is located in "the place where meaning grows."[15] So it is that Ricoeur can relate and expand this pattern in the context of *Soi-même comme un autre*:

> In the application of literature to life what we transfer and transpose in the exegesis of ourselves is the dialectic of *ipse* and *idem*. In it resides the purgative virtue of thought experiments carried out by literature, not only on the plane of theoretical reflection, but on that of existence.[16]

But the crucial question for me concerns the actual viability of this composite of the *narrative self*, born of the dialectic of *ipse* and *idem*. In what way is it an answer to the deflated pretensions of an essentialist or egocentric self, on one hand, or alternately, the aberrations of the decentered postmodern subject? My ruminations on this subject have been greatly aided by movements in contemporary feminist thought, in this particular instance by the work of Jane Flax, in her book *Thinking Fragments: Psychoanalysis, Feminism and Postmodernism in the Contemporary West*.[17]

Flax's work mirrors the growing unease that many feminists have with the postmodern rejection of subjectivity and its concomitant dismissal of any notion of agency. Insofar as women are just beginning to come into their own in terms of self-definition, the wholesale abandonment by significant male scholars of the concept of self-determination could be construed as just one more stratagem, under the subterfuge of scholarship, to deprive women of any voice in their own narratives.

But, on closer examination, the rejection may not be as resounding as it is often described. The work of such postmodern luminaries as Foucault and Derrida does not advocate an irrevocable eradication of subjectivity or reference, as has been inferred by some of their more fervid admirers. A sensitive reading of their work reveals that what they wish to dislodge is any assumption of im-med-iate access to a self that is authorial and has pretensions to an atemporal closure. As evidence of this, in an interview with Richard Kearney, Derrida states:

> The other, which is beyond language and which summons language, is perhaps not a "referent" in the normal sense which linguists have attached to this term. But to distance oneself thus from the habitual structure of reference, to challenge or complicate our common assumptions about it, does not amount to saying that there is *nothing* beyond language.[18]

This is the Derrida that constantly interrogates false or assumed dogmatic positions. Such an interpretation of Derrida is eloquently presented by John Caputo in his book, *Radical Hermeneutics*.[19] Here Derrida is portrayed as akin to Meister Eckhart, Kierkegaard and other tricksters who have repudiated received dogmas because for them the ultimate truth or mystery will always evade conceptual encapsulation.

In a vein comparable to Derrida, Foucault describes his position regarding subjectivity:

> I have not denied—far from it—the possibility of changing discourse: I have deprived the sovereignty of the subject of the exclusive and instantaneous right to it.[20]

This is not the Nietzschean Foucault as found in the work of Gilles Deleuze, but more the "ecstatic thinker" who continually challenges us beyond our present confinements. Like Caputo who aligns Derrida with forces that continually call into question assumed or imposed constructs, James Bernauer, in his book *Michel Foucault's Force of Flight* shows that Foucault's final aesthetic of existence wishes to emphasize the need for eccentric imaginative variations in all our constructs of thought and life, including those of narrative.[21] For Foucault, these imaginative formations have too long been relegated to aesthetics and regarded as an inferior form of knowledge. Foucault wishes to reclaim such aesthetic practices as part of a hermeneutic of the self. Thus, Foucault's final volumes concerning the *practices of the self* as he calls them, do provide grounds for a fruitful future comparison with Ricoeur's hermeneutic narrative of identity.

Such questioning, if not thoroughgoing distrust of all objective presumptions, does not utterly abolish a possible recuperation of a chastened format of subjectivity. Such a revised subjectivity can indeed feature as an agent or medium for change of outmoded and oppressive structures. Indeed, inherent in the work of both Foucault and Derrida is an unthematized notion of subjectivity that operates along these lines. As Flax observes:

> For, though they denounce any essentialist or universalist notion of human nature, their work also incorporates a profoundly romantic/aesthetic dimension.[22]

This aesthetic aspect of subjectivity functions as a participant in a movement by which it both constructs yet suspects itself at the same time. Thus, though both Derrida and Foucault consciously advocate the construction of a playing field where the game of identity is deployed in a fast and loose fashion, what can be observed in this game is that there is, nonetheless, a sense of continuity involved that in fact cultivates and is cultivated by the game itself.

Flax's own observation on the type of subjectivity employed here reflects her work as a psychotherapist which she conducts concomitantly with her academic research as a political scientist. Flax comments:

> Those who celebrate or call for a "decentered" self seem self-deceptively naive and unaware of the basic cohesion within themselves that makes the fragmentation of experiences something other than a terrifying slide into psychosis.[23]

Flax's work with psychotic patients, whose every effort is to try to establish some tenuous toehold on a configuration of self, illuminates the gratuitously assumed self-cohesion on the part of postmodernists who can so cavalierly dispense with all configurations of the self. Flax discerns in this apparent inconsistency a failure to distinguish between two different understandings of self or identity:

> Postmodernists seem to confuse two different and logically distinct concepts of the self: a "unitary" and a "core" one. All possible forms of self are confounded with the unitary, mentalist, deeroticized, masterful and positional selves they rightfully criticize.[24]

It is this core sense of self (as distinct from the duly criticized unitary one), Flax is trying to recuperate in her work with psychotics and feels is particularly pertinent for contemporary feminists who are trying to delineate an appropriate sense of identity. And this is where I believe Ricoeur's and Flax's diagnoses of the situation have marked affinities which are in need of greater exploration. For Flax's *unitary* sense of self approximates in some measure Ricoeur's description of *idem*, while the *core* sense parallels the notion of *ipse*. It is in their therapeutics, however, that the emphasis varies. It is not possible to pursue this aspect further with reference to Flax's work in this context, but it is a topic that merits detailed comparison. Suffice it to say that Ricoeur posits that a constructive view of the self can be fashioned from the productive exchanges of *idem* and *ipse*. In contrast Flax obviously grounds her observations in the painstaking work of personal therapy.

However this is not to say that Ricoeur's discussion here must be regarded as merely abstract and irrelevant theorizing, removed from the process of actual existence and its therapeutic interventions. The narrative process, as outlined above, entails a continuous movement from theory to praxis, so that the *narrative self* is firmly grounded in lived experience. For Ricoeur, it is this practical and pragmatic exercise that prevents the *narrative self* from being absorbed into the interminable dislocations that mark the postmodern position. From this perspective, the conflation of *idem* and *ipse* can be understood as the indicator of the unitary temptation to use objective data as the sole indicator of permanence that will always haunt our projects of self-delineation. This urge is constantly in need of disruption, so that the differentiation between *idem* and *ipse,* necessary for the emergence of an existential appreciation of identity in time, may occur. To achieve this separation, so as to arrive at an awareness of the two disparate understandings of identity, even deconstructive tactics (as employed by Caputo's and Bernauer's readings of Derrida and Foucault respectively) could be employed effectively and thus be incorporated into the moment of critique. For it could be said that it is this very distinction in identity between *idem* and *ipse* that both Foucault and Derrida wish to effect.

In Ricoeur's model, however, this disruption is supplied not by deconstructive pyrotechnics but by the disjunction of *ipse* and *idem* that questions any easy congruence of theory and life-world. Yet, at the same time, and I believe this is the core of Ricoeur's insight, this incompatibility is witness to a type of existential disposition that persists in change and that is not to be confused with objective components or universals. Ricoeur's appeal to a sense of self that issues in and through the narrative mode can thus be understood as holding in tension the divergent elements that at once encourage and discourage the formation of any ideal self. In this sense, Ricoeur's work can be appreciated as a measured response to the critique posed by the work of Derrida and Foucault, as it avoids the pitfalls they all-too-tellingly detect in traditional assumptions of identity.

Yet these components of changeless uniformity and irreparable dissemination at work in the formation of *narrative identity* need not be tabled under the headings of modernity versus postmodernity, where they appear as two diametrically opposed options. I believe that they constitute instead the paradox of any consciously lived existence and the always inadequate attempts to depict such vicissitudes in words. Ricoeur has provided a vital portrait of this ongoing adventure in a way that does justice to these complexities, without leaving us stranded with hypothetical intangibles that bear no relation to the aspirations or limitations of our lives.

Narrative identity can be understood as a more realistic endeavor to reflect the actualities of existence and to build a base from which concrete responses to contemporary political and social challenges can be organized. This *poietic* resolution to the problematic of identity is thus intimately connected to a practical and critical commitment to change, not just with regard to one's perception of oneself, but with regard to that of the world. There is no implication that this undertaking is an easy one, for it is fraught with the dissonance/consonance variables of time, place and other contingencies that delimit the realization of our ownmost possibilities.

In establishing *narrative identity* as a hermeneutic exercise, Ricoeur has provided the grounds for further critical evaluation and appreciation of the narratives (both fictional and historical) by which women in particular are today trying to give voice to the dilemmas of their existence and the formation of a self that does not necessarily mirror the male model. In this work, women are being both creative and critical in that they are contesting received versions of plot, character and theme, i.e., the meta-narratives of the past which have all-too-often prescribed their roles for them. This development is beset by the temptation to reject the inherited tradition as irrevocably flawed and compromised. But, as Ricoeur and, in a more qualified fashion, Flax, have shown, we do not live in an abstract vacuum. Nor can we presume to create identity *ex nihilo*. Postulates of identity reflect an ongoing interrogation with the theoretical and practical conditions that demarcate our lives.

Unfortunately, the resolution of this predicament has habitually been posed in mutually exclusive options. It is in this regard that our Western heritage seems inclined to encourage such polarization by its allegiance to oppositional formulas that reach definitions by means of separation or exclusion. Such differentiation does not automatically lead to the appreciation of difference. In this sense, deconstruction can be read as an attempt to break down this dichotomous mindset by trying to allow difference, if not the differentiating process itself, to be thought. Ricoeur does not adopt this counter-strategy, particularly in its subversive excesses, but introduces another prospect. The dialectic, or rather dialogical, model that Ricoeur promotes allows for a constant interaction of different terms, of participants, in all their modulations of heterogeneity. These exchanges of discrepant views occur in a social context where life is never held hostage to theory. It is thus that Ricoeur's own dialectic and its mediating function provides a practical grounding that wholesale abandonment to deconstructive devices preclude. As a result of Ricoeur's interventions, there is a dynamic process introduced, where a range of variability, both theoretical and practical, is taken into consideration. In such a setting, feminist as well as other contemporary discussions of identity need not remain fixated in an antithetical posturing but must explore the innovative insights that an open-ended conversation in a pluralist mode encourages. For making such a discussion available and for indicating a route beyond a seeming impasse, I am indebted to the work of Paul Ricoeur.

NOTES

1.   P. Ricoeur, *Oneself as Another*, trans. K. Blamey (Chicago: University of Chicago Press, 1992).

2.   P. Ricoeur, *Time and Narrative*, Vol. 3, trans. K. Blamey and D. Pellauer (Chicago: University of Chicago Press, 1988), 246.

3.   P. Ricoeur, "Heidegger and the Question of the Subject," in *The Conflict of Interpretations: Essays in Hermeneutics,* ed. D. Ihde (Evanston: Northwestern University Press, 1974), 223-35; "The Question of the Subject: The Challenge of Semiology," in *Conflict*, 236–66.

4.   P. Ricoeur, *Time and Narrative*, 3 vols. (Chicago: University of Chicago Press, 1984–88).

5.   P. Ricoeur, "Narrative Identity," *Philosophy Today* 35 (1991), 73.

6.   "Narrative Identity," 74.

7.   "Narrative Identity," 75.

8.   P. Ricoeur, *Freedom and Nature: The Voluntary and the Involuntary*, trans. E. V. Kohák (Evanston: Northwestern University Press, 1966).

9.   P. Ricoeur, *Fallible Man*, trans. C. A. Kelbley (New York: Fordham University Press, 1965; reprint, 1988).

10.   *Fallible Man*, 78.

11.   P. Ricoeur, *Oneself as Another*, 149.

12.   P. Ricoeur, "Narrative Identity," 75.

13.   P. Ricoeur, *The Rule of Metaphor*, trans. R. Czerny, K. McLaughlin et al. (Toronto: University of Toronto Press, 1977).

14. For a basic idea of Ricoeur's notion of suspicion see *Freud and Philosophy: An Essay on Interpretation*, trans. D. Savage (New Haven: Yale University Press, 1970), 3–36.

15. P. Ricoeur, *The Rule of Metaphor*, 308–9.

16. P. Ricoeur, "Narrative Identity," 79.

17. J. Flax, *Thinking Fragments: Psychoanalysis, Feminism and Postmodernism in the Contemporary West* (Berkeley: University of California Press, 1990).

18. R. Kearney, "Derrida," in *Dialogues with Contemporary Continental Thinkers* (Manchester: Manchester University Press, 1987), 123–4.

19. J. Caputo, *Radical Hermeneutics* (Bloomington: Indiana University Press, 1987).

20. M. Foucault, *The Archaeology of Knowledge* (New York: Pantheon Books, 1972), 209.

21. J. Bernauer, *Michel Foucault's Force of Flight* (Atlantic Highlands, N.J.: Humanities Press, 1990).

22. J. Flax, *Thinking Fragments*, 216.

23. *Thinking Fragments*, 218–19.

24. *Thinking Fragments*, 218.

EMMANUEL LÉVINAS
AND THE IRONY OF A/THEISM

Richard Cooper
Montreal

The title of this paper owes a double vote of thanks, if not of apologies, to J. C. McLelland and Mark Taylor: to the former for the subtitle of his book *Prometheus Rebound* and to the latter for the peculiar spelling of a/theism which is analogous to his spelling of a/theology.[1] Throughout my discussion I distinguish "atheism" in the ordinary, if not unproblematic sense from a/theism with a slash as indicative of any particular theism (a theism). That there is a homonymous play on the words is a way of eliciting synoptically and diacritically a paradox that hovers over the thought of Emmanuel Lévinas, as it does over a great deal of modern and postmodern theological and religious thinking. But when the doubleness that makes possible the paradox is seen, then there is the possibility of irony.

If any particular theism by the very nature of its inscription into a system of categories consequently limits that which it attempts to articulate, then, inherently, it opens itself to the possibility of atheism, of a positive denial of the theological coherence of its project. That which is by definition transcendent—that which absolutely surpasses yet founds the categories of its articulation—is not subject to any analytic or constitutive schematism. And this means equally that it can neither be affirmed nor denied within the modalities of pure reason, or metaphysical logos. Such is the substance of Kant's critique of metaphysical reason and the classical proofs of theism. The attempt to argue the ontological necessity of God, or the gods, is equally and justly balanced by the counterargument against any such necessity. Rational theism is *ab ovo* complicitous with rational atheism. The problem appears to be that no matter what the degree of universalization, theism *qua* theism is *a* theism, just as atheism is the denial of any and every theism. That which is transcendent is translated into the logical, articulatable, thematizable categories of the non-transcendent. And it matters little whether this translation leaves a remainder, as in the case of the play of the transcendent and the immanent, for any remainder might just as well not be at all, except insofar as it serves a sleight-of-mind or the silence-riddled language of mystagogy.

In brief, then, the logical complicity of any theism and atheism underscores the crisis of Reason that is one of the distinctive traits of modernity. Thence follows a reaction in the form of a series of divorces between God and the world, eternity and time, infinity and finitude, reason and will, the self and the other, the *res cogitans* and the *res extensa*. The list of dualisms could be considerably extended. But the crisis of Reason, because it is thus structured in terms of binaries, also gives rise to the impetus towards the overcoming of binaries, towards unification and unity. In the history of modern philosophy there seems to be a pattern of stand-offs between various forms of dualism and monism, between, as it were, Descartes and Spinoza, Kant and Schelling. And this pattern, moreover, engenders almost automatically, and even within the thinkers just mentioned, a hyperawareness of limits and the seductive call for mediation. That this seemingly endless repetition of the problem of the One and the Many manifests itself in the metaphors of opposition, conflict, strategy, and debate and in the countervailing metaphors of reconciliation, negotiation, dialogue, and mediation is indicative of what we might call in a Freudian way the return of the philosophical repressed. Just how one is to characterize this "repressed" is a subject that needs constantly to be raised within philosophic discourse itself, for it is by no means apparent just what "it" is that is being repressed.[2] In my view, much of Lévinas's thought is concerned with this question of the repressed of Western philosophy, and this paper is an attempt to explore some of the implications of his questioning.

The repressed can never, of course, be elicited directly, but only through metaphors, images, gestures, and linguistic patterns, and then perhaps only partially and tentatively, for the symptoms can conceal as much as they reveal. The most general pattern that runs throughout Lévinas's thinking is the pattern of juxtaposition and opposition.

One of the fascinating things about the titles of many books that belong to or come out of the phenomenological tradition in twentieth-century philosophy is their use of the conjunction "and." This conjunction encapsulates the pattern of juxtaposition and opposition, whether it be, for example, in *Being and Time*,

Being and Nothingness, or *Totality and Infinity*. For purposes of this discussion, I am concentrating on Lévinas's major work, *Totalité et Infini* (1961). In many ways, *Totality and Infinity* brings to a crisis the phenomenological and post-phenomenological project of a double vision which works through juxtaposition and opposition to an alternative way of thinking that plays over, against, and with the natural attitude. If in so doing it returns to an empiricism, as Lévinas suggests and Derrida explicates,[3] this empiricism is a radical, non-positivistic, and pluralist empiricism, a philosophy of experience that is won through the critique of philosophies of metaphysical totality, but also by means of the presuppositions, methodologies, and discourses of those philosophies—particularly, in the case of *Totality and Infinity*, of transcendental phenomenology (Husserl) and fundamental ontology (the earlier Heidegger). But these are matters of anticipation, just as is the question, which Derrida emphasizes, of the degree of the complicity of Lévinas's critique with the philosophies which it criticizes.

What is of immediate concern is the situation of a serious, philosophical irony that emerges out of the juxtaposition and opposition of philosophies of totality, that is, systematic philosophies in the strong sense, on the one hand, and philosophies of experience, on the other. The "and" both divides and conjoins, and the degree of division or conjunction is presupposed by the horizon of the future which each kind of philosophy projects—the "future perfect," the seemingly paradoxical yet grammatically constantly invoked structure of a future memory. The degree to which any system can totalize is thus always already deferred. What Lévinas does is to project this movement of deferral, which Derrida will later call *différance*, beyond phenomenological temporalization onto the constantly receding horizon of the Infinite, an Infinite which for Lévinas must be positively apprehended in order to avoid the regression of "bad infinity." Hence an Infinite which can usefully be thought of, with the necessary precautions of analogy, in anthropomorphic images. When any philosophy of totality seeks to close off the horizon of infinity, it paradoxically relativizes itself; yet without this closure it cannot be a philosophy of totality.

If this debate seems redolent of Kierkegaard's strictures on the Hegelian System, it is perhaps because it is a repetition of a recurrent pattern in philosophical thinking rather than primarily a matter of influences. The pattern is similar to that which Harold Bloom has described in the history of poetry as the "anxiety of influence," that is, the way in which self-consciously "original" poets subject their powerful precursors to strong *misreadings* in order to ensure the distinctiveness of their own voices.[4] What is repressed in such strong misreading is the actual repetition of the past, and this gives rise to the anxiety that accompanies the repression, indeed constitutes it—the anxiety that the past will be merely repeated. This pattern is structurally analogous to Lévinas's descriptions of desire and need. True desire is always unfulfilled, for it is desire for the Infinite; desires which are fulfilled, which aim at a *telos*, are properly speaking not desires at all, but needs. Any philosophical desire that aims short of infinity can be fulfilled in a totalizing system and fills a need which may not in itself be philosophical. A philosophical need can thus be the final hypostatization of the self, of the state, of art, or of philosophy itself. Nonetheless, what a philosophical need has repressed in aiming at fulfilment is the unending movement of thinking as such. Only the *unendlich* as the matter of the process of thinking and speaking, which for Lévinas are the same, can be projected as the horizon of real philosophic thought precisely because it cannot be subsumed under any concept, object, or category and still retain what is essential to its meaning.

Thus there is always in the history of philosophy a juxtaposition and conjunction between philosophies of totality and philosophies of infinity. And where there is juxtaposition and conjunction, there is conflict. Moreover, when philosophies of totality dominate there is exclusion of philosophies of infinity. Indeed, they are most often relegated to the nebulous realm of non-philosophy or, more precisely, to the status of being extra-metaphysical. Besides this, the internal conflict of philosophies of totality results not only in the irony of their relativization, as has already been mentioned, but also in the paradigmatic situation of the struggle for domination, which is the state of war. As Lévinas asks in the Preface to *Totality and Infinity*: "Does not lucidity, the mind's openness upon the true, consist in catching sight of the permanent possibility of war?" And, further, he states: "The visage [*face*] of being that shows itself in war is fixed in the concept of totality, which dominates Western philosophy."[5]

War is the metaphor that concretizes the pattern of juxtaposition and conjunction under the dialectical aspect of both conflict and reconciliation. Against the "ontology of war" Lévinas poses the "eschatology of messianic peace" (22/6). The latter is, for Lévinas, the only justification for morality just because it belongs to an unrealized but anamnetic or symbolically enacted future. In order to break the pattern of juxtaposition and conjunction, and hence the ontology of war, Lévinas proposes an irreconcilable pattern of radical disjunction, a pattern of radical alterity. Alterity encompasses both the neutral other (*l'autre*) and the personal other (*autrui*), though the latter is privileged because the only access that human beings have to a *positively* meaningful infinity is in the absolute nudity of the face of another person. The highest disjunction, that which makes possible and radicalizes every other alterity, is the absolute difference between all that is (the totality of beings *qua* being) and the

Infinite. Since the term "difference" itself poses problems, as in Heidegger's "ontological difference" (the difference between Being and beings), it is necessary to emphasize that the difference between totality and the Infinite is *absolute* in the peculiar sense that Lévinas attributes to the word as meaning "absolved from all relation."

At this point the objection could be raised that if the Infinite is as radically separated from Being as Lévinas maintains it is, then how could there be any thought or experience of the Infinite at all? Lévinas's way out of this quandary is to appeal to Descartes' idea of infinity as the one idea that we as thinking substances could not conceive of for ourselves. It must be given from without, from the realm of absolute exteriority. Whether this solution is convincing is not a question which I wish to pursue at present. Rather, I wish to join, as Lévinas does, the idea of infinity, which in itself is *not* a manipulatable concept, to the experience of the face-to-face encounter with another person and to speech.

It is not Lévinas's task to destroy metaphysics, but rather to displace ontology from the centre of metaphysics and to replace it with ethics. Indeed, Lévinas defines metaphysics as ethics:

> Metaphysics, transcendence, the welcoming of the other [*l'Autre*] by the same, of the Other [*Autrui*] by me, is concretely produced as the calling into question of the same by the other [*l'Autre*], that is, as the ethics that accomplishes the critical essence of knowledge. And as critique precedes dogmatism, metaphysics precedes ontology. (43/33)

Ethics, as the enactment of critique, is then, to use the traditional term, first philosophy.

The metaphysical notion par excellence is not the idea of the same, of identity, of "I=I," which, according to Lévinas, is the foundation of ontology. Instead, it is the idea of the other, and pre-eminently of the other as infinitely other, of the Other as Infinite. The recognition of this absolute, transcendent separation of the same and the other, of an other that is other without (exterior to) the sameness of the same ought to result in a deference and deferral of the same *vis-à-vis* the other. In terms of the idea of infinity, the other points to Plato's mysterious Good that is "beyond being" (*epekeina tēs ousias*); in terms of the human experience of the infinite in concrete relationships of thought and action, the Other is encountered *indirectly* through the scriptures, myths, and traditions of religion as God, and *directly* as every other person who elicits one's attention and affords the possibility of a speech situation, that is, potentially every other person. These latter human experiences are personal and interpersonal; they point out of and away from the self in its identical sameness. They also point to the infinite uniqueness of each person and hence not only to the respect but to the service that is due to each person, and to personhood taken to its infinite power, which is God. The idea of the Good, on the other hand, functions chiefly as an indicator (a mark or "trace") that disallows the identification of any particular good with the Good, just as the idea of infinity prohibits the identification of any finite entity with the Infinite. The latter identification, of course, is exactly the one that Lévinas thinks philosophies of totality make.

The idea of the Good must always serve as a check on any finite experience one has or may think that one has of God. On the other hand, human experiences of God, as well as of other people, if they are met with humility in the face of the Infinite, can be revelatory of the direction of the movement towards the Good. The idea of infinity, as Descartes knew, breeds humility—or, to give this difficult word more content, the wonder in which Aristotle, ironically the great totalizer, saw philosophy beginning. Humility is my word. Lévinas himself better describes the relationship between God and human beings and among human beings as one of extreme dissymmetry: the Other is always "higher" than I; the Other is indeed the Most High. The supreme ethical duty is to welcome with hospitality and generosity the stranger, the widow, and the orphan, for in so doing one is welcoming God. Or, if I may put it this way, the supreme ethical duty is the "preferential option for the poor," provided we do not call them poor and do not keep them that way.

The point of this somewhat facetious, if actually quite serious remark is to stress that in Lévinas's view ethics is intrinsically and at once both personal and social. The social aspect of his thinking comes out in his concern with justice, around which clusters a whole series of images and allusions drawn from the Hebrew Scriptures and the Talmud. Lévinas's great criticism of Heidegger's fundamental ontology is that it "affirms the primacy of freedom over ethics" (45/36). Thus one might say that already in *Sein und Zeit* Heidegger's thinking is implicitly aesthetic in the way that much modern philosophy often carries a repressed aesthetic bias or inspiration. Like Plato, Lévinas is a great enemy of art and rhetoric, and like Plato, too, he is a very accomplished writer of persuasive prose. But that is only one of several ironies under review here.

To return to the question of justice, it must be acknowledged that for Lévinas justice is primarily a matter of the interpretation and application of the Law (Torah and by extension all positive law). What keeps this from being a legal totalism or positivism is, first, that it is a law under the aegis of the Infinite, thus there can in good faith be no dogmatism on any point of the Law, for the spirit of dogmatism contradicts the infinite inspiration of the Good, of the choice of life that is obedience to the Law. Secondly, the tradition of interpretation and commentary ensures that any tendency towards ossification of the Law in practice is subjected to critique. One might even say that critical philosophy originates with the rabbis.

More important than questions of legalism, however, is the possibility provided by the Law of giving an account of oneself and of one's thought and actions. In French, Lévinas calls this possibility *une apologie*, which his translator Lingis somewhat inadequately renders into English as "an apology." I prefer to call it an *apologia* or defence. The situation of judgement obviously involves an asymmetrical relationship between the judge who sits on high and the defendant who stands below. Yet the occasion offered to the defendant to speak for himself, to give an account of his actions, brings the judge under judgement, under the necessity of accounting for his judgement, on the one hand, and under the infinite judgement that the Law embodies, if only partially, on the other.

The situation of justice, of judgement based on the Law but open to accountability and the possibility of defence, may thus serve as a paradigmatic instance of the relationships to the Other and to others. It also illustrates the way in which Lévinas thinks of the speech situation.

The primordial locus of the ethical relation is the encounter in which speech becomes possible. As in the case of judgement, this is an asymmetrical relationship that is founded on the absolute alterity of speaker and listener as interlocutor. It is primarily and *a fortiori* the direct act of speaking in the face-to-face encounter with the other; other forms of discourse are derivative. The dominant image that Lévinas uses for the speech situation is the relationship of teaching—of being taught by the Other (51/43). Instruction, rather than dialogue or debate, is the paradigmatic relation of speech. The dissymmetry between the teacher and the person being instructed ensures, according to Lévinas, a relationship of respect between persons, however different, opposed, and alien their beliefs or ways of life may be. Lévinas's main criticism of Buber's I-Thou relation is that it is a formalism that does not determine any concrete structure; it does not enable us to account for any kind of life other than friendship: "it can unite man to things as much as man to man" (68-69/64-65). However much one might wish to question this reading of Buber, one understands Lévinas's point about the respect that arises from the condition of separation. Speech is the "interpellation" (69/65) to the Other; it is the being present and making present of the actual—the "actualization of the actual," which is "expression." But it is not chiefly an expression of the self or the same, but an expression of the process of clarification of actuality, of ideas and facts. "Speech . . . is essentially magisterial" (69/65). Thus the teacher is he who has mastered speech, but only through the service of speech as a *presentation* of actuality to a welcomed interlocutor. "The master, the coinciding of the teaching and the teacher, is not in turn a fact among others. The present of the manifestation of the master who teaches overcomes the anarchy of facts" (69-70/66).

We have surveyed briefly three of the main images—images which give rise to metaphors—in *Totality and Infinity*. They are war, justice, and teaching. Each is structured by a pattern of radical separation in order to foreclose the option of mediation which could transform each into the possible basis of a totalistic philosophy. There is a fourth cluster of images and metaphors, those drawn from erotic and familial relationships, which are structured in the same way. These, however, I wish to defer to the end of my discussion in order to return at present to the subject with which I began: the irony of a/theism.

Though in dealing with Lévinas's thought, one ought always to be suspicious of the Odyssean theme of return, let us look at atheism through a kind of Kierkegaardian repetition. In terms of religion, Lévinas's thought denies the possibility of any participation by the finite in the Infinite. He says, "For the relation between the being here below and the transcendent being that results in no community of concept or totality—a relation without relation—we reserve the term religion. . . . Religion, where relationship subsists between the same and the other [*l'Autre*] despite the impossibility of the Whole—the idea of Infinity—is the ultimate structure" (80/78-79). And later he remarks: "Society with God is not an addition to God nor a disappearance of the interval that separates God from the creature. By contrast with totalization we have called it religion" (104/107).

What is interesting, if not particularly original, in Lévinas's thought is the way in which atheism is construed in nearly the same terms as religion. For example:

> One can call atheism this separation so complete that the separated being maintains itself in existence all by itself, without participating in the Being from which it is separated—eventually capable of adhering to it by belief. The break with participation is implied in this capability. One lives outside of God, at home with oneself; one is an I, an egoism. The soul, the dimension of the psychic, being an accomplishment of separation, is naturally atheist. By atheism we thus understand a position prior to both the negation and the affirmation of the divine, the breaking with participation by which the I posits itself as the same and as I. (58/52)

Lévinas immediately proceeds to designate by the term "will" this "being capable of atheism, a being which, without having been *causa sui*, has an independent view and word and is at home with itself" (58-59/52). Among the

book to have been written by a woman unique in the history of metaphysical writing?"[6] One might charitably suspect Derrida of a certain irony here, for he goes on to raise the question of whether it might be the case that "metaphysical desire is essentially virile." It is nonetheless true that Lévinas dissociates the "feminine" from the "feminine sex" and hence reduces woman even in her alterity to an aspect of the masculine (158/169). The results of this reduction come out in particular near the end of *Totality and Infinity* (278-80/310-13) in Lévinas's discussion of paternity, filiality and fraternity, in which the relation of maternity oddly appears to be almost incidental. The particularity of being a woman, the radical Other of a man, is subsumed stereotypically within the phenomenology of the body which is both "above" and "below" speech.

Instead, however, of engaging in a diatribe against Lévinas's sexism and heterosexism, I should like to underline a couple of ironic implications of his discourse on sexuality. One of the main strands in feminist thought is the advocacy of an alterity as radical as that found in Lévinas. It might even be seen as the inverted contrary of Lévinas's opposition of the masculine and feminine but without the theme of erotic fecundity on which Lévinas focuses his discussion. This development within feminism could thus be seen as an instantiation of the war between the sexes which Lévinas attempts, perhaps too proleptically, to obviate through shifting the description away from the metaphysical nudity of the face and onto the nudity of the body. The result is precisely the abjection and subjection of the physical in the face of the metaphysical. But this is the recourse of the whole pattern of Lévinas's thought. It ensures, however, an area opaque to the ethical just where one would like to invoke the ethical relation most strongly.

On the other hand, there has recently been a trend in feminist thought and philosophies of sexuality and gender that endeavours to establish a double vision that encompasses synoptically yet diacritically both the same and the other (the *homo* and the *hetero*) in the full validity of their separation and opposition. These views have been advanced to mitigate without mediating the intense contemporary debate between essentialism and constructivism.[7] There is thus the on-going possibility arising from the power-laden dissymmetries between binary opposites for resistance and a shift in valorization. But there is also the possibility for a separate respect beyond suspicion and beyond the alienation that evades discourse as the interpellation of the radically other by the same and of the identically same by the other. Across the profoundly bodily abyss of persons a voice speaks and is silent.

NOTES

1.   See Joseph C. McLelland, *Prometheus Rebound: The Irony of Atheism*, Editions SR 10 (Waterloo, ON: Wilfrid Laurier University Press, 1988); Mark C. Taylor, *Erring: A Postmodern A/theology* (Chicago: University of Chicago Press, 1984) and *Altarity* (Chicago: University of Chicago Press, 1987). I owe in more ways than could be readily specified a special debt of gratitude to Professor McLelland. Thanks also go to the students of the McGill University Department of Philosophy who participated with me in a Lévinas discussion group during the 1991 Winter Term: Alexandra Diebel, Aden Evens, Jeremy Grundy, and David Stevenson.

2.   Derrida's critical conclusion in his major essay on Lévinas ("Violence and Metaphysics") that it is violence that is at the very opening of speech and hence of metaphysics seems to me just one explication of the repressed, though a very important one. It is interesting that Lévinas has recently stated that "I always say that justice is the primary violence" (Raoul Mortley, *French Philosophers in Conversation* [London and New York: Routledge, 1991], 18).

3.   Jacques Derrida, "Violence and Metaphysics: An Essay on the Thought of Emmanuel Lévinas," in *Writing and Difference*, trans. Alan Bass (Chicago: University of Chicago Press, 1978), 79-153.

4.   See Harold Bloom, *The Anxiety of Influence: A Theory of Poetry* (New York: Oxford University Press, 1973) and *A Map of Misreading* (New York: Oxford University Press, 1975).

5.   Emmanuel Lévinas, *Totality and Infinity: An Essay on Exteriority*, trans. Alphonso Lingis (Pittsburgh: Duquesne University Press, 1969), 21; *Totalité et Infini: Essai sur l'extériorité* (Paris: Livre de Poche, 1990; orig. pub. The Hague: Martinus Nijhoff, 1961), 5-6. Subsequent references are within the text; the first page numbers refer to the translation, those after the slash to the French text.

6.   Derrida, 321, n. 92.

7.   Cf. Jonathan Dollimore, *Sexual Dissidence: Augustine to Wilde, Freud to Foucault* (Oxford: Clarendon, 1991).

PART II

THEOLOGY

THE REFORMATION:
A Paradigm for Christian Theology

Alister E. McGrath
Oxford University

The contributions to this volume are a testimony both to the breadth and depth of Joseph McClelland's theological interests. Not only is the honorand of this volume one of Canada's most distinguished Reformation scholars; he has also made some highly suggestive and creative contributions to the wider field of Christian theology as a whole. It is the purpose of this essay to explore the interface between these two concerns. In what way can the Reformation provide a stimulus to modern theology? Or can it provide more than that, by allowing us to recover insights, values or methods which had become lost or neglected in the dust and heat of modern debates?

I remember how, as a small boy, one of my greatest pleasures was rummaging through my grandparents' attic. For me, the room was something of a treasure house, full of books, paintings and household items dating back to the first decades of the twentieth century. Situated at the top of a rambling Victorian house, this room had long served as a repository for all kinds of items which, although old, nobody had the heart to throw away. "They might come in useful sometime" was the homespun philosophy which lay beneath this reluctance to discard anything of potential value or use.

I have since come to discover that this same attitude underlies the best in Christian thinking. Responsible Christian theology and spirituality regard the ideas and values of the past, not as obsolete, but as items with a potential continued distinguished history of use. The Reformation, like many other formative periods in Christian history, has much to offer us today. The use to which Martin Luther has been put in modern theology will illustrate this point. Jürgen Moltmann's *The Crucified God* is a superb contemporary exposition of the contemporary relevance of Luther's theology of the cross, bringing out the potential continued history of use of this notion in the modern world.[1] McGill's distinguished theologian Douglas John Hall has also explored this theological approach with great flair,[2] relating it particularly to the North American situation which he knows so well. And in a magisterial study, Gerhard Ebeling has brought out both the manner and the remarkable extent to which Karl Barth has drawn upon Luther in the construction of his own theological system.[3]

To study the theology of the Reformation is thus not to luxuriate in romanticism. It is not to look back in nostalgia, like some old-timer hankering after the good old days when everything was better than it is now. It is not like the sentimental scrutiny of sepia-tinted photographs, nor the wistful recollection of days of lost innocence, a longing for a bygone period and its security. Rather, it is a hard-headed examination of past events, individuals and ideas, with a view to exploiting their present potential. It is to reach into our Christian past, and recover some of its riches. It is a critical awareness that not everything in the Christian present is quite what it could be, linked with a willingness to consider alternative possibilities with a distinguished history of use within the Christian tradition.

So what might the Reformation have to say to contemporary theology? Clearly, I shall have to be selective in my approach. I shall single out some areas in which my own thinking has been influenced by the Reformation, in the hope that others will be stimulated by the same considerations. I begin by dealing with the matter of theology itself.

1. The relevance of theology

Richard John Neuhaus, author of the highly-acclaimed volume *The Naked Public Square*, puts his finger on one of the weak points of modern theology. Surveying the output of one leading North American religious publishing house, he remarks: "most clergy, never mind lay people, have given up reading theology."[4] Why? Two reasons may easily be given:

1. Much modern theology is written in a style and using a vocabulary which is alien to the vast majority of its potential reading public.

2. Much modern theology addresses issues which seem to bear little relation to the concerns of the Christian public.

Let me explore the second point further with reference to the novels of David Lodge. Lodge, formerly professor of English at the University of Birmingham, is a distinguished student of postmodern literature. His novel *Small World* (1984) is a witty and elegant exploration of the inner inconsistencies of deconstruction. A more recent novel, *Nice Work* (1988),[5] asks us to imagine a collision of worlds—the world of a small business in Birmingham, specializing in the manufacture of machine parts, and that of a junior lecturer in the Department of English at the University of Birmingham, who is deeply influenced by Jacques Derrida. In a marvellously narrated section, Lodge describes the latter's gradual realization that the vital issues of her life—deconstruction, the arbitrariness of the relation between the signifier and signified—are an utter irrelevance to 99.9% of the human race. It is a painful realization, which alters her outlook upon the academic world.

It is a sad and simple fact of life, that probably a comparable proportion of academic theology is perceived as totally pointless, not just by the general public, but even by educated lay Christians. Its vocabulary and concerns seem to belong to a different planet. Yet the Reformation offers us a vision of a time when theology was directed towards the issues which concerned the Christian public.

As a university teacher of theology at Oxford, I cannot help but notice the reaction of theology students to my lectures on Reformation thought. "We can understand what these guys are talking about!" is a typical response from students who have been bewildered by the verbal prolixity (often, it has to be said, masking a conceptual shallowness) of the writings of some recent theologians. "They're dealing with real questions" is another response, grounded in a growing impatience with an academic theology which seems bent on pursuing questions of purely academic interest.

The issues which are today treated with what often approaches polite contempt by academic theologians were regarded as of vital importance by sixteenth century writers—issues such as the nature of the true church, the proper relation of the church and state, the grounds of Christian assurance, and a direct answer to the age-old question, "What must I do to be saved?"

These issues are still debated today. But they are largely debated outside the academy, in local church study groups, in university Bible studies, and in many North American seminaries. The academy has become seriously isolated from the heartbeat of North American Christianity.

2. The status of the theologian

In the Middle Ages, theologians were often equally isolated from the community of faith. They were generally individuals, like the great Thomas Aquinas, who were based in the majestic monasteries of Europe. They were closeted within the confines of the monastic life, and wrote—when they wrote at all—for an audience of their fellow monks. It is rare—but happily, as the example of Thomas à Kempis reminds us, not totally unknown—to find a medieval theologian operating outside this context. In our own day and age, theologians have become increasingly detached from the communities which they are meant to serve. They have become more and more professionalized, isolated within academic theological faculties, and becoming vulnerable to the charge of dwelling within ivory towers. Professionalization has tended to remove theologians from within the communities of faith, and placed them within the narrow confines of the universities. Secularization has led to a separation of personal faith and academic life; the professional academic theologian need not have any commitment to the faith or life of the church.

The Reformation bridges the gap between these two unsatisfactory approaches to the function of theology. The reformers, however diverse their origins may have been, were individuals who were based in the cities of Europe, living within the communities which they served, and sharing their faith. They were isolated by neither monastery nor university from the people who looked to them for guidance. Their task was to interpret and apply the gospel to the concrete situations in which they found themselves—above all, in relating to the lives of ordinary people.

Perhaps one of the most important moments of the Reformation may be traced to 1520, when Luther made the momentous and dramatic decision to cease being a purely academic reformer, addressing academic issues and audiences, and instead to make a direct and passionate appeal to the religious hopes and faith of the German people. Luther became both a preacher and a pastor—and his pastoral concern and experience shows up, time and time again, in his theology. Luther read and interpreted the New Testament as one who believed that this document was of vital and continuing relevance to the life of the Christian community (another stark contrast between the theologians of the Reformation period and the manner in which this document is handled in much modern academia). Here is a genuine pastoral theology, a theology which addresses the needs and concerns of ordinary believers, and those who seek to minister to them.

Similarly, throughout Calvin's writings, we find a determination to engage with the real world of everyday life in the city of Geneva, along with all the problems and possibilities this brings with it. Calvin addresses real and specific human situations—social, political and economic—with all the risks that this precision entails. Here is no abstract theorizing, conducted in the refined atmosphere of an ivory tower. Rather, here is a theologian sharing the life of his people, and attempting to interpret and apply the gospel in that situation. Calvin wrote, worshipped and preached as a member of the community which he addressed. He was not apart from them; he was not above them; rather, he wrote from within his community, as part of it, sharing its life and its problems. Here is no theology imposed from above or from outside, but a theology generated within a community, with the needs, possibilities and aspirations of that community in mind.

Is there not a model here which has relevance and appeal for today? Again and again, ordinary Christians today comment on how irrelevant they consider theologians to be. "They seem so distant." "They don't seem to understand the problems of everyday life." "They seem to have a totally different agenda from ordinary believers." "We can't understand what they are going on about." While teaching as a visiting professor in the United States in 1990, I even heard the following criticism of certain theologians teaching at major North American seminaries: "These guys don't even go to church—why should we listen to them?" "There is no way that these people present us with role models suitable for Christian ministry."

In brief, academic theology gets a very bad popular press. These comments are deeply revealing, indicating the considerable gulf that has opened up between the academy and the church. Surely, many ask, there must me a more satisfactory way of conceiving the task, calling and responsibilities of the theologian? It is thus vitally important to note that the Reformation offers a very different model, with a distinguished history of application within the Christian tradition. The theologian operates within the community, addressing its needs and concerns. (There are strong echoes and endorsements here of the Eastern Orthodox idea of the theologian as one who prays properly.) In short: the theologian is one who is called to serve the community of faith from within. Part of that service is criticism of its ideas and outlooks—but it is a loving and caring criticism on the basis of shared Christian beliefs and commitments, rather than the modern criticism of the Christian community by academic "theologians" on the basis of secular beliefs and values, often radically agnostic or atheistic, which that community feels no pressing reason to share. Criticism of a community is a sign and a consequence of commitment to that community.

This approach was developed by the Marxist writer Antonio Gramsci, who used the Reformation as a paradigm for his notion of the "organic intellectual." This idea, which originates at the time of the Reformation, is of considerable importance to my theme. Gramsci argues that two distinct types of intellectuals can be discerned. In the first place, there are those who are imposed upon a community by an external authority. These "institutional intellectuals" were not chosen by that community, and have influence only in so far as that authority is forced upon the community. In contrast to this, Gramsci notes—and commends—the idea of an "organic intellectual." The organic intellectual is one who arises within a community, and who gains authority on account of his or her being seen to represent the outlook of that community. His or her authority emerges naturally, and reflects the esteem in which the community holds them.

This model of the theologian is enormously helpful, and seems to be true to experience. If I might be allowed to reflect on the situation in England, it resonates well with the experience of evangelicalism within the Church of England, which has always regarded institutionally-imposed authorities with some suspicion. Evangelical theologians earn their spurs in the evangelical constituency, gradually gaining respect and commanding authority on account of their observable fidelity to Scripture, ability to express themselves, and concern for the well-being of the church. John Stott—an excellent example of an "organic intellectual"—has no institutional authority worth speaking of, but enjoys enormous status within the worldwide evangelical community (and beyond) on account of his having *earned* that respect. Whereas certain bishops and university professors have simply been imposed upon a church which is increasingly weary of their pretensions to authority, Stott and others like him have authority because they have been accepted as being *worthy* of possessing authority.

3. The search for roots

Recognition of the need to recover a sense of Christian identity and purpose pervades the writings of the reformers. There was a feeling that Christianity needed to be reborn and reshaped. It was not merely that medieval forms of Christianity were of limited relevance to the new era of human history then dawning; it was that those medieval forms of Christianity represented distortions of authentic Christianity. Time and time again, the writings of the reformers develop the following theme: there is an urgent need to return to the roots of faith, and reappropriate an authentic form of the Christian gospel. Authenticity is the touchstone of relevance: an authentic gospel will be a relevant and a stable gospel.

The idea of returning to one's roots is as complex as it is powerful, and needs careful examination before its full potential can be appreciated. We can begin to catch a sense of its relevance by considering the importance of this theme for the Italian Renaissance—that great period in European history when, in the words of Paolo Giovio, culture was "born again." The Italian Renaissance is rightly regarded as one of the most important and creative periods in European culture. The art galleries and museums of the world are packed full of exhibits showing the remarkable originality and imagination of the new culture which took hold of northern Italy during the period 1350-1550. By the end of the sixteenth century, virtually all of western Europe had been infected by this astonishing enthusiasm and vision. But what lay behind this magnificent outburst of energy, of incredible artistic excitement, at the time?

The answer to this question is complex. However, a substantial part of that answer can be stated in two Latin words—*ad fontes*, "back to the original sources." Italian culture gained a new sense of purpose and dignity by seeing itself as the modern heir and champion of the long-dead culture of classical Rome. The Italian Renaissance could be said to be about bringing the culture of ancient Rome back to life in the modern period. The imaginations of artists, architects, poets, writers and theologians were seized by this vision. Imagine being able to allow the glory of the past to interact with the cultural void of fourteenth century Italy! And as the process of recollection began, Italy began to gain a reputation as the cradle of a new civilization in Europe.

It is no accident that Italy was the birthplace and cradle of the Renaissance. The Italian writers of the period appear to have seen themselves as returning to their cultural roots, in the world of classical Rome. A stream, they argued, was purest at its source; why not return to that source, instead of being satisfied with the muddy and stagnant waters of existing medieval culture? The past was seen as a resource, a foundational influence, whose greatness demanded that it should be allowed a voice in the present. The Italian Renaissance arose through a decision to allow the historic roots of Italian culture to impose upon the present, to inform it, to stimulate it—and to transform it. The explosion of creativity which resulted is an eloquent and powerful witness to the potential effects of returning to cultural roots, and allowing them to impact upon the present. The excitement of the Renaissance rediscovery of the past was tempered only by the awareness that only the smallest part of classical culture had been reclaimed; the vast bulk, it was realized, had been lost for ever. But what remained had a profound impact upon the Renaissance.

The history of the United States of America shows up a phenomenon of central importance to Reformation spirituality. Roots matter to people—especially to people exiled from their homeland. Ethnic groupings, faced with the threat of being overwhelmed by a larger, more amorphous culture, choose to resist this development. How? By asserting their distinctiveness. And that distinctiveness is often specifically linked with an appeal to the past. To lose one's distinctiveness is to lose something irreplaceable and identity-giving, evoking a sense of loss of place and purpose in the world.

This general phenomenon can be traced throughout modern America. Irish-Americans, anxious to preserve their cultural identity, celebrate their Irish roots with a degree of commitment and enthusiasm which is always something of a mystery to those who chose to stay behind in Ireland. Many recent American presidents have found it to be electorally important to discover that they have links—however distant—with the Emerald Isle. St. Patrick's Day is celebrated with far greater fervor in New York than it is in Dublin. Why? Because it preserves the identity of a group which would otherwise lose its distinctive character. The same is true of the American Jewish community, which finds in the Passover celebrations a focus for its sense of identity. The new interest in the rediscovery of the African roots of black American culture is yet another illustration of this general principle of a return to cultural roots. Alex Haley's novel of the 1970s, *Roots*, made a deep and emotive appeal to this same sense of being rooted in the past. And as the constituent states of the former Soviet Union try to regain a sense of national identity, the rediscovery of roots—roots that had been suppressed during the period of Stalinization—has proceeded apace. The recollection of past roots aids the preservation of present individuality. Who you are is partly determined by where you come from.

For the reformers, the past possesses a capacity to illuminate, interpret—and even to transform—the present. The relevance of the crucifixion lies not in the fact that it is past, but because it is foundational, charged with interpretative and existential power.

Let me invite you to consider once more Renaissance Italy. The Renaissance was a period of perhaps unparalleled creativity in European culture. The Renaissance seemed to breathe new life and fresh vitality into the life of humanity. Yet, as Roberto Weiss suggests,[6] this came about through both a physical and cultural encounter with the past. The past breathed fresh air into the stagnant atmosphere of medieval Europe. Through wrestling with this cultural heritage, a period of outstanding creativity and originality dawned. The same is true of other periods. An excellent example might be the Oxford Movement within the Church of England, which traces its origins to 1833.

The Oxford Movement drew its inspiration from the apostolic church. The critical comparison between the contemporary and actual church of the nineteenth century with the historic and ideal church of the apostles proved to be enormously creative, providing a stimulus to development and innovation which led to what can only be described as a renaissance in religious life in England and far beyond. The vitality and life of that movement was due to a willingness to allow the present to be challenged and nourished by its historical roots. Past roots contributed a powerful impetus to present reflection and recollection, and future transformation.

There is a theological parallel here for our own day and age. I do not wish to labour this point; it is perhaps too evident to require me to do so. Yet it seems to me, as it seems to many others, that the most exciting things now happening in the fields of Christian theology and spirituality today involve a willingness and an ability to engage with the central and foundational resources of the Christian faith—the cross and resurrection of Jesus Christ. And that is certainly the direction in which Reformation spirituality is pointing us, urging us to achieve a fusion of the horizons of the past and present.

Roots are important for continuity and stability; they nurture the conditions under which growth and maturity may develop. Tradition encourages wariness, through exercising a restraining influence upon innovation. An enduring tradition, firmly located in history and taken seriously by those who claim to be its heirs, ensures caution and continuity within that community. Faithfulness to one's roots is not inconsistent with addressing contemporary needs and opportunities. At first sight, this respect for roots might seem to be a recipe for encouraging unoriginality and the stifling of creativity. But there is another side to this story. Commitment to a tradition is not equivalent to an encrusted dogmatism, a denial of the freedom to think or of the importance of creativity. Freedom to think without an accompanying commitment to a tradition can lead to little more than an unanchored chaos. The twentieth century has provided us with ample historical examples of what happens when a society breaks free from the restraining force of tradition. Nazi Germany and the Stalinist Soviet Union are excellent illustrations of the unacceptable consequences of a break with tradition. Walter Benjamin's "Theses on the Philosophy of History" reflect his despair at the totalitarianism which results when a civilized society chooses to break with its traditional values. It is very easy to break with one's roots; but, as the cultural history of the Soviet Union in recent years makes clear, it is very difficult to pick up those roots, once broken. Perhaps this has been one of the most worrying aspects of some recent liberal theological writings: a tendency to emphasize present individual religious experience over and against past corporate roots, a matter to which we may proceed immediately.

4. Theological Reflection within a Tradition

The writers of the magisterial Reformation insisted that they were not creating a new religious tradition, but reforming one which already existed. Theology, they argued, is concerned with the criticism of a tradition from within, by a sustained process of inquiry concerning what that tradition purports to represent, and the degree to which it succeeds in this task. Throughout the writings of Luther and Calvin one may discern an affirmation that theology does not, indeed cannot, begin *de novo*; rather, its starting point is fixed for it by a community tradition, which acts as a matrix within which criticical reflection can proceed. This approach has found new relevance today, as the movement which has come to be known as "postliberalism" gains momentum in the academic theological world.

One of the most significant developments in theology since about 1980 has been a growing scepticism over the plausibility of a liberal worldview. Accompanying this retreat from liberalism have been a number of developments, perhaps most important of which has been the repristination of more conservative viewpoints. One such development has been postliberalism, which has become especially associated with Yale Divinity School. Its central foundations are narrative approaches to theology, such as those developed by Hans Frei, and to the schools of social interpretation which stress the importance of culture and language in the generation and interpretation of experience and thought.[7]

Building upon the work of philosophers such as Alasdair MacIntyre, postliberalism rejects both the traditional Enlightenment appeal to a "universal rationality" and the liberal assumption of an immediate religious experience common to all humanity. Arguing that all thought and experience is historically and socially mediated, postliberalism bases its theological programme upon a return to religious traditions, whose values are inwardly appropriated. Post-liberalism is thus anti-foundational (in that it rejects the notion of a universal foundation of knowledge), communitarian (in that it appeals to the values, experiences and language of a community, rather than prioritizing the individual), and historicist (in that it insists upon the importance of traditions and their associated historical communities in the shaping of experience and thought).

Postliberalism is of particular importance in relation to two areas of Christian theology.

1. Systematic Theology. Theology is understood to be primarily a descriptive discipline, concerned with the exploration of the normative foundations of the Christian tradition, which are mediated through the scriptural narrative of Jesus Christ. Truth can be, at least in part, equated with fidelity to the distinctive doctrinal traditions of the Christian faith. This has caused critics of postliberalism to accuse it of retreating from the public arena into some kind of Christian ghetto. If Christian theology, as postliberalism suggests, is intrasystemic (that is, concerned with the exploration of the internal relationships of the Christian tradition), its validity is to be judged with reference to its own internal standards, rather than some publicly agreed or universal criteria. Once more, this has prompted criticism from those who suggest that theology ought to have external criteria, subject to public scrutiny, by which its validity can be tested.

2. Christian Ethics. Stanley Hauerwas is one of a number of writers to explore postliberal approaches to ethics. Rejecting the Enlightenment idea of a universal set of moral ideals or values, Hauerwas argues that Christian ethics is concerned with the identification of the moral vision of a historical community (the church), and with bringing that vision to actualization in the lives of its members. Thus ethics is intrasystemic, in that it concerns the study of the internal moral values of a community. To be moral is to identify the moral vision of a specific historical community, to appropriate its moral values, and to practice them within that community.[8]

The most significant statement of the postliberal agenda remains George Lindbeck's *Nature of Doctrine*.[9] Rejecting "cognitive-propositional" approaches to doctrine as pre-modern, and liberal "experiential-expressive" theories as failing to take account of both human experiential diversity and the mediating role of culture in human thought and experience, Lindbeck develops a "cultural-linguistic" approach which embodies the leading features of postliberalism.

The "cultural-linguistic" approach denies that there is some universal un-mediated human experience, which exists apart from human language and culture. Rather, it stresses that the heart of religion lies in living within a specific historical religious tradition, and interiorizing its ideas and values. This tradition rests upon a historically-mediated set of ideas, for which the narrative is an especially suitable means of transmission.

There are strong resonances here with the Reformation tradition. (Indeed, it is no accident that George Lindbeck, one of the most distinguished representatives of the movement, is himself a specialist in the field of Reformation theology.) For example, Luther's "theology of the cross" can be interpreted as an affirmation of the priority of narrative over metaphysics.[10] As the debate over the theological merits of postliberalism gains momentum, the Reformation may continue to serve as a reference point and resource for signficant debates in the modern period.

5. *The link between theology and spirituality*

Caricatures die hard, and perhaps one of the most influential caricatures of Christian history lies in the nineteenth-century suggestion that the Reformation and its inheritance were devoid of any spirituality. The very phrase "Reformation spirituality" was alleged to be an oxymoron, a blatant self-contradiction. It is a pleasure to be able to write this contribution in the knowledge that this crude stereotype is in what is to be hoped to be irreversible decline. Recent scholarship has revealed many of the leading figures of the Reformation as individuals with a passionate concern for the pastoral, spiritual and social well-being of their people, concerned to ground their theologies firmly in the realities of everyday life. Their search for an authentically Christian spirituality was grounded in their belief that true knowledge of God was transformative, capable of deeply changing the mental, experiential and social worlds of those who grasped it.[11]

The basic insight I wish to explore here is the following: Spirituality rests upon theological foundations. Reformation spirituality insists that the quest for human identity, authenticity and fulfillment cannot be undertaken in isolation from God. To find out *who* we are—and *why* we are—is to find out who God is, and what he is like. Calvin states this principle with characteristic lucidity in the opening sentence of the 1559 edition of his *Institutes of the Christian Religion*: "nearly all the wisdom we possess, that is to say, true and sound wisdom, consists of two parts: the knowledge of God and of ourselves. . . . We never achieve a clear knowledge of ourselves until we have first looked upon God's face, and then descend from contemplating him to examine ourselves." Any notion of spirituality as a quest for heightened religious experience as an end in itself is totally alien to the outlook of the Reformation. Equally, any idea that it is possible to have a detached or disinterested knowledge of God is excluded. To know God is to be changed by God.

There is thus a substantial doctrinal foundation to Reformation spirituality. Nevertheless, an interest in doctrine is not necessarily regarded as equivalent to an interest in spirituality. For example, both Luther and Calvin strongly criticized scholastic theology, on account of its tendency to drive a wedge between theological reflection and spirituality, between the head and the heart, on the one hand, and its failure to relate to the existential aspects of faith on the other.

There can be no cerebralization of faith. As Calvin stated this point in the 1539 edition of the *Institutes*:

> Doctrine is not a matter of the tongue, but of life. It is not apprehended only by the intellect and memory, like other branches of learning, but is received only when it possesses the whole soul. . . . We assign priority to doctrine, in which our religion is contained, since by it our salvation begins; but it must be transfused into our hearts, and pass into our conduct, and thus transform us into itself. . . . The gospel ought to penetrate the innermost feelings of the heart, fix its seat in the soul, and pervade the entire person a hundred times more than the frigid writings of the philosophers.

Calvin's emphasis upon the experiential aspects of our knowledge of God (a serious embarrassment, incidentally, to those who stolidly persist in portraying him as insensitive to spiritual experience, or woodenly intellectualist or cerebral) reflects the common Reformation belief: to know God is to experience the power of God. To know God is to be changed by God. "The knowledge of God which we are invited to develop is not the sort that is content with empty speculation, which just rattles around inside our heads, but a knowledge which proves to be substantial and fruitful in our hearts."

Knowledge of God is thus like a vital force, capable of changing those who possess it and are possessed by it. True knowledge of God moves us to worship, obedience and the hope of eternal life. Calvin stresses that there is no knowledge of God where there is no faith and worship of God. It is only in knowing God that we come to know ourselves—although, as Calvin pointed out with equal vigour, it is only by knowing ourselves fully that we come to know God fully. Knowledge of ourselves and knowledge of God are given together—or they are not given at all.

My fundamental point here is simply this: psychology is not theology. To draw upon insights concerning the human condition is only half of the story that Christian spirituality is concerned to tell; indeed, if only half of that story is told, it has not been properly and authentically told at all. Knowledge of God and knowledge of ourselves are the essential components of an authentic and responsible spirituality, according to the Reformation tradition. To base a spirituality solely upon the insights of secular psychology or psychotherapy is to forfeit both the use of the term "Christian," and the insights which the Christian knowledge of God in Christ brings in its wake. Psychology alone cannot, and should not be allowed to, become the fundamental resource of Christian spirituality. If the Reformation has anything to say to the present generation, it is simply this: don't lose sight of God. Pop psychology makes sloppy theology which makes for mushy Christianity. A vigorous dose of real theology gives intellectual backbone and stamina to faith. And faith needs such reinforcement, in the muddled and confused world of the late twentieth century.

I must conclude. My thesis is that the Reformation can function as a paradigm for modern theology in a number of ways. Through reminding us of the ease with which academic theology can become divorced from the life of the Christian community, it offers us an invitation to reconsider the nature of theology and the status of the theologian. It reminds us of the importance of valuing our roots, and working within a tradition. And it also obliges us to ask hard questions about the proliferations of "spiritualities" which lack any real foundation in Christian doctrine. And in doing this, it asks the kind of questions that need to be asked, if theology is to continue to be relevant to the life of the church. For a theology which is not seen to be relevant in this way will become seriously marginalized by ordinary Christians, who may well turn to others for guidance and inspiration. That would be a tragedy, for both academy and church. Happily, it is a tragedy which can be avoided. The Reformation offers us some hints as to how.

NOTES

1.   Jürgen Moltmann, *The Crucified God* (Philadelphia: Westminster, 1974). For a critical assessment of Moltmann's relation to Luther, see Pierre Bühler, *Kreuz und Eschatologie: Eine Auseinandersetzung mit der politischen Theologie im Anschluß an Luthers theologia crucis* (Tübingen: Mohr, 1981).

2.   See Douglas John Hall, *God and Human Suffering: An Exercise in the Theology of the Cross* (Minneapolis: Augsburg, 1986).

3.   Gerhard Ebeling, "Karl Barths Ringen mit Luther", in *Lutherstudien III* (Tübingen: Mohr, 1985), 428-73.

4.   Richard John Neuhaus, in *First Things*, October 1991, 71.

5.   David Lodge, *Nice Work* (London/New York: Penguin, 1988).

6.   Roberto Weiss, *The Renaissance Rediscovery of Classical Antiquity*, 2d ed. (Oxford: Blackwell, 1988).

7.   See William C. Placher, *Unapologetic Theology: A Christian Voice in a Pluralistic Conversation* (Louisville: Westminster/John Knox, 1989); Hans W. Frei, *The Eclipse of Biblical Narrative* (New Haven: Yale University Press, 1974); R. F. Thiemann, *Revelation and Theology: The Gospel as Narrated Promise* (Notre Dame: University of Notre Dame Press, 1985).

8.   See Stanley Hauerwas, *Against the Nations* (Minneapolis: Winston, 1985), 11-12.

9.   G. A. Lindbeck, *The Nature of Doctrine: Religion and Theology in a Postliberal Age* (Philadelphia: Fortress, 1984).

10. See Alister E. McGrath, *The Genesis of Doctrine* (Oxford: Blackwell, 1990), 64-6.

11. See Alister E. McGrath, *Roots that Refresh: A Celebration of Reformation Spirituality* (London: Hodder & Stoughton, 1992).

FOR AND AGAINST JOHN MILBANK

Gregory Baum
McGill University

In this paper I want to engage in critical conversation with the new, orginal theological approach introduced by John Milbank. This learned young English-man, a postmodern radical theologian, claims with a Barthian vehemence that there is no good society, no valid ethics and no true wisdom apart from the life and message of Jesus Christ. In his book, *Theology and Social Theory*,[1] John Milbank repudiates the entire history of freedom associated with the Enlightenment project, repudiates the social sciences in their entirety, repudi-ates—on Christian, not on Marxist grounds—the capitalist system and its cultural implications, repudiates every form of universal reason, classical and modern, that pretends to define a common humanity—and all this in the name of the life and message of Jesus Christ, who with his counter-practice and counter-discourse interrupted the logic of violence operative in human history.

Yet Milbank is not Karl Barth redivivus. The newness brought by Jesus Christ, according to Milbank, is the practice, not the proclamation of God's approaching reign. Jesus brought a new praxis of love, forgiveness and peace, a community-creating way of life that saved and saves his followers from the violence implicit in their culture. The new practice generated social actions and cultural expressions that were "coded"—this is how our postmodern theologian puts it—that bore the imprint of the Gospel, a new message that called for articulation and gave rise to attentive reflection. Here praxis precedes kerygma and theology. Milbank is an Anabaptist or Mennonite Barth.

A few words about the nature of *Theology and Social Theory*. It is an original, brilliant and enormously erudite treatise. From his own perspective of the primacy of practice, Milbank re-reads the classical authors, especially Plato and Aristotle, re-reads Augustine and Thomas Aquinas, re-reads the political theorists of the Enlightenment and the sociologists of the 19th and early 20th century, re-reads Maurice Blondel and more recent Roman Catholic theologians, re-reads Heidegger, Derrida, Foucault and the postmodern philosophers. The book also offers Milbank's own, original, daring, postmodern theology. The work is an overwhelming intellectual achievement, carried through with great passion, conceptual precision, and a marvellously readable prose. The book moved me deeply. I often felt at home with the author, but, since the postmodern deconstruction of reason and truth does not convince me, the book also enraged me.

In this essay I wish to focus only on one of the many issues raised by the British theologian, namely his critique of liberation theology. While Milbank affirms the primacy of practice—as do liberation theologians—and presents himself as a Christian socialist offering a devastating critique of capitalism, he believes that liberation theology has strayed from the true sense of the Gospel. Milbank's arguments deserve a hearing.

In the first part of his book Milbank, following the reasoning of postmodern thought, offers a learned repudiation of the social sciences and all forms of universal reason. Therefore the churches and their theologians are in error, Milbank argues, when they engage in dialogue with sociology and use sociological theories to interpret the power and meaning of the Christian Gospel. This is Milbank's first argument against liberation theology, an argument I wish to present and question in the first part of this essay.

In the second part of his book containing his affirmation of the supernatural, Milbank offers more properly theological arguments against liberation theology: first, it follows an erroneous christology, secondly, it reduces the impact of the Gospel to personal motivation, and thirdly, it derives its concept of freedom from the Enlightenment tradition.

1. The Repudiation of Social Science

Milbank begins by arguing that "the secular" is an arbitrary construction of modernity. Ordinary human life, he argues, is always and everywhere deeply shaped by symbols and stories that are in some way related to an absolute. Classical philosophy recognized this. For Plato and Aristotle human actions were intrinsically related to a transcendent dimension, the Idea of the Good or the ultimate Telos. The Stoics were the first to confine the religious dimension to the inner life of individuals. With the coming of Christianity, the new coded practice of Jesus Christ, people's daily interactions were again understood as shaped by God's revealed presence. While Augustine's approach to God through the soul's interior journey anticipated the notion of an external world from which God was absent, he himself provided an alternative imagination, especially in his major work, *The City of God*. Only in the Renaissance and the subsequent Enlightenment, Milbank argues, did philosophers propose the idea that ordinary, day-to-day human activity was "secular," i.e. unrelated to a myth that gave it meaning, and consequently that religion came upon the secular as an *additum*, as brief interruptions in moments of prayer.

This change of theory reflected a change of practice: people increasingly saw themselves as defined by their struggle to survive, promote their own advantage and do better than their neighbour. As life in modern society defined itself increasingly in terms of personal freedom and scientific rationality, people set aside the religious *additum* altogether. The Comtean proposal of the gradual emancipation of humanity from religious fables was paradigmatic for the orientation of modern society.

The so-called secular, Milbank insists, designates the sphere of people's historical existence independent of any relation to an absolute. What defined secular existence for many Enlightenment thinkers was the "conatus" of self-preservation, the struggle for survival, success and security, sustained by the desire for freedom from outside interference. Here human life was understood apart from its relation to good and evil. Milbank wants to show that this secularity is not an historical reality observed and presented by modern thinkers, but an arbitrary, anti-theological construction made by them, relying on the myth of secular reason. The concept of the secular thus reflects the modern meta-narrative of man's emancipatory self-creation through an ever renewed application of scientific rationality.

Modern thought defined the human being against classical wisdom and Christian faith. Milbank argues that secular reason operative in the social sciences is founded upon a non-demonstrable, anti-Christian stance that cannot make a greater claim to truth than does the supernatural stance it sought to replace, God's self-revelation in Jesus Christ.

Milbank begins his detailed study of modern scientific thought with the political philosophers of the Enlightenment, for whom human beings were defined by the "conatus" to survive, protect their life and property, and improve their position in the world. This possessive individualism reflected the practice of the emerging middle class.

But Milbank has no more sympathy for the 19th century sociologists in the French tradition of Auguste Comte and Emile Durkheim who, reacting against

Enlightenment individualism, adopted a collectivist perspective. For them, the individual was embedded in and shaped by society. They held that society steered people's lives through the power of symbols, assigning them their place and their social roles for the benefit of the entire body. These symbols, Milbank argues, represented a false theology. Since these sociologists divinized the finite, they emptied religion of its transcendent meaning and reduced it to the function it supposedly exercised in developing and stabilizing society. The meta-narrative behind their sociological perspective was therefore also the rational orientation of society toward ever greater progress.

Curiously enough, Milbank does not offer a more sympathetic reading of sociologists in the German tradition, Max Weber in particular, even though they rejected the Durkheimian trend of divinizing society and lamented the decline of culture produced by modernity. What Milbank regrets in Max Weber's work is his return to the individualism of the early Enlightenment, his concept of man defined by the "conatus" for self-preservation, and his radical separation of sociology from social ethics. When humans are no longer defined by their relation to good and evil, Milbank reasons correctly, then social peace can only be conceived as an unstable compromise between conflicting interests or as an order imposed upon citizens by an all-powerful state.

According to Milbank, sociology in the French and German tradition reflects the practice of modernity, coded by scientific reason—a practice at odds with the counter- practice initiated by Jesus Christ. Milbank repudiates the validity of the social sciences. He refuses to enter into dialogue with sociology; and he scolds contemporary theologians who make critical use of sociological theories in their theology. Milbank recognizes of course that theologians must offer critiques of church and society, but he firmly believes that such crtiques can be derived from the new practice introduced by Jesus Christ and continued by the community of his disciples.

While Milbank calls "For and Against Hegel" his chapter on this German philosopher and "For and Against Marx" his chapter on this political thinker, he refuses to engage in a dialogue "for and against" the social sciences. Milbank would have my full support if he rejected the positivistic social sciences which suppose that human actions follow scientifically discoverable laws, that these actions are fully determined by antecedent causes and that they are therefore in principle predictable. But Milbank repudiates also the hermeneutical social sciences which recognize only strong trends—not laws—in society, acknowledge only probable causes and understand history as forever open to the unexpected. In my opinion, Milbank's reading of Max Weber does not do him justice. Rejecting all of sociology in principle, Milbank makes the bold proposal that the only valid insights into social developments, insights theology must take seriously, are derived from historical narratives. History, not social science, deserves the attention of the theologian.

While this is not the place to offer all my objections to Milbank's analysis of sociology, I will make a few critical remarks. It seems to me that the English theologian and other postmodern thinkers—following Durkheim, whom they do not honour—exaggerate the extent to which human beings are constructed by the myth of their society. For these thinkers nothing of human existence is a given, there is no human nature, human existence is constructed by social and linguistic practice founded upon some meta-narrative. These thinkers overlook that human beings live at the intersection of certain given orientations and several narratives that affect their minds. For instance, the "conatus" for self-preservation is a given impulse (not a construction of modernity) that is to some degree operative in people's lives, even when they are deeply involved in the religious myth of their society.

Let me give an example from the Bible. When the people of Israel, threatened by enemies from the North, asked God for a king to rule over them and protect them, Samuel tried to persuade them to change their mind (cf. I Samuel 8:10-18). He did not plead with them to remain faithful to the egalitarian confederation God had given them to remind them that God alone was their king and to protect their society from becoming another Egypt, a system of structured inequality. Samuel did not offer the people arguments taken from their meta-narrative. Instead, Samuel warned the people that if they have a king set over them, he will force their sons to do burdensome duties as soldiers and labourers, he will oblige their daughters to enter his service as maids and cooks, and he will take away their most valued fields and vineyards to hand them over to his officers. Samuel offered the people a secular argument, appealing to the conatus of self-preservation.

People are complex: they live out of more than one story and are prompted to action by mixed motivations. Max Weber recognized this. He also acknowledged that sometimes people, drawing upon hidden resources or sudden charisms, were able to transcend their culture.

Samuel's famous speech recorded in Scripture anticipates sociological theory in an intuitive, pre-scientific manner. Samuel applies his theory that monarchies produce class distinction and class exploitation to the particular historical situation of the Israelites. His argument goes further than simple historical narrative. His argument includes a certain generalization, without of course claiming that this establishes a law. Samuel regards exploitation as a trend in monarchical regimes that is likely to manifest itself, though he does not deny that this trend may be overcome by an unusual king who loves justice.

Let me add that Milbank occasionally does enter into dialogue with sociology. When he discusses the work of Norman Gottwald and Wayne Meeks who applied sociological theory to the interpretation of Scripture (see pp. 111-21), Milbank appreciates the light their research has shed on the social practice of the biblical community and hence on the meaning of the biblical message; he criticizes the conclusions of these scholars only for the element of positivism that remains in them. Because, with Weber, Milbank affirms the openness of history to the unexpected, he improves Gottwald's and Meeks's conclusions by pointing to the possibility of unpredictable human creativity which the two authors underestimated. Here Milbank involves himself "for and against sociology." Why then the categorical repudiation?

Milbank wants to demonstrate that the Church in its practice and proclamation cannot learn anything from sociology and, more generally, from the critiques offered by Enlightenment thinkers. The Church, he argues, has its own sources of self-criticism. "Because historical narration is the true mode of social knowledge, theology no longer has any need, like Ricoeur, to concede the foundationalist suspicion of Marx, Freud and sociology, and appropriate this as a supposed mode of the *via negativa*, or as a way of purifying the true subject matter of theology itself" (p. 268). Milbank, as we shall see, pays a high price for his refusal to listen to the modern critics.

Since Milbank makes the thought of St. Augustine central to his theological proposal, I wish to mention an instance, also of interest to Milbank, where the pastoral approach of the great African bishop tragically failed because he had no access to sociological theory. His failure is an allegory for many contemporary failures. In his ongoing struggle against the Donatists, Augustine never recognized one important reason why the Donatists were so harsh in their judgement of the bishops who had betrayed their faith during the persecution and why they refused to recognize them when they repented and were reconciled with the Church. The Donatists were drawn from the ethnic population of North Africa that had been pushed by the Roman colonists from the fertile stretches of land along the Mediterranean coast to settle in the mountainous, less fertile regions of the interior. These people refused integration in the culture of the Roman Empire. They stood aloof from the assimilated Christians of North Africa, like Augustine, who lived as Christians in a society whose language and to a certain extent whose culture they shared. While the Latinized Christians found the idolatrous surrender to Emperor in times of persecution a sin that could be forgiven, the Donatists looked upon this apostasy as an irreparable break with the Church, pouring into this judgment their historical resentment against the material and cultural oppression inflicted upon them by the Empire. Because he lacked such a social analysis, Augustine was unable to address the Donatists in a manner that acknowledged their suffering.

Milbank strengthens his rejection of the social sciences by making it a part of the wider repudiation of all forms of reason that claim universal validity. Milbank here follows the French deconstructionists and postmodern philosophers who believe that all truth claims are expressions of power within a given society and that universal truth claims are related to an intention of imperialistic control. Here as everywhere practice precedes theory. Milbank agrees with the postmodern thinkers that modernity was created by the meta-narratives of the Enlightenment, first the liberal story of continual progress through science, technology and democracy, and then the Marxist story, also relying on science and technology, that expected the revolution to overcome liberal society and man's exploitation of man. What has happened in the present, the postmoderns and Milbank argue, is that these meta-narratives have lost their power. Not only did they fail to deliver what they promised, they also generated forms of totalitarian rule, like all stories claiming universal validity.

Milbank thus looks upon reason as an instrument of violence. He applies this not only to modern, secular rationality but also, reluctantly, to classical reason, even though classical reason did recognize the orientation of humans toward the good and expressed the practice of justice in the ideal republic. To show that even classical reason remains an instrument of violence, Milbank analyses the contradiction between the practice of the "polis," defined by justice, and the practice of the "oikos," the household, which was exploitative (pp. 364-69). For the household, providing the material basis for the men engaged in the "polis," reduced women, children and slaves to an inferior status. Hence even classical reason offered legitimation for violence. Jesus alone brought a counter-practice of compassion and forgiveness, destined to overcome the regimes of violence and transcend the rationalties associated with them.

Milbank's postmodern repudiation of universal reason, we note, is not an ideology critique followed by a retrieval in a new key. He specifically disagrees with the philosophers of the Frankfurt School who lament the collapse of Enlightenment reason into instrumental rationality—"the dialectic of the Enlightenment"—but who still have enough hope to revive and reaffirm the ethical dimension present in the emancipatory project of the Enlightenment. With the postmodern thinkers, Milbank opposes the Frankfurt School because of their continuing trust in context-transcending ethical reason. At this point, as we shall see, I part company with Milbank for reasons that are ultimately theological.

Milbank is not only "for" postmodern thought, he is also "against" it. According to his analysis, postmodern philosophies inevitably lead to the deconstruction of all ethical values and the legitimation of arbitrary violence. Milbank offers a passionate argument that the one choice confronting the contemporary generation is between postmodern nihilism and Christian faith.

Against Milbank, I resist the postmodern theorists according to whom a truth claim is always and everywhere an attempt to impose an order on society. They see truth as a child of violence. Yet if we assume that this is so, then the affirmation of their truth is also the child of violence and hence there is no reason why we should trust postmodern reasoning more than the thought they seek to replace. Or again, if truth is always contextual, and if there is no common "ratio" among different cultural contexts and hence no context-transcending dialogue, then why do postmodern thinkers speak to us? Is not discourse addressed to others always based on the hope that these others are capable of understanding it? A French postmodernist has claimed that for the author of a book the readers are really a nuisance: writing a book is like placing a message into a bottle and throwing it into the ocean.[2] But who will believe him? An author writes books and invents provocative images in order to be heard. The very act of communication makes an implicit affirmation that subsequent denials cannot invalidate.

Since Milbank looks upon secular reason as an instrument of violence, he discards the critical ideas of Marx, Freud and other thinkers, which reveal the dark powers operative on a deep and often hidden level in human self-making, personal and social. These critiques, Milbank argues, are part and parcel of the secular project, the construction of a society unrelated to the good and to ultimate meaning, and therefore these critiques contain elements of violence. Milbank also recognizes violence present in the postmodern denial of universal reason and their deconstruction of the great philosophical and ethical traditions. But the question Milbank does not ask is whether the Christian meta-narrative contains a grain of violence that might have to be overcome in the Church's history. We shall return to this topic further on.

2. The Affirmation of the Supernatural

(1) An Erroneous Christology?

Milbank uses the term "the supernatural" as is done in Roman Catholic theology, to refer to the revelation brought by Jesus Christ and the transformation it engenders in humanity. Milbank praises the development of twentieth century Roman Catholic theology which has come to acknowledge that God's grace affects the whole of human existence, not only spiritual but also earthly life, not only the individual but also the collectivity. Milbank calls this "integralism" (not to be confused with "intégrisme," the French word for fundamentalism.) Integralist theology acknowledges that the radical newness brought by Jesus was a new personal and social practice, the bearer of a new message.

Milbank studies two different currents of integralism in Roman Catholic theology. The first current considers the supernatural as the Christ-given fulfilment of the natural order that by itself and apart from Christ remains intrinsically frustrated, and the second current—less sound, according to Milbank—regards the Christ-event as elevating the whole of human history to the supernatural. The first current is associated with several French theologians, especially Maurice Blondel and Henri de Lubac, as well as Urs von Balthasar, and the second current with Karl Rahner, German political theology and Latin American liberation theology.

Milbank associates himself with the first current. According to his reading, these theologians hold that the human response to the divine initiative takes place in surrender, discipleship and action, which for Milbank means especially the practice of love, forgiveness and peace. These theologians look upon human nature as essentially frustated, unable to find fulfilment within the limits of its own powers. Humans overcome this frustration only through the gratuitous encounter with the supernatural. These theologians are critical of Scholastic theology which distinguished between two levels of existence, the natural and the supernatural, where the natural constituted an internally consistent whole and the supernatural appeared as added extrinsically as it were to a fully equipped human existence. These theologians rejected this "extrinsicism." For them the Gospel was not a complement to human nature but a way of life and a message that rescued human nature from its contradictions and lifted it to its true vocation.

In a sinful world marked by competition, power and violence, the Gospel, according to this theology, is the only entry into peace. Apart from Jesus Christ there is only darkness. Such a christology is often called "exclusivist." Yet this theology, we note, offers an integralist interpretation of the supernatural: it recognizes the power of divine grace to transform the entire human context and hence presents a non-individualistic, social theory of human existence.

At the same time, this theology sets Christians apart from the rest of humanity. Christians enlivened and enlightened by the supernatural have nothing to learn from outsiders, because outsiders are people caught in cultures, religions and philosophical traditions that inevitably reflect practices of domination.

Authentic social theology is ecclesiology. Because Milbank defends this radical thesis with brilliant intelligence and extraordinary erudition, I have called him an Anabaptist Barth. At the same time, Milbank repudiates any wisdom apart from Jesus not so much on biblical grounds—as did Karl Barth—as on grounds drawn from the postmodern analysis of the human condition.

The second current of contemporary Roman Catholic theology is severely criticized by Milbank. It is based on a christology often called "inclusivist." For Karl Rahner, the redemption brought by Jesus Christ assures the presence of divine grace in the community of believers as well as the whole of sinful humanity. Now it is Christ, and no longer Adam, who defines the situation of the human family. The divine mercy revealed in Christ is believed, proclaimed and celebrated only in the Christian Church, but in a hidden way this redeeming grace is operative wherever people are, offering them freedom from their sins and supporting their quest for truth and justice.

Because history itself is here seen as lifted to the supernatural order, the practice of Christians—their faith, their love of neighbour, their commitment to justice—does not necessarily differ from the practice of others who thanks to God's grace have become trusting, loving and justice-oriented. In the light of this inclusivist christology, there exists a common human nature, wounded by sin, yet under the impact of divine grace. Here creation and redemption are held to intersect in the lives of people and their common history.

This theological current, we note, also overcomes the "extrinsicism" of Scholastic thought since here the supernatural is seen as rescuing, elevating and transforming the damaged resources of human nature. Yet this current of theology differs significantly from the preceding since it insists that the gift of divine grace creates human solidarity and provides the foundation for the cooperation of all in the ever-to-be renewed effort to overcome injustice, senseless human suffering and violence.

Milbank rejects this inclusivist christology not on biblical grounds as many theologians want to do, but rather on the strength of postmodern arguments that deconstruct any univerally shared truths and values. According to Milbank, Rahner and theologians (like myself) who in one way or another follow him, have been seduced by secular Enlightenment reason. These theologians falsely believe that the insights of the Enlightenment are reliable and can be used critically in the exercise of theology. In the first part of his book, Milbank tried to demonstrate that secular reason is neither objective nor a universally shared capacity but a subjective construction reflecting a myth or meta-narrative of world domination. Secular reason is therefore unable to make a greater claim to truth than the Christian Story. Here meta-narrative stands against meta-narrative, faith against reason, Jesus against Enlightenment.

(2) A Collapse into Secular Reason?

The second current of integralist theology, Milbank argues, has been taken up by liberation theology and by theological approaches influenced by it: here human history itself, not just the Church, is seen as the locus of the supernatural. What Milbank does not mention is that liberation theologians share with him a strong sense, not found in Karl Rahner, that divine redemption still remains incomplete: for them, the "not yet" is much more pronounced than the "always already." Still, their inclusivist christology does have an affinity with Karl Rahner.

On the basis of this christology, liberation theologians believe the divine grace is operative in social movements that struggle for emancipation. For them, these struggles echo the tradition of the prophets, recorded in Scripture. These theologians hold that the Gospel summons Christians to stand in solidarity with these movements and to integrate into their theology the Enlightenment insights expressed in these movements.

Milbank disapproves of this. The content of these movements, he argues, is totally determined by secular aspirations and ideas so that the Christian contribution to these movements is simply the religious motivation in people's hearts. Thus while the theology of liberation pretends to be social, Milbank insists, it actually turns out to be exclusively personal, revealing its own inner contradiction.

Milbank also criticizes liberation theology because it wants to purify the Christian tradition with the help of modern critical reflection, because it uses Marxist social theory to clarify the Church's pastoral mission, and because it accepts the modern idea that people are meant to be free subjects of their personal and social existence. According to Milbank, this represents a switch from the Christian Story generating love, peace and forgiveness to another myth or meta-narrative, the secular one, oriented toward conquest, universal control and ultimately violence. Milbank argues that liberation theology has accepted the Enlightenment idea of freedom, freedom from interference and for self-determination, which is an "empty" freedom, that is to say simply the power or capacity to do as one wishes or to please oneself, a path that eventually leads to injustice and domination. Liberation theology, Milbank argues, transfers this "liberal" idea of freedom to the struggle of groups or classes against oppression.

Are Milbank's accusations justified? The British theologian is mistaken when he argues that liberation theology confines the impact of the Gospel to the creation of personal religious motivation. Milbank misreads the starting point of liberation theology, which is practice—a practice called "the preferential option for the poor" and understood as the contemporary form of discipleship. This option implies a double commitment, to look at society from the perspective of its victims and to act in solidarity with their struggle for social justice.

The preferential option based on Christian faith and love is different from any secular emancipatory commitment. The content of the preferential option affects the mode of the social struggle, the ethics that guides it, the relationships among the comrades, and the attitude toward the oppressor. Here faith and love remain operative throughout the struggle for social justice. Christians involved with secular men and women in resistance movements or liberation struggles give witness to this love and often influence the actions and ideas of their cells and groups. Testimonies of this abound.

Two decades ago, when Franco was still the ruler of Spain, the Spanish theologian, Casiano Floristan, exercised his ministry and shared his life with Catholic socialist workers in Madrid. At an editorial meeting of the international Catholic theological review, *Concilium*, to which he and I then belonged, he was asked how his Catholic workers differed from the atheist socialists with whom they shared the same struggle. After a long reflection he offered a reply. First, the Catholic workers had a greater sense of humour because they retained a certain distance from their social engagement. Since ultimate struggle had been won by Jesus Christ, their own historical struggle was only penultimate. Secondly, the Catholic workers were less crushed by the failure of their common action. Since they evaluated their struggle in terms of fidelity, not success, they were able to cheer up their atheist comrades. Thirdly, Casiano Floristan told us, when their spies in the police force informed them that the next day large numbers of labour activists would be arrested, the Catholic workers gathered at night for the eucharist to celebrate a victory that could not be taken away from them. As they sang and played the guitar, their atheist friends stood in the back because they liked the music.

The preferential option not only influences present behaviour, it also acts as a transcendent principle that remains valid after the reconstruction of society. Here it offers a critical perspective on the newly created society and generates solidarity with the men and women who now find themselves at the margin. Thus we read that after the victory in Nicaragua, the Christian base communities demanded that the revolutionary government extend forgiveness to the soldiers who had fought and killed for the deposed dictator, Somosa.[3] I find it ironic that despite his emphasis on practice, Milbank is a professor who judges the world on the basis of theories.

Milbank also errs when he accuses liberation theology of embracing a "liberal" notion of freedom. The above remarks have already shown that the preferential option for the poor contains a vision of society. Liberation theology, critical as it is of liberalism, is well aware that Christian freedom is not an empty freedom from interference that allows people to please themselves, but a coded freedom for doing good that enables people to overcome evil and create conditions of justice and peace. Following Paolo Freire, liberation theologians recognize that the great temptation of the oppressed is to envy their oppressor, to wish to conquer him and to put themselves in his place. That is why liberation theology describes the society of the future not in terms of the power exercised by the formerly oppressed (as in Marxism, the dictatorship of the proletariate) but rather in ethical terms of social and economic justice, tempered by forgiveness. Liberation theology recognizes that justice alone is not sufficient for creating a peaceful society: for if the correction of unjust structures is not qualified by mercy it will produce conditions that again provoke resentment and give rise to social unrest.

This defense of liberation theology, I wish to add, must be proposed with great humility since secular men and women active in emancipatory movements are also touched by God's grace and hence are often deeply transformed by love and generosity, whatever the shortcomings of their theory. I regard this as an important point. In my writings I have called this "the irony of the Gospel."[4] Again and again we encounter non-Christian people who are more transformed by faith, hope and love than we are. We marvel at their goodness because we recognize in it the presence of God's grace.

The last paragraph takes us back to the difference between the inclusivist christology, with which I am identified, and the exclusivist christology which Milbank shares with many important theologians. It is not my intention in this paper to offer a defense of the inclusivist christology, to show that it is rooted in certain biblical texts and in a stream within the Catholic tradition, and to demonstrate that since Vatican Council II it has been widely accepted within Roman Catholicism and even acknowledged in this quotation from John Paul II. "By his incarnation, the Son of God has united himself in a certain way with every human being. . . . Every person without exception has been redeemed by Christ. Christ is united in a certain way with every person—without any exception whatever—even if that person is unaware of it."[5]

Instead of defending inclusivist christology, I wish to raise some problems implicit in Milbank's exclusivist christology.

(3) Is Violence Implicit in Christian Discourse?

Because of his christology and his postmodern analysis of human existence, Milbank looks upon the cultural, philosophical and religious traditions outside the Church in terms of their blindness and sin. This is not done lightly. He offers the most extended philosophical analyses, with an erudition that amazes the reader, revealing that operative in these traditions have always been myths or meta-narratives that legitimated practices of domination and oppression and thus generated violence in one form or another. On these terms, Milbank discards secular reason operative in sociology and social theory, discards the tradition of classical reason, and discards—with the postmodern thinkers—any form of universal reason and any claim of universal truth. The one exception to this rule is the claim of Jesus Christ, the divine break-through in human history, whose message of universal relevance is encoded in his counter-practice of love, forgiveness and peace, a practice that inverts the violence of the world and mediates friendship and reconciliation.

Yet with postmodern thinkers Milbank exaggerates the extent to which people's practices and ideas are constructed by the myth implicit in their cultural tradition. In my opinion, as I mentioned above, this exaggeration is derived from Emile Durkheim's structuralist imagination, powerfully present in the French intellectual tradition, even if postmodern thinkers reject Durkheim's scientific project. For Milbank and the postmoderns, nothing is simply given and then discovered. Thus there is no human nature. All is constructed by the meta-narrative of the culture to which people belong.

Yet in reality, people live at the intersection of several orientations, some determined by their nature, and others derived from stories and cultural traditions. No one, except a few fanatics, lives out of a single meta-narrative.

Let us look, for instance, at the exercise of hospitality, a virtue praised and practised in many ancient cultures and religions. People have followed this ideal promoted by their cultural and religious stories for several reasons. The practice of hospitality expresses their awareness of mutual interdependence, their respect for human beings and the compassion they feel faced with human vulnerability. One supposes that elements of legitimate self-interest, cultural conformity, religious conviction and personal generosity (responding to some inner call) co-exist in the magnificent practice of hospitality, which Christians cannot but admire.

Yet Milbank's approach would oblige us to understand this practice only as an expression of people's culture or religion and hence purely and simply as a reflection of the respective meta-narrative. Since Milbank interprets the meta-narratives other than the Christian Story as myths legitimating domination, he would want us to interpret the practice of hospitality beyond the Church as an expression of violence. I am puzzled by Milbank's inability to marvel at goodness found beyond the Christian community. He has no sense of what I have called "the irony of the Gospel." Like Jonah, John Milbank does not want to believe that God can be merciful to Nineveh.

Basing himself on postmodern theory and his exclusivist christology, Milbank rejects all dialogue across the boundaries of the Church. Postmodern thinkers argue dialogue presupposes that the partners have something in common, some boundary-transcending "ratio," a presupposition the postmoderns reject as a modern illusion. They hold instead that people belong to differently constructed cultural spheres that are incommensurable. There is no common ground, no shared human nature, no solidarity in a joint struggle for justice. Endorsing this postmodern position, Milbank argues that Christians should not join non-Christians in defense of a just cause. Since all practice is coded by the meta-narrative that guides it, the actions of non-believers on behalf of a good cause are engendered, despite appearances, by the religious or secular culture to which they belong and hence, inevitably, open the door to violence.

In an article analysing the hidden, imperialist implications, derived from secular reason, present in the contemporary dialogue of Christians with members of other religions, Milbank argues that the Church's stance towards the world religions should be—not dialogue but suspicion.[6] In my opinion, articulating such a position in contemporary England, troubled by religious and racial conflicts, Milbank—despite his theoretical commitment to peace—creates a discourse or linguistic practice that encourages violence.

This takes us to Milbank's fateful decision, for postmodern and christological reasons, to dispense the Church from the critiques of modernity uttered by Marx, Freud, Nietzsche and many others. The critiques derived from secular reason, he argues, perpetuate the violence implicit in the Enlightenment project. What John Milbank, committed pacifist, fails to recognize is that the Christian practice itself, almost from the beginning, contained dimensions of violence, dimensions that were brought to light only in the Church's subsequent history, in part because of outbursts of visible violence and in part because of the arrival of the Enlightenment's emancipatory rationality.

Symbolic of the dark dimension of Christian practice is the negation of Jewish existence in action and theory, associated from the beginning with the proclamation of Jesus as Lord. In her study of Christian origins and the Church's subsequent preaching, Rosemary Ruether has called Christian antisemitism "the left hand of christology."[7] The violence present in the Christian meta-narrative escaped the Christian churches and their preachers for centuries. It was only after the Holocaust that the churches were ready to face the implications of their own linguistic practice about the Jews. The Holocaust as Christian challenge was an historical experience, one among several, that created the socio-cultural context for Karl Rahner's inclusivist christology and its rapid spread in one form or another among church people and theologians. This christology allowed Christians for the first time to honour Jewish religion. Eventually the Church purified its liturgy of the detrimental references to the people to whom Jesus belonged.

The Church remains forever in need of critiques uttered by people who have been adversely affected by Christian discourse and practice. Milbank who presents himself as a feminist seems to believe that the practice of Jesus alone provides an adequate critique of the Church's patriarchal tradition. He makes no reference to feminist critical theory. Against Milbank, I hold very strongly that the Church is in need of critiques derived from Enlightenment thought.

If Milbank listened to these critics, he would have to deal, for example, with serious questions regarding the stance of pacifism. Depth psychology has revealed the possibility that a self-willed pacifism represses hostile impulses which may return in unexpected ways, especially as paranoia. The ancient Christian hostility to Jewish religion may be a case in point. Milbank suffers from the illusion shared by sects and monasteries that it is possible to have a community defined *ad intra* by love and peace while relating itself *ad extra* by distance and non-reception. This illusion is the theme of the novel, *Peace Shall Destroy Many*[8] by Rudy Wiebe, the great Canadian Mennonite author, which examines the harsh indifference of a Mennonite community in regard to the Metis people living near them. To do penance for his own participation in this prejudice, Rudi Wiebe wrote two historical novels celebrating the courage and determination of Native heroes, Big Bear and Louis Riel.[9] Rejection of dialogue and indifference to the suffering of outsiders are self-damaging to the members of the loving community. This principle has been grasped by the Mennonite Central Committee of Canada and the United States when they extended their ministry of justice and reconciliation to peoples in conflict anywhere in the world.

A Church damages itself when it refuses to hear God's Word sounding in the cries of victims and the critical wisdom of humanity. For Milbank, Christian socialist and feminist, all of these messages are already contained in the practice of Jesus. But does he give sufficient evidence for this belief? I think Milbank could learn a great deal from listening to secular critical theory and liberation theology.

NOTES

1.   John Milbank, *Theology and Social Theory: Beyond Secular Reason* (Oxford and Cambridge, MA: Basil Blackwell, 1990).

2.   Jean-François Lyotard, *Just Gaming* (Minneapolis: University of Minnesota Press, 1985), 5-6.

3.   James McGinnis, *Solidarity with the People of Nicaragua* (Maryknoll, NY: Orbis, 1985), 124-27.

4.   Gregory Baum, *Man Becoming* (New York: Herder and Herder, 1971), 67.

5.   John Paul II, *Redemptor hominis* (1979), par. 8, 14, *Proclaiming Justice and Peace*, ed. M. Walsh and B. Davies (Mystic, CT: Twenty-Third Publications, 1991), 326, 333.

6.   John Milbank, "The End of Dialogue" in *Christian Uniqueness Reconsidered*, ed. Gavin D'Costa (Maryknoll, NY: Orbis, 1990), 174-91, 190.

7.   Rosemary Ruether, *Faith and Fratricide: The Theological Roots of Antisemitism* (New York: Seabury, 1974).

8.   Rudy Wiebe, *Peace Shall Destroy Many* (Toronto: McClelland and Stewart, 1962).

9.   Rudy Wiebe, *The Temptations of Big Bear* (Toronto: McClelland and Stewart, 1973) and *Scorched Wood People* (Toronto: McClelland and Stewart, 1977).

REFORMATION STUDIES
AND CHRISTIAN THEOLOGY

Douglas John Hall
McGill University

The question to which I shall seek to respond in this paper is: Why is an ongoing contemplation of the Reformation mandatory for Christian theology? My response will be in three parts: first, I shall try to characterize the situation—namely, the *present* theological context—in which the question is being asked; second, I shall consider briefly what seems to me to be the core of the 16th Century Reformation so far as Christian "self-definition" is concerned; and third, I shall return to the term "studied contemplation" as a way of speaking about the relation of theology to this particular past.

1. Whatever Became of Protestantism?

A visitor to earth from that very convenient imaginary planet entertained by earth-bound scholars from time to time, a sphere where everything about our planet and its history is fully understood, would have one question in particular to ask about the Christian religion in its North American expression. That question would be: "Whatever became of Protestantism?" This mythic visitor would not be deterred from his impertinent question when it was pointed out to him that there are in fact some four thousand "Protestant" denominations bustling about on this continent. He would certainly not desist, but would become all the more adamant in his demands, were he invited to view any number of Protestant "evangelical" television programs. And I suspect that he

141

would find little reason to qualify the starkness of his question were he to spend a year or two of Sundays going from one worship service to another in our once-mainline Protestant churches. Or perhaps, alas, he would feel after that experience that he had had his question answered, and would make his way back to his own intellectual utopia shaking his head.

Naturally, theologians and biblical scholars in our many seminaries and colleges would want to detain him. They would draw his attention to the considerable theological ferment in and around their institutions—the many theological movements, the endless stream of new publications, the development of whole new fields of discourse, and (of course!) the continuing presence in theological curricula of "Reformation Studies"! Would this satisfy our visitor that Protestantism was indeed still alive and well in North America?

One hopes it might give him pause. But I wonder. When Wilhelm Pauck of blessed memory was asked by a frustrated undergraduate student of self-confessed conservative leanings, "But where do *you* stand, Professor Pauck?", the great historian of the Reformation answered with a characteristic chuckle, "I have one foot in the Reformation, and the other . . . on a banana peel." Sometimes today one is tempted to think that all that is left is the banana peel.

This seems to be the conclusion of a prominent contemporary German scholar about the entire theological scene in the West. In his book, *Zur Freiheit eines Christenmenschen*, in which he discusses "Luther's Significance for Contempoary Theology," the Tübingen theologian Ernst Jüngel writes:

> . . . one of the most striking characteristics of contemporary theology is its lack of orientation. This is indicated in the capriciousness of its themes. Contemporary theology speaks to everything and everyone. But by doing so, it has less and less specifically theological to say. It has no *thema probandum* (theme needing testing) of its own.[1]

That is perhaps an overly critical assessment by a person not noted for his modesty;[2] yet it points to some realities that should not be ignored. At least from the vantage-point of the Reformation, theology today often does appear to lack an "orientation" of its own. It responds more consistently than it initiates. It tends to align itself with some other discipline or movement or "issue," to become the theistic or generally religious dimension of that phenomenon, and to test its authenticity by noting its acceptability to others associated with that same point of view—or, conversely, its *un*acceptability to the enemies of that point of view. Thus, one is a *liberation* theologian, or a *feminist* theologian, or a *black* theologian, or a *narrative* theologian or a theologian concerned with issues of the environment, or justice, or inter-faith dialogue, etc. One's program is associated in an explicit way with the adjectives qualifying the nouns "theologian" or "theology," or with the subject upon which one concentrates. These adjectives and subjects of concentration define what one is doing. So that it is a ludicrous thing, in contemporary theological discourse, if anyone announces: "I am a Christian theologian." The statement immediately begs for us the question, "But what *sort* of Christian theology do you profess?"

And that is no doubt a pertinent question, since a great many terrible things have been put forward under the name of Christian theology! In a world where nearly every right-wing political party bears the adjective "Christian" in its nomenclature, this word is probably more suspect than ever before in history. And yet the Reformers would certainly have found it strange that we wish now to identify ourselves in these quite programatic ways. Luther, were he, all unawares, to enter one of our contemporary theological consultations, say, the American Academy of Religion, might well naively introduce himself in the way that he regularly did in his own time—for instance, this: "As for me, I regard myself as a Christian. Nevertheless, I know how difficult it has been for me, and still is, to apprehend and to keep this cornerstone [Christ]. But they certainly do me wrong [who call me a Lutheran]. . . ."[3]

Professor Jüngel's complaint is that we have no *thema probandum*, that we lack an "orientation" that is "specifically theological," that arises from our being, simply, "Christian." We may remind him, of course, that Christianity has never been "pure."[4] It has always been thoroughly mixed up with other points of view, philosophies, religions, causes—hellenism or hellenistic judaism, gnost-icism, platonism, aristotelianism. The Reformation itself, we could mention, is inconceivable apart from the movements of which it was part. Only think of the role of Germanic mysticism and of nominalism in the case of Luther, or humanism in the formation of Zwingli, Melanchthon, Calvin, Oecolampadius and many others. Not to mention the rise of nationalisms of every hue! Is it not a pure construct, in fact, this "Christianity" that we attribute to our Protestant saints?

Beyond that, did they not themselves teach us to be a *responding* discipline, or at least foster, in their own ways, the methodology of response that was in fact present from the newer Testament onwards? They spoke much about "the Word of God," but even when they accentuated the discontinuity principle to the full—perhaps especially then!—did they not in fact do so for the purpose of *answering* what was already there in the world. A negative answer, like Karl Barth's famous "Nein!", is still an answer—a response. There is, behind it, a heightened consciousness of what is "going on" in the world. It does not seek to make *positive* contact with other movements and trends in the historical situation, but it certainly intends to respond, and very decisively! What indeed could the name "Protestant" mean apart from such an intention at the heart of this movement? We have turned it into something extremely innocuous; we should pronounce it "Pro*test*-ant." What Tillich called "the Protestant principle" is a pro*test*ing, ergo a *responding* principle. When therefore contemporary theological movements form themselves around this or that pressing socio-historical reality—for instance one of what Charles Birch called the "three great instabilities" of the age, injustice, unpeace, and the disintegration of creation—are they not following in the footsteps also of the Reformers?

Perhaps. But only, I think, perhaps! The determining question is whether our response issues from anything reasonably understood as the *core* of the faith, as *kerygma*. Nearly every imaginable response to every imaginable worldly reality can fit itself out with a language drawn from "Christian" sources, including the Bible—which in any case, as Luther put it, "has a wax nose." Indeed, one would be hard pressed in the "Christian" West to find any responses by anyone to almost anything which did not have some trace, however obscure, of Christianity in it. The great question is: Does a response issue from some fresh wrestling with the heart of the matter called Christian? Is the Christian community, confronted by the ever-changing specifics of historical existence, driven back to its *foundations*? Is it even conscious of these foundations, or of the necessity continuously to return to them, reassess them, reassess itself in relation to them, rediscover the meaning of "gospel" as it lives in the tension between them and its context?

This, I think, is what Jüngel means by "orientation": namely, being turned towards the *fundamentum*, the foundation. And when he speaks of "the capriciousness" of our contemporary theological "themes" he is saying, not that they lack liveliness, or significance, or even religious and ethical pertinence, but that they lack the kind of struggle with the foundational profession of faith that could give them a frame of reference of their own and prevent them from being *merely* responsive.

The question that this, in turn, raises is of course, What precisely *are* these foundations? After all, one church's cornerstone may be another's millstone! I have just used the Latin word, *fundamentum*, and who in North America can speak about "fundamentals" without immediately conjuring up in everyone's mind the 1895 Niagara conferences, where the enemies of liberal Christianity determined there were to be exactly *five* "fundamentals"—and every one of them a stumbling-block to contemporary intelligence!

This points to the truth that the Truth under which we live, as Christians, is not reducible to truths. It is a living truth and must therefore always be discovered, encountered, anew. There is only one corner-stone—and it is not "christology," it is Jesus Christ.

Yet there have been moments in the evolution of this faith when the foundations were—not coded! but—described, clarified. Moments when the Christian community, precisely in being *denied* further access to its familiar codification of truth, found itself encountered by the living Truth that it could not reduce to doctrine. That these moments were themselves regularly domesticated by the immediately subsequent cohorts of Christians; that their "creative chaos" (Tillich) was conquered by an all-too-predictable sort of ordering—this is a truism of history. But the moments themselves are still clarifying, if we can make our way back to them through all the welter of events and words. And amongst these moments, none, I think, is quite so clarifying *for us* as what we call the Reformation.

2. The Reformation as Christian "Definition"

The authority of the Reformation for theology ought not to be located in confessional ties that bind some denominations of the church to these beginnings. To honour Luther because one is a Lutheran, or Knox and Calvin because one is a Presbyterian, or Wyclif and Cranmer because one is an Anglican: these are shabby grounds indeed, hardly rising above the most primitive chauvinism. They are also unnecessary. The legitimate authority of the Reformation for Christian theology of all varieties has to do with the innate power of its *definition* of the Christian faith; and this in turn is connected, externally speaking, with its "timing," and internally with the persuasiveness of the account which, under the pressure of these temporal conditions, the Christian movement was able to give of its message.

(Before I proceed to elaborate on this hypothesis, let me in parenthesis comment on the word "definition" which will play a somewhat important part in what follows: it is employed here in a manner consistent with the *first* meaning of the *Oxford English Dictionary*, which, though considered obsolete, is precisely suggestive of what I mean: "The setting of bounds or limits." This meaning, following from the Middle English and Old French, *definer* (to bound), retains the idea of needing boundaries within which a given phenomenon may be experienced or known, without implying the kind of *precision* or *exactness* intended by the *modern* use of the word "definition." It would be better for Christian doctrine as a whole if *this* conception of the verb "to define" were still in vogue!)

To return from the parenthesis: Let me illustrate what I mean by "timing" by referring to three dimensions of the Reformation which constitute the beginnings of realities with which Christianity still lives and in relation to which it is still in process of discovering *how* it ought to live.

(1) *The Reformation occurred at a time in the evolution of European civilization when the Christian movement began to find it necessary to distinguish itself from other intellectual and spiritual currents, which by the 16th Century had become genuine alternatives to an explicitly Christian faith.* Under these conditions, it became necessary for Christians to inquire in more engaged and practical ways than they had done formerly how their belief was to be understood *vis-à-vis* the general experience of humanity. This meant of course the necessity of rethinking the relation of faith to human rationality—in a way an ancient inquiry, but now an inquiry with new dimensions.

For nearly a thousand years, Christianity had been able to depend upon dialogue with a Reason which, if not inherently predisposed towards itself, could at least be persuaded or caused to seem so. Moreover, during this long and formative period, the public preeminence of the Christian religion could hardly be said to be dependent upon the outcome of the attempts of the theological academy to demonstrate and retain Reason's favour. With the appearance of a new or renewed aristotelianism in the thirteenth century, and (at first) under the auspices of rival faiths, Christianity was as it were "given notice" that its monopoly on the mind (at least the mind!) of Europe could no longer be presumed upon.[5] Through the genius of the Dominicans, Albertus Magnus and Thomas Aquinas, a synthesis of faith with aristotelian rationality was devised to supplement or replace the old augustinian synthesis. But in this new concordat reason's independence was consistently upheld, and its support of faith, while perhaps strong (for a time) in the area of a generally theistic belief, was (to say the least) limited where an explicitly christocentric theism is concerned. The nominalists, and particularly Occam, not only further circumscribed the role of reason in the life of faith but presented the primary data of revelation in such a way as to be inaccessible to rationality. By the time of Luther and Zwingli, if not already with the pre-Reformers, the outcome of the dialogue of intellectuals on the subject of reason and faith was no longer confined to the intelligentsia but was having its effects on the general populace and upon social and political institutions.

We live still with the epistemological questions which first emerged for Christians in a prominent way at this time; and while we cannot simply repeat the Reformers' answers to these questions, we must nevertheless submit ourselves to their struggle with them—and especially if we wish to avoid foolish repetitions of the *simplistic* answers that were given by later schools of Christian thought, both conservative and liberal.

(2) The second historical factor which seems to me to oblige theology today to sustain an active contemplation of the Reformation of the sixteenth century is that *the Reformation marks, if not the beginning then at least the first decisive recognition on the part of the Christian movement (or let us say its cutting edge) that theology must always strive to distinguish the "essence" of the faith from its historical accretions, its **accidens**, and that, in order to arrive at the essence of a faith which is centred in an historically concretized understanding of revelation, it is necessary to have access to the most reliable accounts of Christian beginnings.*

This observation is related to one that I shall make presently about the so-called "formal principle" of the Reformation; but for the moment I only wish to point out that with the Reformation—at its very centre, in fact—we encounter the beginnings of a problem that distinguishes modern from pre-modern theology and is still very much with us. It could of course be said that the quest for the essence of the faith has been an aspect of Christian theology throughout its history. While that is true in an important sense (in Anselm's sense, for instance, that since faith, if genuine, is innately driven to the quest for understanding it is inherently bound to distinguish the kernel from the husk), a great difference is made, nonetheless, at that point in time where faith's essence is no longer defined and protected by effective sacred and even secular authorities but must establish itself in the heat of dialogue between representatives of differing experiences and points of view, and always, therefore, temporarily. That point is the Reformation. From the Reformation onwards, the question, "What *is* Christianity?"—von Harnack's question—has been unavoidable, and as an *original* question, one which requires original work of each new generation.

(3) The third and perhaps, in the last analysis, the most important historical factor establishing the significance of the Reformation for all subsequent Christian theology is that *it marks the beginning of the expulsion of the Christian movement from its constantinian cocoon*. If the second observation is associated especially with the Reformers who were trained in the humanistic tradition—Zwingli, Melanchthon and Calvin particularly—the implications of the whole Reformation for the disestablishment of the Christian religion are best seen in the destiny of the Reformation's radical wing. For the most part, the main Reformers seem not to have questioned the constantinian arrangement—or rather, they seemed content to adapt it to the new, largely national centres of power with which they were perhaps inevitably associated; and this despite the fact that the seeds of Christendom's disruption were present in their own most

characteristic teachings. Luther's "theology of the cross" could never have served as the cultic undergirding of empire, and if it had been pursued by the Germanic peoples as fervently as German Protestants pursued a truncated ("cheap") version of Luther's "justification by grace" the *theologia crucis* would have at least exercised a critical function in the face of German political and cultural triumphalism. Calvin's doctrine of the sovereignty of God *alone* also contains something inimical to the purposes of *Kulturreligion*, as may be more conspicuous in the work of John Knox than of Calvin himself. Such anti-establishmentarian emphases were neglected by the central Reform on account of their embrace by the powers that were; but the radicals had to learn to live outside of the imperial household, and for that reason alone (not to mention others) their story, so long neglected by mainstream Christianity, may be more important for us today than many other aspects of the Reformation. As the Christian movement throughout the western world finds itself pushed out of the centre and onto the periphery, it is obliged to seek historical models of diaspora faith; and amongst these the various models presented by the Reformation's left wing should by no means be despised.

While in these and other ways we are bound to the Reformation by its sheer "timing," its positioning at the point of rending between classical-medieval and modern Christianity, we should not find these historical connections so intriguing as they are were it not for the internal clarity of the response that was drawn from those whose personal experience of being jostled between the spirit of the times and the Spirit of God forced them to rethink the faith. Any brief attempt at an exposition of that claim is doomed to superficiality; but at least to rescue the claim from obscurity I shall again illustrate what I mean by referring to what the older Lutheran dogmatics called the "material" and the "formal" principles of Reformation faith.

(1) The slogan, "justification by grace through faith," does not, it is true, capture the whole substance of the Christian message as it was grasped by the Reformers, particularly Luther.[6] Without the presupposition, *per Christum solum*, the *sola gratia* and *sola fide* are in fact incomplete and misleading. Moreover, all three components of the slogan—"justification," "grace," and "faith"—require careful interpretation if they are to convey *to us* what the Reformers intended them to convey. And yet as a way of expressing what is *basic* or *definitive*, this doctrinal symbol is one whose comprehensiveness and lucidity cannot be overlooked without loss.[7]

To begin with, "justification by grace through faith" should not be construed simply as "a doctrine." It cuts across all the major doctrinal dimensions of the tradition and attempts a summation of them which is at the same time theoretical and practical—today we could speak of *praxis*. For this reason, Tillich called it "a principle":

> . . . I call it not only a doctrine and an article among others but also a principle, because it is the first and basic expression of the Protestant principle itself. It is only for unavoidable reasons of expedience a particular doctrine and should, at the same time, be regarded as the principle which permeates every single assertion of the theological system. It should be regarded as the Protestant principle that, in relation to God, God alone can act and that no human claim, especially no religious claim, no intellectual or moral or devotional "work," can reunite us with him. . . . In this sense the doctrine of justification is the universal principle of Protestant theology. . . .[8]

As Tillich's statement implies, the justification "principle" articulates the Christian message both positively and negatively. *Via negativa* (and we may begin there because, historically, that *is*, in a real sense, the beginning), it enters a permanent criticism against legalistic, moralistic religion. Such a critique is perennially necessary, because the essence of the "religious" heresy is the human propensity to acquire divine (and human) acceptability through allegedly "righteous" or "just" behaviour. In fact, Hendrikus Berkhof, in a wonderfully informative small-print discussion of the history of the justification principle, proposes that " . . . the reason for the early demise of [Paul's justification teachings] in the history of the church, without leaving much of a trace behind them" is related precisely to its debunking of presumed righteousness. "The morally blameless man considers it offence that his righteousness before God should rest totally on the righteousness of Christ."[9]

The principle of justification by grace through faith is by no means, however, a category of critical theology only; it contains a highly positive statement both about God and humanity. It insists that the fundamental posture of God in relation to the creature is one of unambiguous favour; that the "Absolute" *vis-à-vis* whom our lives are lived is not only "with us" but also "for us" (*pro nobis*). Though we are unworthy, we are pursued by a love that will not let us go—will indeed sacrifice itself rather than permit our self-destruction. From the perspective of human worth, a more positive conception of deity could hardly be imagined. As for humanity, while the justification principle assumes (on the negative side) the universality of sin and the helplessness of the sinner, on the positive side it presupposes a capacity for *fiducia*—that is, for a trust which is stronger than alienation and can live towards reconciliation. This trust is not "natural" to us, according to the Reformers, but it may nevertheless be achieved by the divine Spirit working within us; it may become in some genuine

sense ours—not as a permanent possession, but as a gift and struggle continuous
ly renewed.[10]

We shall return to the question of the *meaning* of "justification" later. We
turn now to the "formal principle."

(2) The *sola scriptura* of the Reformation, contrary to popular opinion, was
never intended to *displace* tradition but rather to become the authenticating mark
of divine revelation, the first principle of Christian knowing. It was the
principium cognoscendi or *principium cognoscendi externum*, corresponding to
the *principium cognoscendi internum* of faith, which as we have just noted is the
consequence of the "internal testimony of the Holy Spirit," the *principium
essendi* or essential foundation of divine revelation.

For Luther himself, the scriptures were not to be regarded as the object of
belief but only the indispensable *means* through which, given the Spirit's
testimony and faith's reception of it, the divine Word might be heard. Those
trained in the traditions of the new humanism were all of them, it seems to me,
at least *tempted* to believe *in* the Bible and not only *through* the Bible; and this
is true even of Luther's most illustrious theological companion, Melanchthon,
who maintained his Erasmian connection throughout his life, who lacked any
"mystical" sense, and who was given to a kind of "doctrinalism" that was
foreign to the spirit of Luther himself.[11] At least in the case of Luther, scripture
should not be considered the *substance* of belief but the primary external witness
to and enabler of belief—hence, the "formal" and not "material" principle.

Nevertheless, from the perspective of all the reformers, as well as Occam,
Wyclif, Hus and many who preceded the Reformation proper, the Scriptures of
the older and newer Testaments, considered as *Holy* Scripture, are (in our sense)
"definitive" of faith. And once again there is a negative as well as a positive
connotation implied in the *sola scriptura* principle. Without in the style of
biblicism *discounting* the accumulated traditions of (at that time) fifteen centuries
or more, the *sola Scriptura* relegates all traditions to a secondary place. Calvin
expressly rejects the notion that the authority of Scripture is dependent upon the
Church and insists, on the contrary, that the opposite is the case:

> It is a very false notion . . . that the power of judging of the Scripture belongs to
> the Church, so as to make the certainty of it dependent on the Church's will.
> Wherefore, when the Church receives it, and seals it with her suffrage, she does not
> authenticate a thing otherwise dubious or controvertible; but, knowing it to be the
> truth of her God, performs a duty of piety, by treating it with immediate veneration.
> But, with regard to the question, How shall we be persuaded of its divine original,
> unless we have recourse to the decree of the Church? this is just as if any one
> should inquire, How shall we learn to distinguish light from darkness, white from

black, sweet from bitter? For the Scripture exhibits as clear evidence of its truth, as white and black things do of their colour, or sweet and bitter things of their taste.[12]

The critical function of the formal principle of the Reformation has perhaps been overstressed, historically, and while there are very good reasons why this is the case, Daniel Migliori seems to me to be on the right track when he insists that "For the sixteenth-century Reformers, the authority of Scripture was rooted in its *liberating* message. . . . The Bible was experienced not as an arbitrary or despotic authority but as a source of renewal, freedom, and joy." In this vein, he goes on to propose: "Thus, a major task of theology today is to develop a liberative understanding of the authority of Scripture."[13]

With this necessarily limited summation of the Reformation's "definition" of Christianity, I turn now to the third and final major question: How does the studied contemplation of the Reformation make for theological wisdom?

3. Theological Wisdom and the Studied Contemplation of the Reformation

Like every other historical expression of the Christian faith, the heritage of the Reformation is coloured by the realities, obvious and obscure, of the context in which it occurred and of which it was part. We have become unusually conscious of the relativity of truth, especially religious truth, and in the past two decades this consciousness has been aggravated by the recognition that putative truth often serves questionable interests. Today from a great many perspectives critical questions are put to this heritage—questions which make everyone conscious of its thoroughly conditioned character. African, Asian, Latin American and even some North American theological communities lump the Reformation together with all the long tradition of european Christendom and ask, "Why should we be governed by this foreign history?" African-American and indigenous Canadian and American peoples testify to the oppressiveness of this tradition, how it has been used, just as often as european Catholicism, to destroy their own cultic and cultural heritages. Women who are inclined to do so have little difficulty documenting, from the annals of Reformation history and theology, their general thesis concerning the male domination and patriarchalism of the whole Judeo-Christian tradition.[14] Moreover, the mood of the churches of the West—churches which owe their existence, in one way or another, to the Reformation of the sixteenth century—is hardly conducive to a studied contemplation of the Reformation heritage. Particularly in North America, even where the atmosphere is not one of sheer historical ignorance and forgetfulness, the formerly mainline Protestants frequently relegate the remembrance and promulgation of the Reformation tradition to the most reactionary elements within Protestantism, which render the teachings of the Reformers all the more arcane and anachronistic, if not through outright misinterpretation, then through the failure to engage in hermeneutical consideration of the question how best to translate into late 20th century language the thoughts of sixteenth century people.

To this we might add, I think, a certain uninvited "spin-off" from the ecumenical movement and the concern for sensitivity to the plurality of religious traditions. Without intending it, ecumenicity and inter-faith dialogue have created in many Protestants, particularly liberal Protestants, a kind of hesitancy about the pursuit of their Protestant roots. Four or five centuries of denominational hostility and mistrust, together with the more recent recognition of Christian exclusivity and imperialism, have suggested to the consciences of sensitive people in all churches that it would be better to minimize the explicit dogmas and practices of their various traditions and to look instead for common contemporary concerns around which new expressions of mutuality could be woven.

For these and other reasons, the question that Paul Tillich asked fifty years ago, far from being passé, is all the more appropriate today: "Will the Protestant era come to an end?"[15] We might even press beyond this and ask, whether it has perhaps come to an end already? Are the many churches which still claim this nomenclature in fact pursuing something quite different from what the Reformation stood for? And if and insofar as they are, what should we think about the Protestant *message*? Is it, too, a relic of the past?

My own response to these questions will be a variation on the one that Tillich gave in *The Protestant Era*. In the *first* place, we should recognize—above all, knowledgeable Protestants themselves should recognize—that Protestantism as an historical phenomenon, as the characteristic expression of Christian faith and life in the midst of specific cultures and peoples, neither *is* nor should be considered permanent. It is foreign to the spirit of Protestantism to attribute finality to any historical expression of Christian faith. To set ourselves the task of preserving this or that form of the Protestant church, and to approach the contemplation of the Reformation with such a goal in mind, would be unworthy of the best insights of the Reformation itself, which sought (precisely!) to re-form the church, not to establish and sustain another church.

Secondly, it may even be asked—and perhaps at this juncture in the history of Protestantism we can no longer refuse to ask quite openly—whether at its heart Reformation Protestantism was ever truly compatible with the concept of "church" according to the connotation of that term current in Europe since the Constantinian-Theodosian establishment: namely, "church" as the official cult of a whole civilization and whole nations and cultures. Protestantism in its major expressions was certainly recruited for just such an office; but did it not, as Kierkegaard and Overbeck proposed, forfeit something of its very *essence* when it permitted itself to take up that role? At the heart of Protestantism stands (to use Tillich's formula) "the Protestant principle"—a principle which, as I have endeavoured to show in the previous section, informs in a rudimentary way both the material and formal principles of the Protestant message, a principle which must *protest* the perennial religious and human substitution of the finite for the infinite, the conditioned for the unconditional, the relative for the absolute. This critical principle, which is not the property of historical Protestantism but is the inheritance of Christianity from the prophetic tradition of Israel, by no means precludes the enucleation of specific communal expressions of the faith and of positive dogma. But it functions continuously to probe these, and to prevent their elevation to ultimacy. And precisely this function is—and has been!—a threat to every form of Christian establishment, whose whole logic is the preservation and buttressing of existing structures and values. Was Protestantism—Pro-*test*antism!—ever really fit for establishment? Was it from the beginning suited rather to the office of a critical minority, operating prophetically *within* the larger Christian and human communities?[16]

Thirdly, to the question whether the Protestant *message* must be subjected to the same critical assessment as I have just applied to the Protestant churches or "era," it is necessary to answer both yes and no. If, as I have done in the foregoing, we take the so-called material and formal principles of the Reformation as constituting a reasonable and defendable attempt to "define" this message, then we must certainly recognize in both cases the historical limitations of the language in which they are expressed. In the case of the material principle, the whole conception of "justification" may be, as Tillich suggests, incomprehensible to our contemporaries—even, he says, to most church-going Protestants and theological scholars.[17] For one thing, "justification by grace through faith" was conceived under the impact of an abiding sense of guilt before God; and if, as Tillich elsewhere insists (it seems to me quite rightly), the anxiety prevalent in contemporary Western society is not that of guilt but of "meaninglessness and despair," a gospel which addresses the guilty will not engage our culture at its cutting edge. Perhaps even Tillich's own "translation" of justification into the concept of "acceptance" is not quite appropriate to an age which—increasingly since his death—has demonstrated an incapacity for entertaining the significance of human creaturehood.

As for the formal principle, it would be irresponsible of Christians today simply to repeat the formula *sola scriptura* in the fashion of the Reformers. For, as Brunner amongst others has shown,[18] since the Reformation there has come to be a powerful, distorted form of the principle of scriptural authority, a form with which the Reformers themselves did not have to contend but which has so persuasively attached itself to Protestantism that the whole idea of the Bible's unique authority has been entirely coloured by it:

> Now . . . , what is or should be the basis of the Reformation principle of Scripture? To this question Reformation theology has only been able to give an inadequate answer, because in this theology, alongside of the right view of the authority of Scripture, which distinguishes the revelation in Jesus Christ from the Biblical testimony to it, an erroneous, "orthodox" doctrine of the authority of Scripture was at work, which became increasingly effective.[19]

In these and other ways we recognize that also the *message* of the Reformation must be subjected to "the Protestant principle": nothing—*nothing!*—temporal and finite may be accorded the status of ultimacy. In what sense, then, may we insist that the message of the Reformation nevertheless *transcends* its doctrinal articulations and deserves our studied contemplation as a particular source of theological wisdom?

I would like to respond to this question on two levels, one having more to do with content and the other with method. In connection with content, I would say that whatever language it may use now or in the future, a community wittingly accepting the designation "Christian" would have to sustain the *intention* both of the material and formal principles of the Reformation. It would not legitimately cling to that designation, in other words, were it (a) to lose touch with the belief that, in Jesus Christ, God has come and comes to be "with us" as One whose acceptance of us is not dependent upon our achievements but may be appropriated by us through a Spirit-inspired relation of trust, and (b) to cease to regard the scriptures of the older and newer Testaments as the primary external witness to what Christians profess. In this, it seems to me, the Reformation has correctly "defined" what is essential to this profession of faith, and therefore its struggle to do so, under the unique conditions of the emergence of Modernity, is permanently significant to the theological reflection of the Christian community.

The methodological observation may be more to the point, however, in our present context. It is bound up with the thought expressed in the previous sentence: the *struggle* of the Reformation to define essential Christianity. Without detracting from the importance of the "definition" that was actually put forward, I want to be able to say that the "struggle" for the definition is itself of the essence. In both its material and the formal principles, but particularly in the former, what the Reformation was about was an attempt to grasp the *centre*, the *core*, the *kerygma*. Whoever studies this immense and complex period called "Reformation" knows perfectly well that many subjects were explored, many questions probed, many answers given. For the reformers, nothing is uninteresting or unimportant—think of the variety of Luther's letters of spiritual counsel! Think of the organizational activities of the Swiss reformers! They are Christians, and therefore everything about the world—in it and beyond it!—constitutes their subject matter. And yet throughout there is a quest for the centre; for it is realized—for the most part, I think, intuitively, but also because of the historical factors to which I drew some attention earlier—that without a centre the rest also collapses.

With this observation I return, in conclusion, to the place where I began. If for the sake of getting wisdom, theologically, contemporary Christians are counselled to contemplate the Reformation of the sixteenth century, then it is this persistent quest for the centre that we should in particular concentrate upon. This centre may not be described in permanently valid *doctrina*; this foundation (to resort to an earlier metaphor) may not be unearthed once and for all, laid claim to, and built upon as something taken for granted. It may only be exposed through disciplined study, persistent prayer, and the readiness to "suffer" the insight to which it leads. But the *quest* for it is the condition without which the Christian movement will always lack an "orientation" (Jüngel); and then, even if it speaks to everything and everyone, it will have nothing "definitive" to say.

NOTES

1.   *The Freedom of a Christian: Luther's Significance for Contemporary Theology*, trans. Roy A. Harrisville (Minneapolis: Augsburg, 1988), 22.

2.   In the same work, he quotes with obvious delight Goethe's opinion that "only rascals are modest," and comments: "And where theology is involved, I would rather be taken for immodest than for a rascal" (*Freedom of a Christian*, 17).

3.   WA 31, I: 174, 26.

4.   " . . . there is no abstract Christian message. It is always embodied in a particular culture." Paul Tillich, *Systematic Theology*, Vol. III (Chicago: University of Chicago Press, 1963), 193.

5.   While the principal thinkers of Islam and Judaism in whom this aristotelian "renaissance" first occurred all lived earlier (in the case of Avicenna [980-1037], much earlier), the impact of their work upon Christianity seems to date from about the year 1230 at the earliest. In

1256, Pope Alexander IV asked Albertus Magnus to study the teachings of Averroes [1126-1198], particularly as relating to the nature of the intellect. Maimonides, who attempted to correlate Aristotle's teachings with *Jewish* revelatory faith, died in 1204.

6.   Luther wrote: "Der Artikel von der Rechtfertigung ist ein Meister und Fürst über alle Arten von Lehre und er regiert alles Gewissen und die Kirche. Ohne ihn ist die Welt fade und lauter Finsternis." Kurt Aland, ed., *Lutherlexikon* (Göttingen: Vandenhoeck & Ruprecht, 1983), 269.

7.   See Daniel L. Migliori, *Faith Seeking Understanding: An Introduction to Christian Theology* (Grand Rapids: Eerdman's, 1991), 175-77. Migliori writes: "While the doctrine of justification was the centerpiece of the theology of Luther and has been called 'the article by which the church stands or falls' [Carl E. Braaten], it would be a mistake to suggest that all Christian doctrine can be reduced to this single truth. The fullness of the event of Jesus Christ does not find expression simply in the doctrine of justification." He goes on to admit, however, that it would nevertheless "be folly to think that this doctrine is an outmoded teaching."
   This is a fair assessment, but it is mistaken in one thing, and that one thing is of singular importance: "justification by grace through faith" is not primarily "a doctrine"—or rather, if it becomes "a doctrine," as it tends to do with Melanchthon's interpretation of it (See Wilhelm Pauck, *From Luther to Tillich: The Reformers and Their Heirs* [San Francisco: Harper & Row, 1984], 51), the point of its being (in Migliori's term) Luther's "centerpiece" is missed.

8.   *Systematic Theology*, Vol. III (Chicago: University of Chicago Press, 1963), 223-24.

9.   Berkhof finds the Pauline theology of justification by grace through faith surfaces only *rarely* in the history of Christian thought—to wit, in Augustine, Luther, Calvin (to some extent), Wesley, the nineteenth century Reformed theologian, H.F. Kohlbrugge (1803-1875), and Karl Barth. He also relates that, according to a certain tradition (which he does not identify), " . . . Luther, at the end of his life, refering to the doctrine of justification, said, 'Soon after our death this doctrine will be obscured.' That [Berkhof continues] has indeed happened, not only then, but after each subsequent explosion, also in our own century. To live as a sinner from the faith that salvation is purely God's free gift is something which in the long run proves too demanding." *Christian Faith: An Introduction to the Study of the Faith*, trans. Sierd Woudstra (Grand Rapids: Eerdmans, 1979), 438.

10.   "Luther, at the same time that he speaks of faith as a work of God, has also described faith as a continuous and persistent struggle, and has spoken of its bold *dennoch*, its 'nevertheless.' Faith exists as a militant and praying faith, which can exist and continue only by being constantly won anew. There is always something of this element in faith: Lord, I will not let you go unless you bless me." Gustav Aulen, *The Faith of the Christian Church*, trans. Eric H. Wahlstrom and G. Everett Arden (Philadelphia: Muhlenberg, 1948), 320.

11.   On this subject see Wilhelm Pauck's excellent essay, "Luther and Melanchthon," in *From Luther to Tillich*, 39-65.

12.   *Institutes*, Book I, Chap. VII, II.

13.   Migliori, 40.

14. In this connection, however, see Jane Dempsey Douglas's essay, "Women and the Continental Reformation" in *Religion and Sexism: Images of Women in the Jewish and Christian Traditions*, ed. Rosemary Radford Ruether (New York: Simon and Schuster, 1974), 292-318.

15. *The Protestant Era*, trans. James Luther Adams (Chicago: The University of Chicago Press, 1948), xii.

16. In his third "way," marking the conclusion of his essay, "The End of the Protestant Era?", Tillich implies an affirmative answer to this question; at least, he assumes that the minority-diaspora status will have to be the way of the Protestant future, and may already be our reality: "This third way requires that Protestantism appear as the prophetic spirit which lists where it will, without ecclesiastical conditions, organization, and traditions. Thus it will operate through Catholicism as well as through orthodoxy, through fascism as well as through communism; and in all these movements it will take the form of resistance against the distortion of humanity and divinity which necessarily is connected with the rise of the new systems of authority." Tillich does not think of this as a merely formless or amorphous "trend," but assumes a degree of organization: " . . . this imperative [to resist distortions of humanity and divinity] would remain a very idealistic demand if there were no living group which could be bearer of this spirit. Such a group could not be described adequately as a sect. It would approximate more closely an order or fellowship and would constitute an active group, aiming to realize, first, in itself that transformation of Protestantism which cannot be realized either by the present churches or by the movements of retreat and defense. It would therefore be a group in which the Christian message would be understood as the reintegrating principle in the disintegrating world situation of today." *The Protestant Era*, 232.

17. "Protestantism was born out of the struggle for the doctrine of justification by faith. This idea is strange to the man of today and even to Protestant people in the churches; indeed, as I have over and over again had the opportunity to learn, it is so strange to the modern man that there is scarcely any way of making it intelligible to him. And yet this doctrine of justification by faith has divided the old unity of Christendom. . . . We have here a breaking-down of tradition that has few parallels. And we should not imagine that it will be possible in some simple fashion to leap over this gulf and resume our connection with the Reformation again." *The Protestant Era*, 196.

18. *Dogmatics*, Vol. I (*The Christian Doctrine of God*), trans. Olive Wyon (London: Lutterworth, 1949), 44ff.

19. *Dogmatics*, Vol. I, 45.

Iconoclast or Regenerator?
The Work of Andreas Bodenstein in Reforming the Church of the Sixteenth Century

Edward J. Furcha
McGill University

In recent analyses of persons on the sidelines of history, stark alternatives like the one implied in the title of this paper have seemed to be the only way of getting the attention of one's colleagues in the field. Even when we know from experience that life is never as neat as we manage to arrange it in lectures and symposia, we tend to allot such persons a place of singular importance in the scale of things. And we then proceed by a sleight of archival hands to demonstrate beyond the shadow of a doubt that these agents of change had to be exactly the way we perceive them and that they stood for either right or wrong, truth or falsehood, the good or the evil side, in everything they wrote or said. At the end of our deliberations we come away with the illusion of having scored an important point in our field of scholarship. Of course, we will be subject to the criticism of those who do not agree with our conclusions and, whether or not we will have succeeded in correcting misconceptions or will, in the process, have contributed toward a better understanding of the person under scrutiny, remains a matter for further question.

In focussing on the reform work of Andreas Bodenstein, 1486-1541, from the town of Karlstadt in Lower Franconia, I could be accused of having tried just such a scholarly trick. My primary objective is to rescue Carlstadt from being perceived negatively as an iconoclast. I hope to achieve that task by juxtaposing

159

two of his previously recognized contributions which, at a first glance, seem to be contradictory: his alleged iconoclasm during his Wittenberg years and his emphasis on personal and social regeneration, which came to full fruition during his years in Zurich and Basel toward the end of his life. If my reading of Carlstadt is valid, these two aspects of his work complement each other: his iconoclasm being but a first step toward making the inner spiritual regeneration visible in externals.[1]

Andreas Bodenstein who, from an early stage in his career liked to be known as Carlstadt (after his birthplace), invites our scrutiny. Until the ground-breaking work of Hermann Barge most histories dwelt on Carlstadt's iconoclastic activities at Wittenberg (choosing to ignore his later work in Zurich and Basel or treating it as no more deserving of attention than his years as "new lay person" from around 1523 onward). Recently Ulrich Bubenheimer, Ronald Sider and Calvin Pater have undertaken more nuanced re-examinations of the sources and, as a result, have highlighted Carlstadt's contribution as regenerator.

In juxtaposing what I consider to be Carlstadt's two major contributions to ecclesiastical and social reforms, I am proceeding from the premise that our own attitude significantly colours how we assess the work of this somewhat enigmatic scholar. Thus, if we take Luther as the norm for our judgement, Carlstadt will look more like a destroyer of his reforms than a healer of religious and social ills, or like an antagonist, rather than an innovator. If, on the other hand, we are prepared to examine his work on its own merit and to read his arguments sympathetically, we may come to recognize the depth of his concern for discipline and discipleship (which he espoused by both training and disposition). Before I dwell in greater detail on the two key contributions I mentioned, let me briefly sketch some significant moments in Carlstadt's life.

Since a recent discovery by Bubenheimer[2] we know that Carlstadt was actually younger than Luther by three years. This fact may explain, at least in part, why Luther so readily gained the upper hand in their rivalry during the Wittenberg period and why, when Luther returned from the Wartburg where he had been kept in hiding, he blamed this erstwhile colleague for the near chaos that had ensued in his absence.[3] Like Luther, Carlstadt had been given a professorship at the fledgling University in Wittenberg. People obviously looked to Luther as the elder statesman and chief exponent of evangelical reform with whom Melanchthon and Carlstadt were expected to toe the line. A certain degree of unanimity would therefore have been expected. When, for reasons we may never fully know, Carlstadt was judged to be the odd man out, the latter had no choice but to leave Wittenberg.

His dismissal undoubtedly had political as well as religious implications. The long-established notion of the corpus christianorum, according to which temporal rulers had rights and obligations and spiritual rulers worked together with them in guiding the flock within clearly understood boundaries, had to be preserved in an evangelically reformed territory. Disagreements among spiritual leaders would be seen as bringing disunity to the flock and as a threat to the careful balance between the temporal and the spiritual sword. Carlstadt's identification with rebellious elements in Wittenberg was judged, as a result, to be the consequence of his doctrinally unsound and politically dangerous enthusiasm. Under different circumstances, Carlstadt would probably have agreed with such perceptions. What he failed to see in the matter of the prompt removal of "idolatrous objects and practices" was that his view of how temporal and spiritual authority ought to converge in towns and cities differed from Luther's.[4]

In the three reform tracts of 1520 (*To the German Nobility, The Babylonian Captivity of the Church*, and *The Freedom of the Christian*) Luther places responsibility for temporal authority squarely with princes and rulers and assigns spiritual authority to an evangelically reformed papacy (note his Preface to Pope Leo X).[5] In other words, Luther still works with the principle of an authenticated magisterium, although he seems to have sensed that simply continuing old structures would not result in the needed reforms.

By contrast, Carlstadt had begun to see that radical reform would have to originate in communities of Christians who, prompted by the spirit of God, would learn to live by the letter of the written word of God.

The rift between them brought about Carlstadt's almost instant dismissal from Electoral Saxony and with it the loss of his livelihood. Fortunately for him and his family, the land his wife had inherited allowed him to work the soil for a while—a chore for which he obviously had no aptitude. In the ensuing years he lived as a "new lay person," travelling widely and establishing numerous contacts in the Lowlands, in Silesia, in Denmark and in South Germany. Finally in 1530 he settled in Zurich as chaplain and supply preacher at the Greatminster and as instructor in Zwingli's *Prophezei*.

By 1534 Carlstadt was appointed to a teaching position at Basel where he became heavily involved in revamping the educational system. During his time there he served as respected professor, dean of the theological faculty and, for a term, as rector of the University. At the age of forty eight Carlstadt, therefore, achieved what he had probably envisaged in his Wittenberg days—to be a doctor of a truly reformed church and, as such, a "truthful" transmitter of the very word of God which he believed to be the source of the renewal of individuals and their structures. His career had come full circle.

In light of this career it seems rhetorical to ask whether Carlstadt was merely an iconoclast. His numerous contributions toward change and renewal suggest that he also had a role as regenerator of Christendom in the early sixteenth century. To appreciate how his work as iconoclast—the manner of his attack on deceptive externals—contained the seed of his contribution toward regeneration, a careful re-examination of his writings would be essential. In the context of this paper I can merely suggest the direction such examination may take by looking in some detail at three of Carlstadt's writings.[6] In addition, I wish to suggest that his activities in Zurich and Basel where he spent the last eleven years of his life, rather than reflecting yet another ideological shift, are integral to Carlstadt's intellectual development and proof positive that he was more than an unrepentant enthusiast and troublemaker. In fact, were I a determinist I might suggest that his return to academic life was the inevitable apex of a rich and variegated life "under the word." Certainly Carlstadt's work in Zurich and Basel gives us significant clues about the nature of his reform work.

This line of defence is not without its problems, of course. The first difficulty Carlstadt presents to the historian comes when we attempt to fit him into one of the three categories that have generally been used to classify sixteenth century reformers: 1. magisterial reformers, 2. defenders of the established order, and 3. radicals or enthusiasts. Carlstadt cannot easily be placed into any of the above without careful qualifications. Although Heinold Fast (with some obvious unease) includes him among enthusiasts, and although Calvin Pater has attempted to show him as progenitor of Anabaptists, Carlstadt is neither enthusiast nor Anabaptist.[7] Nor can he be identified with Luther's cause, either in his ecclesiology or in his understanding of baptism and the eucharist.

On the basis of his apparent identification with the cause of Zwingli and Bullinger during the last career change he undertook, we might wish to align Carlstadt with the Reformed cause in Zurich and Basel. But even that association is not problem-free, for Carlstadt is demonstrably not a Zwinglian. Perhaps the fairest treatment we can give him is to see him as an evangelical individualist. This obliges us to take him seriously enough to come to terms with his writings and to allow that the last word on Carlstadt's place in history has not been written or spoken.

When we look at Carlstadt's tract On the Removal of Images *Von Abtuhung der Bilder* we realize that the major rift between Luther and Carlstadt had less to do with the place of images in evangelically reformed churches, than it did with the nature of biblical authority. During Luther's absence from Wittenberg in 1521/22 Carlstadt—who had been rather reluctant to become involved in militant reform activities—was drawn, along with Melanchthon, into the forceful and generally destructive removal of statues and images from Wittenberg sanctuaries. His *Von Abtuhung der Bilder* of February 1522 is Carlstadt's spirited justification of the radical removal of statues and images, based on texts from both the Old and the New Testaments.

Three things gave rise to the pamphlet which, incidentally, he dedicated to the Count of Passau, Wolf Schlick, probably to prod him into similar action: 1. a recently promulgated regional Church Order according to which the Mass was to be distributed to the laity in both kinds; 2. an order to remove images from churches, and 3. a mandate to care for the poor in the city of Wittenberg.[8]

Carlstadt obviously took the fact that reforms were to be carried out on order of a rightfully instituted temporal authority as a sign of the soundness of evangelical reforms in Electoral Saxony. It would seem appropriate to him, as a doctor of the Christian community there, to provide the authoritative biblical foundation for the reforms. Unlike Emser and Eck who strongly advocated retention in chapels and churches of the "picture books for the laity,"[9] Carlstadt urged the removal of images as a way of protecting "weak consciences" from irreparable harm.

Contrary to the allegations of his detractors, Carlstadt's intention was not to incite to rioting, but rather to show with Scripture that, while radical change would have to cut to the quick, it would, at the same time, "preserve true Christian order."[10] Incidentally, he frequently used the metaphor of spiritual circumcision (or, circumcision of the heart) to allude to the radical surgery required at the onset of the new life.

Beginning with the first commandment, and continuing with the warnings against misplaced devotion found in selected prophetic sayings, Carlstadt proceeded to postulate that sanctuaries are places of prayer to God alone. Any homage rendered to saints was to give to human beings what was exclusively God's. And since true worship was a disposition of the heart rather than rituals carried out in front of objects of wood or stone, reverence for images was sheer idolatry. "To worship God through images is to worship falsehoods."[11] So confident was Carlstadt of the divine displeasure with external worship in any form that he would exclaim, "God prohibited images no less and with no less fervour than murder, robbery, adultery and such like."[12] Indeed, "no one who honours images, comes to God."[13]

Carlstadt's use of Scripture shows him to be a near biblicist. As such he does not greatly differ from Luther or many another of his contemporaries. However, his appeal to the text of Scripture is tempered by what he defines in *On the Manifoldness of the Singular, One Will of God* of 1523 as "probing the spirit of the letter" which alone reveals the will of God.[14] Although such searching for the spirit of the letter of biblical texts may appear to be arbitrary and individualistic, Carlstadt promotes it as the only acceptable way of becoming attuned to the internal Word of God—a process of discernment reserved to those Christians who are truly *gelassen* in God. Externals are not totally excluded in such discerning, but are merely expressions in the public arena of the obedient believer's internal responses to God's bidding—actions which serve as testimony to the world, but are not essential to the God-human relationship.

Carlstadt's readers were probably not unfamiliar with the notion of *Gelassenheit* (detachment, surrender, yieldedness),[15] when he published his *Von Abtuhung*. His first tract on the matter—somewhat in the form of an *apologia pro vita sua*—had appeared as early as 1519 and had been reprinted at least twice since then. A more elaborate treatise was to appear a year or so later in 1523. Within a few years *Gelassenheit* was to become a stock phrase in Anabaptist circles and among radical reformers of the period. In my reading of Carlstadt's thought *Gelassenheit* is a fundamental notion which he both advocates and seeks to live by. I shall now turn to the two tracts in which this concept is developed in some detail.[16]

When Carlstadt published *Tract on the Supreme Virtue of Detachment*—some sixteen pages in translation—he was about thirty-three years of age, full of anxiety over the "roaring of the Florentine Lion" (a not-so-veiled reference to the Florentine Medici, Pope Leo X[17]) and deeply concerned with the well-intentioned efforts of his mother and family to protect him from the possible consequences his rash involvement in change and reform might have.[18] In explaining to them why he is prepared to accept any suffering he must endure for swimming against the stream, he describes the two forms of death one can suffer: 1. destruction of the spirit (which has eternal consequences) and 2. death of the flesh (a temporary moment). The former he ties to following the demands of an "indoctus Papa," the latter he sees to be the inevitable lot of anyone who obeys Scripture.

As we noted in his justification of the removal of images, here too the spiritual reading or hearing of God's Word is the key to Carlstadt's action. As defined in the tract, surrender or yieldedness is far from being a coward's escape from responsible action. Rather, such *Gelassenheit* calls for a discernment of the Truth and how it is received, a certainty of one's authority, and a willingness to accept consequences which could affect one's career, one's social relationships and even one's physical life.

Carlstadt, it would seem, had arrived at a position in which the authority of the Pope would be accepted only if it corresponded with his own understanding of where truth was to be found—a rather specific application of the *sola*

Scriptura principle. He leaves little doubt that an unlearned, unscriptural pope was none other than an antichrist.[19] With some conviction he can assert, "If the Pope is righteous and a Christian, let him show me Scripture and overcome my teaching with the word of God."[20] And a little later in the Tract, "Papa lupus, non pater" clearly caps his considered opinion of a christless pretender to spiritual authority.

What must have been particularly hurtful to his mother and his family was Carlstadt's rigorous denunciation of their friendship and love insofar as he saw it interfering with his doing of God's will and living in imitatio Christi. He tells them, "Therefore, dear friends, I have to be against you, if you should try to draw me away from the word of God."[21]

In a rigorous Christian stance such as his, detachment extends not only to material things, but to human relationships—indeed, to oneself. Carlstadt harbours no doubt when he states, "Not only must I detach myself from you, but from myself as well. I must have no regard for body and soul." His definition of the virtue of detachment or surrender is all-encompassing. It contains both a passive "letting-go" and an act of the will. He writes,

> I know that there is no greater virtue on earth and in heaven than detachment, when a person leaves behind all possessions, honour, friends, body and soul. Even if I should burn in the midst of the flames, but if I have no detachment, my suffering would be of no merit to me, i.e., if I did not love God and place my trust, comfort, faith, and hope in him, I would be like a sounding bell (1 Cor 13).

In greater detail and more nuanced than in his tract of 1519, Carlstadt developed his understanding of yieldedness in the 1523 tract entitled, *The Meaning of the Term "Detached" (gelassen) and where in Holy Scripture it is found*. Much in his life had changed. He had renounced academic status and honours, had donned the garb of the peasant and had partially withdrawn to his wife's land which he attempted to work—unsuccessfully, as we noted earlier. Detachment was no longer a principle to be discussed academically. It had become reality in Carlstadt's own experience—external testimony to a radically changed inner disposition. Carlstadt understood his state of yieldedness as having been wrought by God's grace in his inner being—a divine action he "suffered" but to which he, in turn, had given his fullest assent.

Through his reading, particularly of the *German Theology,* and through his life changes and experience, Carlstadt had gained added insights on the truly *gelassen* state. These he would now pass on, through his publications, to earnest inquirers, and to a wider audience.

Noteworthy is the link Carlstadt makes in this particular tract between yieldedness and circumcision of the heart or spiritual circumcision—between, on the one hand, "immersion of the soul in the unfathomable will of God"[22] and, on the other, total detachment from desire, material things, yes, even from oneself. Carlstadt now sees these two apparent opposites as inextricably and paradoxically linked in true *Gelassenheit*.

The contrasting state is agreeableness or unyieldedness—the human inclination to seek honour from others, and to follow the dictates of one's own will. In such a state, Carlstadt holds, it is impossible to believe in God.[23] Not surprisingly perhaps he detects this tendency in people like himself who, more than simple Christians, rely on their own wisdom and strength, rather than putting their trust in God. In fact, in a section of this pamphlet, entitled "Higher Education" he reaches an acute state of pessimism in his exposure of academics as prime examples of those who readily incline toward agreeableness. For readers less sophisticated than himself, the exaggerated self-deprecation implied in this view led to anti-intellectualism; regrettably, such disdain of intellectual prowess has often tainted many otherwise discerning radicals.

Fortunately, Carlstadt himself seems to have suffered from no more than a passing bout of pessimism which was probably fueled, at the time he wrote the tract on detachment, by the circumstances of his expulsion from Electoral Saxony and by the ever-widening gulf between himself and Luther.

Toward the end of this fascinating exposition of genuine "yieldedness" he is able to speak of yieldedness becoming transformed into what he calls "heavenly yieldedness"—a superior spiritual state—the ultimate experience of a person who is wholly "in God." He writes,

> When the spirit of restfulness takes hold of us and fills the house or temple of God, which is the soul, with its splendour, the detachment comes to an end and turns into unyieldedness.

A hasty reader might detect in such an assertion a trace of perfectionism. For Carlstadt these concluding lines were little more than a sincere prayer that God might grant him and his readers that future state of blessedness in which "creaturely detachment becomes divine unyieldedness."[24]

Before such a state would be a possibility for Carlstadt himself, a number of tasks faced him. One, of course, was responsibility for his family. Another was the finding of an arena in which he might carry out, in a reasonably supportive context, his share of building up the household of faith. At such a point, iconoclasm and violent action would no longer be necessary since the agents of reform in their respective communities had truly yielded to the regenerating power within them by which they would then be led to the correct action.

I have argued elsewhere[25] that Carlstadt's balancing of the temporal and spiritual realms more closely approximated Zwingli's reform work in Zurich than that of Luther in Electoral Saxony. In Zurich the temporal power was exercised by a Christian magistrate, fully supported by an evangelically reformed clergy, as custodians of spiritual authority. Similar conditions would prevail for Carlstadt when he moved to Basel in 1534. Having by then attained a tranquil state of mind, and finding himself in a climate of relative openness to renewal, the rebuilding of communities of faith could be undertaken. In such regeneration from within, the word of God alone was to be the norm by which any existing structures would be measured and any new ones established. These would be protected against renewed idolatry by the very spirit of God which in the first creation had brought order out of chaos. I submit that this spirit was for Carlstadt the sole power by which regenerated men and women would be enabled to walk in obedient surrender to the divine will until, at the end of their labours, they would approach the true sabbath of the Almighty when

> creaturely spirits rest firmly and laudably in God when they understand and know . . . that God sanctified them through Christ . . . [t]hey do what ought to be done. They are still and wait for how and when God deigns to sanctify them in conformity to himself. For all that is external is merely a figure and sign of the internal holiness. . . .[26]

NOTES

1.   In other words, obedient submission to the Gospel calls for obedience to the law of God, "You shall have no other gods before me." Thus, law is gospel and gospel is law.

2.   In an article on "Karlstadt" in *TRE*, vol. 17 (1987): 649ff., Bubenheimer shows on the basis of an archival find that Carlstadt was born in 1486, not, as was formerly held, in 1477 and 1480 respectively.

3.   Evidence suggests that Melanchthon would have deserved as much blame for approving or condoning the radical iconoclastic action by students and others. Carlstadt was by far the more reserved of the two and seems to have been reluctant to take radical routes toward ecclesiastical reform, though, as we shall see later, he did in 1522 write in favour of the removal of images.

4.   The precise nature of this difference is difficult to formulate. At the Leipzig Disputation of 1519 Luther's position seems to be very much like Carlstadt's. Both refer to Scripture, relying on Paul and Augustine rather than on the Thomistic view espoused by John Eck. Luther's side of the argument may be found in WA 2. 250-383.

5.   For recent assessments of Luther's changing attitudes to and relationships with the papacy see Scott H. Hendrix, *Luther and the Papacy* (Philadelphia: Fortress, 1981); Remigius Bäumer, *Martin Luther und der Papst* (Münster: Aschendorff, 1970 [1985]) and Peter N. Brooks, *Seven-Headed Luther* (Oxford: Clarendon, 1983). J. Rogge, *Anfänge der Reformation* (Berlin: Evangelische Verlagsanstalt, 1983), proffers some helpful insights.

6.   My translation of fifteen of Carlstadt's tracts will appear in 1994-95 as volume 8 in the series *Classics of the Radical Reformation*, published by the Herald Press. The three tracts which I shall examine here are, *On the removal of Images*, 1522, *Tract on the Supreme Virtue of Detachment*, 1519 and the 1523 publication *The Meaning of the Term "gelassen" and Where in Holy Scripture It Is Found*.

7.   See Heinold Fast, *Der linke Flügel der Reformation* (Bremen: Schünemann, 1962), 250. C. A. Pater's analysis is lucidly developed in *Karlstadt as the Father of the Baptist Movement. The Emergence of Lay Protestantism* (Toronto: University of Toronto Press, 1984).

8.   See N. Müller, "Die Wittenberger Bewegung 1521 und 1522," 2d ed., in *Archive for Reformation History*, Vols. 6, 7, 8 (Göttingen: Gütersloher Verlagshaus, 1908-11). Fredrick the Wise on February 13,1522 put a temporary halt to reforms promulgated by city councils. See R. Bainton, *Here I Stand* (New York: Abingdon-Cokesbury, 1950), chapter XII.

9.   For a recent English translation see *A Reformation Debate: Karlstadt, Emser, and Eck on Sacred Images*, ed. and trans. Bryan Mangrum and Guiseppe Scavizzi. CRRS Translation Series 5 (Toronto: University of Toronto Press, 1991).

10.   Carlstadt, "On the Removal of Images" in "The Essential Carlstadt," ed. and trans. E. J. Furcha (unpublished manuscript, 91).

11.   Carlstadt, "Removal," 107.

12.   Carlstadt, "Removal," 114.

13.   "Removal," 115.

14.   See Document VIII, "The Nature of God's Eternal Will," in E. J. Furcha, "The Essential Carlstadt," 57.

15.   The notion of *gelassenheit* widely used in medieval mysticism was adapted in numerous ways by Radicals of the sixteenth century. In the seventeenth century *ataraxia* became a moral ideal which included elements of tranquility, detachment, imperturbability and moderation. See Richard Tuck, "Skepticism and Toleration in the 17th Century" in *Justifying Toleration*, ed. S. Mendus (Cambridge: Cambridge University Press, 1988), 21-35.

16.   In a paper given at the Sixteenth Century Studies Conference in October 1992 I attempted to show how Carlstadt develops the notion of *gelassenheit* in his own peculiar way going beyond what it might have meant in the writings of medieval mystics.

17.   Before his elevation to the pontificate in March 1513, Leo X was Giovanni de Medici, 1475-1521. While he was supportive of Renaissance and Humanism, he had little regard for the kind of spirituality represented by mystics and Protestant reformers. His complex political engagements caused him to neglect religious matters—one reason why the Reformation succeeded so well.

18. See Document I in "The Essential Carlstadt," 6.

19. See Carlstadt, "On the Manifold, Singular Will of God," Document VIII in "The Essential Carlstadt," 192ff. There Carlstadt describes the pope, bishops and monks as "the devil's procurers."

20. See *On the Supreme Virtue of Detachment*, 9.

21. *Supreme Virtue of Detachment*, 11.

22. *The Meaning of "Detached,"* 153.

23. *The Meaning of "Detached,"* 161, 164.

24. *The Meaning of "Detached,"* 169.

25. See E. J. Furcha, "Zwingli and the Radicals," paper read at the Sixteenth Century Studies Conference, October 1991, Philadelphia.

26. See Carlstadt, "Regarding the Sabbath and Statutory Holy Days," Document XII in "The Essential Carlstadt," 377.

Part III

World Religions

Religious Pluralism
in its Relation to Theology and Philosophy
—and of These Two to Each Other

Wilfred Cantwell Smith
Professor Emeritus of the Comparative History of Religion
Harvard University

"What is an historian doing in this company?", you may well be asking. Certainly I have been asking myself that question, conscious as I am of how unsophisticated is my philosophic background. I waited until my mid-sixties before writing a book with the word "theology" in the title, and even then it was a matter of *"towards"* it. About philosophy I am still more diffident. Yet accept the invitation I did, forthwith and with delight; and I am certainly happy to be here among you.

One answer to my query is that historians too are human beings, and interested in human beings; and I was quick to grasp the opportunity to take part in this affair primarily because Joe McLelland has been and is so eminently a wonderful human being. One is grateful for the chance to attest to that, and to join in honouring him. I have been fortunate enough to know him virtually ever since my wife and I came back from the Orient to Canada, indeed to Montreal, some four decades back. And there has been, in the years since, no letup in my admiration for both him and his work. In fact: for both it has continued to grow.

There is the further point that he not only has been and is both a philosopher and a theologian of impressive power, but has been and is as well, and in relation to that, himself also an historian. The historical consciousness that he has brought to bear on his philosophic-theological thinking has manifestly been decisive, and has given it a substantial share of the richness and the cogency that it has always had. Would that all philosophers and all theologians were as historically grounded and integrated. Would that I were! And: would that all three groups were as aware of, alert to, the pluralism issue. Each of us—certainly I—have a great deal to learn from him.

Religious pluralism is one of the headings under which this conference has been set up, and I was asked to speak under that rubric. I added to it, in the wording of my title, the particularities of the specific topic that I decided to pursue. My presentation might equally, however, have been named "Human history and its relation to theology and to philosophy, and of these two to each other." For human history is, in *my* view, fundamentally religious history; and, in anybody's view unless they wear blinkers, is pluralist. Anyway, my proposal is to proffer a few historical observations. My suggestion is that a contribution to our thinking may perhaps be derived from seeing our particular Western outlooks from the perspective of the cultural history of the world: that these other matters may be illumined by such a move.

In particular, I would toss out for rumination two such observations. One has to do with the development of Western civilization within world history; the other, with that of Islamic. Not unexpectedly, I find the two to be interlinked. Let me begin with the Islamic.

In the Qur'an, Muslims are called "the middle community", and in fact over the centuries their movement developed and spread and constructed a mighty civilization over a sector of our planet where it found itself midway between Europe on its west and especially India on its east. Worth our noting is an aspect, germane to our topic, of the Islamic meeting with Christians and Jews in the one case and with Hindus in the other. In late mediæval Spain, where Muslim culture was sophisticated, tolerant, and much more highly developed than anything else in sight, there was as you know a trilogue, friendly and fruitful, among Muslims, Jews, and Christians. Significant is that what the intelligentsia of all three groups had in common, as they talked to each other, was Aristotle, while what divided them was their diverging forms of faith. This encounter has left the Western world with a firm sense that philosophy is universal, while "religion" is particular. At the other end of the Islamic world, on the other hand, at approximately the same time, Muslims met the Hindu community with a philosophic tradition at least as subtle, as profound, as complex, as intelligent, as is the Greek, yet different. What the two groups there had in common was not conceptual categories or theoretical outlooks, but faith—or spirituality, to speak in the current mode. What then developed there, called *bhakti* on the Hindu side, *Sufi* on the Muslim, was a movement—or a pair of parallel movements—emphasizing personal devotion.

I myself see this sort of piety as one form of faith among others—widespread form though it be (certainly overpassing boundaries of any of the so-called religions); just as I see Western philosophy as one form of rationality among others. The modern comparativist, however, can learn something from both of these historical situations and the perceptions engendered in each.

This leads on to the second of what I have called my observations proffered for rumination, regarding the development of Western civilization seen in the context of human history at large. It is a point that I have made before, and some among you may have heard me on this, or read something where I have adumbrated it. Yet I allow myself to repeat it here, for over the years I have come increasingly to feel its force, and increasingly to find it corroborated through further study and reflection. The perception is this: that a great many Western matters—Christian and other, religious and "secular", theoretical and practical—diverge from their counterparts in other civilizations and owe their characteristic quality—which *we* tend to take for granted—to the peculiar duality of the West, arising from the fact that its civilization has been built on two distinct foundations, one from Greece and Rome, one from Palestine.

Ours is not the only civilization of which something of this general sort has been true: Japanese culture, for instance, has been an amalgam of quite distinct Japanese and Chinese sources; and so on—although Islamic civilization has been more integrated; and China incorporated what it borrowed from India somewhat more unselfconsciously. Yet the West has been unique in its way of relating its two (as well as its two bases being of course themselves quite particular); and that distinctive way of relating them has been consequential. Probably no other major civilization has so strikingly as have we united its foundations without unifying them. Over the centuries the two strands in the Western case have been at times in harmony, at times juxtaposed, at times in conflict; but they have never fused. We might say that they have lived together, but have not married. Or if we wish to think of them as married in the Middle Ages, we see the divorce that followed. (And we to-day are children of that broken home.) One among many results of the West's specific situation is that we have had two traditions of careful, systematic, rationalized thought, two movements one of which we have called philosophy and one of which we have called theology. No one else has done this. The two other centres of mighty rationalist traditions on earth, along with Greece—namely, India and China—have developed their thinking in ways some of which are clearly counterpart to what in our tradition we have called theology; and some, counterpart to what we call philosophy; yet in those cases a distinction between the two has not obtained—to the confusion of Western observers who have imagined that the difference (better: *our* differentiating) is inherent in the nature of things, rather than idiosyncratic.

I shall return to this specific point in a moment; but first we must notice that in fact, we may generalize this fairly widely. There are several areas where this Western sense obtains that the Western way of slicing up human life and society is not, indeed, a slicing up of affairs, but simply an awareness of what is given: of what is natural, inevitable, obvious; is a recognition of the real. Westerners are often heard to say that Muslims are funny people who have "mixed up" politics and religion, as though there were of course different things which it is obtuse to confuse. Similarly the West has put a dividing line between "law" and "religion" (I have put quotations marks here around these Western terms and concepts). In no other major case, Jewish, Islamic, Hindu, Chinese, Japanese, has there been a clear dividing line between these two matters—or rather, between what we call these two; in none of these cultures has there classically been a concept, nor a word, for either of them. What has happened is that the West has its law, its political and economic patterns, its grammar, and various other matters from Greece and Rome, what it calls its religion from Palestine. It has been of massive historical importance that the Islamic community, for example, was responsible for running its own affairs from the start, whereas the Christian Church spent *its* formative few centuries in a society in which other people were responsible for collecting the garbage, maintaining the army and defending the borders, raising taxes, operating the courts, and generally running the government.

Among the many items of the one side of the West's dual heritage, however, our concern here is primarily the Greek philosophic tradition—which I have on occasion called one of the great spiritual traditions of humankind; or one may say also, one of the major religious traditions on our planet. More strictly, I have called φιλοσοφια this, using that "love-of-wisdom" original in order to include the wider legacy of rationalism, idealism, and humanism. I have remarked that the West's problematic question of the relation between faith and reason is better perceived as a relation between faith in God and faith in reason; though I would now add to the latter, faith in ideals, including in an idealized humanity. In this outlook, a rational order was perceived as underlying the universe, as a transcendent pattern; human beings were rational, unlike other animals, in that and insofar as they (we) participate—however partially—in that ultimate. In other words, in this case we human beings are made in its image—however deformed that image be in any given case. Phrased in another way, Reason as the ultimate order has become incarnate on earth—partially, and potentially, in us.

We will not pursue here the argument supporting and elaborating the perception that the classical tradition in Europe has been, like other so-called religious traditions around the world, a particular expression and nurturer of faith. I have given some of that argument elsewhere. Suffice it for the moment to draw a few considerations that impinge on our specific issues here.

As presumably is the case also with the rest of you, the letter that I received inviting me to this conference contained the following sentence: "Historically, Christian theology has always had philosophy as a partner, usually in a positive way as apologetic, often as critic". The wording of this remark illustrates the present-day pluralism issue inadvertently yet interestingly. Naming "theology" as specifically "Christian theology" is nowadays standard (I wonder whether any others among you even noticed the phrase); but in fact is a recent innovation. Traditionally the adjective was not normally affixed: St. Thomas Aquinas, for instance, entitled his great work simply *Summa Theologiae*. Similarly—or shall we say: in contrast—"philosophy" is *not* here called "Western philosophy", although that is what is meant and what alone makes the statement true. This signifies that our theological tradition has entered the consciously pluralist phase that the modern world requires, while our philosophic tradition has not yet done so. The importance of this historical fact is major. It is also, however, subtle. I personally am critical on both sides; concerning the philosophic, quite straightforwardly, recalling that business of the trilogue in mediæval Spain and its Western legacy; in the Christian case wishing to enter caveats to which I will come in a moment.

There are a few exceptions, but on the whole Western philosophers have not yet noticed, certainly have not yet pondered and inwardly digested, the fact that their whole enterprise has been and is one such among others on earth—others equally refined, equally impressive. They have much to learn from the other rationalist traditions; but chiefly, have much to learn, as do theologians, from the sheer fact of diversity, from the finitude of human intellectuality and the resultant variety in our apprehending not only of truth, but of logic, of rationality, of linguistic categories. One consequence of all this is that it gives theologians, long the victims of philosophic critique, the advantage (and duty) of being in a position nowadays to invite their philosophic brethren to come and join us in a modern awareness of pluralism. That awareness is exciting even if painful, enriching even if apparently threatening.

My main point, however, is that the relation between theology and philosophy in the West should henceforth become one neither of apologetics nor of criticism, but as the word "partners" suggests, fellows seeking from distinct backgrounds to understand the complex world, and the over-arching universe, in which we all, jointly, live; and the mysteriously human, in which we all, jointly, participate. This brings us back to the matter of adjectivalized theology. There are Christian theologians; but there is no such thing, there ought to be no such thing, as Christian theology, which ultimately is a contradiction in terms—if not indeed blasphemous. There are Western philosophers, there is a Western philosophic tradition, but ideally the philosophic goal should be to transcend the particularities out of which we come and, learning from them and also from one another and from our very variety, to move towards truth. Similarly, as theologians our goal surely is to understand and to make intelligible conceptually not a, nor the, "Christian" God—whatever that might mean—but God *simpliciter*. More precisely put: to attain the closest approximation to apprehending, conceptually, truth, and God, of which we human beings are at a given moment corporately capable.

This way of perceiving the situation makes theology and philosophy henceforth genuinely partners, each of them confidently humble and humbly confident. There is the further point. Pluralism we may define as the combination of plurality with the awareness of it—the recognition of the fact of plurality and of the requirement of including it in one's interpretation of the universe. This pluralism makes Christian theologians see as their partners in our new task not only, and indeed not primarily, philosophy; but also, and chiefly, the other theologians around the world, and their counterparts. I say "counterparts" because of course Buddhist thinkers on these matters think in terms and categories other than the theistic concept "God", a mundane linguistic matter from which theology has derived its Greek name. And Buddhists have in recent times become Christian theologians' most engaged and most engaging partners. Yet we have also to learn from the Islamic so-called theological tradition and its spokesmen (no women yet), and the Jewish, and from the Hindu theology-and-philosophy continuum, and so on.

This brings me then to the other end, the eastern, of the Islamic inter-religious encounter with which I began: the Muslim-Hindu understanding that what human beings from divergently patterned religious traditions share with one another, and may move towards sharing joyfully, is not theories but a personal relation to God.

I personally have come to feel that of the two, this is the more fundamental. I go so far as to say that the present-day awareness of our world scene and of human history over the millennia not only dethrones for us Western philosophy from its privileged position (just as it has dethroned Christian theology from *its*), but also dethrones philosophy as such from its assumption that truth is primarily within its particular province. To other good things—beauty, moral character, justice—we humans might relate perhaps finally along other avenues; but truth purportedly lay within philosophy's bailiwick. We to-day may see that all good things, including truth, are the province more cardinally of faith.

This assessment has to do with my earlier affirmation that the Western classical tradition of rationality and all was a tradition engendered by, eliciting, and sustaining, faith. Faith in reason, in the course of specifically Western history, has been a significant form of the world-wide human potentiality for and fact of faith. Faith's multiformity, which to-day it is delinquent not to recognize—and some would add, not to celebrate—has included also this.

Faith I have characterized as in general a human recognition of and response to The Transcendent. The Transcendent transcends. He/She/It transcends all our grasp of it, intellectual and other; including, our grasp of and response to revelation. He/She/It transcends the concept, and category, "God", though that concept has played, for theists, a mighty and marvellous role in large sectors of human history. As I have put it, God has used—has richly used—the concept "God" to enter into human lives. He/She/It has also, of course, used other concepts—and many symbolic forms other than concepts—to do so. My contention is that in the case of the Græco-Roman legacy in Western civilization (the rationalist-idealist-humanist), faith has been mediated by that dynamic legacy. Crucial for us is the recognition that in the twentieth century, perhaps especially in the academic world—the Western university has been the chief institution of this tradition—but pervasively now also in our culture at large, faith through this tradition has waned, has almost been altogether lost. A relation between the moral and the intellectual has been at least neglected, if not denied. For centuries one spoke of a "love" of learning, a "respect" for knowledge, the "will" to search for truth, "loyalty" both to an institution and to its goals (how long is it since we have heard the once common phrase "the university that I have the honour to serve"?). There has been a drastic lowering of the idea of truth and knowledge, from something higher than humankind to something lower than we. Classically, universities were in pursuit of a truth that was inherently good (not value-free). Because it was above us, transcended us, it freely won our loyalty and—not so freely—our behaviour: we strove to live—not merely to think—rationally; that is, strove to conform our wills to a rational order higher than our individual persons: something that could be attained at times only at great cost to ourselves, and never without firm discipline—but worth it.

To live in accord with this truth higher than ourselves was often at odds with our lower desires, our baser inclinations, and our "interests"; yet self-fulfilment on a higher plain was made available, through a transcending of one's actual self towards one's true [sic] self. Also, it conferred community. For in the rational order lay a shared truth for corporate living—to which the disparate wills (or "interests") of individuals or particularist groupings were subordinated, and finally transformed into a shared universalism.

The pursuit of truth, the unqualified valuing of reason, the conformity to them of our person and our society, conferred wholeness and meaning on life, justice and peace on the group, and were their own rich reward. In Chrisitan theological terms, Reason was salvific.

These ideals were approximated in actuality, of course, only very partially: in any given instance, perhaps only remotely; and at times hypocrisy was substituted for even a distant loyalty. These are things that religious people, or observers of religious people, know all about. Nonetheless the vision informed and sustained academia for centuries, and there are many persons still living who were touched by it and in some small or large degree transformed. Ideally, education consisted in that transformation.

The shift in recent times has been from this notion of truth that we serve, to a different notion of it as something that serves us. Or, more usually, the new notion is now of knowledge. Reason has moved from being that to which our purposes should conform, to becoming rather that by which they may be implemented—whatever they happen to be. We manufacture knowledge as we manufacture cars, and with similar objectives: to increase our power, pleasure, or profit—or if we are altruistic, to offer it to others that they may increase theirs. Universities have become, in the sorry phrase that I met a while back, "the knowledge industry", its products ours to command, even to buy and sell. From the pursuit of truth to the production of knowledge; yet less kindly one could say that many academics are in pursuit not of truth but of research grants, or of promotion.

With no higher reality to determine what we ought to aim at, to aspire to, purposes replace ideals. Society is impelled by "needs", to whose requirements its institutions respond. Human beings are driven by drives, by motivation, and insofar as our wills are free they are totally free, to will whatever each may choose, with only practical constraints but no theoretical impingements.

Transcendence has generally been banished from the *Weltanschauung* of modern intellectuals: Truth can no longer be spelled with a capital T. Nor Reason with a capital R, now that it is understood as instrumental. And the cognitive and the moral are seen not as integrated but as two discrete things, if not actually in some fashion antithetical.

Certainly my view is that this outlook, with its ontological, epistemological, moral, and personal implications is intellectually in error. I see it as seriously reductionist of reality, of value, of the process of rational learning, of the human;

and seriously disruptive of community. Fundamentally, its fallacy stems from its loss of faith. The Western intellectualist tradition, which I see as deriving from Greece and Rome, was on the right track—or I would say: a right track—so long as it was indeed a spiritual tradition, one of the world's great religious movements; and has been courting disaster once it is ceasing to be so.

What the Islamic movement had in common both with Europeans *and* with Indians—to return to that point—and has had in common indeed with all humankind, was faith. What the Christian Church has had in common with philosophy traditionally, and with other religious communities, is also faith. Unfortunately, neither side recognized this clearly; neither had yet learned that faith—salvific, indispensable for both individual and social life, the greatest gift humanity can receive—comes not only in different degrees for each person, even each day, but also in many apparently diverse forms. There are many hems to the divine garment, which we variously touch.

Further on the relation between theology and philosophy, and specifically Christians' theology and Western philosophy, I said above that the Græco-Roman tradition and the Palestinian tradition in our civilization have been at times in harmony, at times juxtaposed, at times in conflict, while never fused. I toyed with the idea of adding at that point that they have also been at times intertwined; but decided to save that until now. The comparative study of religion discloses that historically all movements on earth that the West has called "the religions", each of which was supposedly self-contained, have in fact been intertwined much more deeply, more decisively, than has ever been perceived. Each, including the Christian, as indeed including all the others, has been what it has been as a result of what the others have been—with so-called influences, borrowing, "syncretisms" and such—to an extent that until our day could hardly be imagined. Each is one strand in the religious history of our race, and each can be understood only in the light of this. (To phrase this point in theological terms, God has dealt with humankind in terms of persons on the one hand, and of our world community moving through time on the other.)

European universities until the modern period were founded by the Church; in North America this was the case right up almost to the end of the 19th century, of most universities and virtually all colleges. Without the Church, after the fall of Rome philosophy would not have survived. In the other direction, without Greek thought theology would not have arisen. The fact that the Church has, and from early on has had, theology, is basically a Græco-Roman contribution. Some, though not all, other major religious groups on earth have had persons whom we may from our perspective call theologians; but no other has "had a theology". After the emancipation of the Jews early last century that group hustled around and tried to get itself one. Under the influence of Greek philosophy the Islamic movement from about the tenth century A.D. produced *kalām*—often translated "theology" although some dispute the legitimacy of that; but in any case most Muslims were highly suspicious of it, to say the least. In both the Jewish and the Islamic instances the primary systematized expression of their form of faith into a coherent formal pattern was not primarily conceptualist but moralist, in *tôrāh* and *sharī'ah*, concepts customarily rendered in Western terms as "law", though that rendering is easily disputed and has been. A consequence, often remarked, is that for both groups the counterpart to what Christians would call "orthodoxy" is rather orthopraxy. (The self-styled "Orthodox" movement in the Jewish case was formed only late last century—or was it early this?—in reaction to the organizing of a "Reform" movement.)

In the Hindu case, as we have said, what we call their philosophic tradition produced some thinkers whom we more readily would see as following under our alternative rubric of "theologians"; but in any case the usual Hindu delight in variety in human responses to transcendence and conviction of its propriety have led to a strong sense that to try to confine either theory or practice to a single form, or to suppose that any one dimension of religious life—the intellectual or the moral or whatever—is paramount or obligatory or is alone "right", seems superficial if not blasphemous. Further, we have that anthropologist's famous observation that "African religion is not thought out but danced out".

In short, the Church is more Greek, and Western philosophy more faithful, than has normally been incorporated into our understanding. The traditional exclusivism of the West led many to be astonished, even perplexed, when told early this century that the Chinese regularly "belong to three religions at the same time". If one is going to use these misleading Western terms, I would contend that many Westerners, certainly intelligent ones, have participated joyfully in the two Western religions.

Certainly I personally like to think of myself as a loyal member of both. I have lived my life as an intellectual; and hope that I have lived it in not too un-Christian a way. Seeing both as traditions rather than fixed entities, however, and seeing the world historically, I am not uncritical of either in the sense that I think it important, even imperative, that the next phase of each movement be a considerable advance over the current phase.

It may seem presumptuous of me as an historian observing the two developments in process, to comment on that new phase: on how they would do well to move. Yet I allow myself, in closing, to proffer two such comments. And each grows out of the evidence that human history, past and present, supplies. The first comment is the obvious one—already suggested, and from me by now trite—that by both the movements, pluralism must be taken seriously, and inwardly digested. Each, I venture to predict, will flounder, if this not be done. Each will be enriched, if it does; and that advance for which we hope will be facilitated and empowered.

The second comment is intimately tied to this first one—though the firm link between the two has not always been discerned. It concerns the need for recognition of, and taking seriously, transcendence: the transcendent dimension of our human life and of our universe. With "recognition of" I include response to it, if integrity is not to be discarded.

Pluralism is a matter of learning not just about others, but about oneself. One might allude to the picture that Jesus gives of one of humanity's besetting sins: "I thank Thee, Lord, that I am not as other men". The Church, of course, has been saying this for centuries, profoundly grateful that we are not like Muslims, Hindus, and the rest: they are lost, we are saved, and their traditions, as well, are ridiculous or perhaps grotesque. Philosophers, especially in recent times, have thanked God at least metaphorically that they are not like those deluded folk, theologians—to say nothing of remote, negligible, and neglected groups like Hindus and Buddhists. I would expect from some of their company at least as much resistance to my trying to classify their work as variations on the theme of faith as from some Christians to being seen as in God's eyes on a par with Muslims and the rest.

My second, transcendence, motif, again for both groups, might appear more congenial to Christian theologians than to modern philosophers; yet one might wonder. The latter group must, I submit, recognize the transcendence of truth as such; but also its transcendence over language, and even over propositions, their beloved location for it. Theologians, too, have tended to treat the Transcendent as having in their case been brought down to earth and within their purview—in another and loftier form, no doubt; but still. . . . They must rather, I submit, recognize it, and God in their vocabulary, as transcendent over an idealized Christianity, and over Christ and all Christian particulars and symbols, and over revelation as such, and too over doctrine as such (even at its conceivable best). No doctrine can be true of God. (Of course, one may add except approximately and metaphorically.) Up to a point we human beings may know God—that is what religious life is all about; but that knowledge is in forms other than verbal. (Love, for instance, is one such form.)

On the particularity business, I return to that unacceptable matter of speaking or thinking of "Christian" theology. One sometimes hears the defeatist notion that the Christian theologian's task is to formulate for our day as lucidly and accurately as possible the inherited faith of the Church—and even, perhaps, to defend that. Surely the task of any theologian, Christian or other, is and ever has been, to formulate in words as lucidly and accurately as possible the truth about God—to render God conceptually available—insofar as human finitude and frailty and the limitations of concepts and of language allow. To achieve this as far as may be feasible one learns from whatever sources be available. Of these, Christian history is certainly one, and important; for Christians, massively important. Yet there are others also—science, for instance, and sunsets, and faith (shall we say, "spirituality"?) wherever it may be found, as in the history of the world's other religious traditions including the Western philosophic, the Buddhist, the so-called primitive (we in North America are just beginning to notice that source)—and at times too among the ostensibly non-religious.

I will not attempt to argue these things here. I have called them presumptuous; you may deem them outrageous. My evidence for them is human history. That is where this presentation began. I began also with a tribute to Joe McLelland; and I end with a hope, however forlorn, that *he* will not find it too intolerably outrageous. I am bold enough to think that perhaps he may not. For although he will be quick to spot my hurried over-simplifications, yet his work shows that he is already into the new phases.

TOWARDS A DIALOGICAL THEOLOGY:
Some Methodological Considerations

David Lochhead
Vancouver School of Theology

"The wind blows where it chooses, and you hear the sound of it, but you do not know where it comes from or where it goes. So it is with everyone who is born of the Spirit." John 3:8

It is a commonplace in discussions about interreligious dialogue that, in any significant conversation with another religious tradition, one's understanding of one's own tradition will be transformed. I agree with this observation, and I will assume that it is true in these remarks. The question that I want to raise is how this transformation can be appropriated theologically. As a Christian, for example, my understanding of my own faith may be significantly transformed by a conversation with Buddhism. As I glimpse what Buddhists mean and have meant by their non-theism, by terms like "emptiness," and the like, my own understanding of Christian faith will not go untouched. My understanding of God and of human nature—to mention the most obvious theological concerns—will be informed and transformed by what I have seen in and through the dialogue. My question is: how are these Buddhist themes appropriated by the theologian? Is the influence of Buddhism—or whatever other tradition may be involved in dialogue with the theologian—made explicit or is it covert? How can the traditions of Buddhism, Hinduism, Islam, etc., become sources for theologians? How can the use of these sources be justified theologically? Is the influence of other traditions incidental to the theological task, a biographical quirk of the individual theologian? Or can one articulate a dialogical agenda for theology that is essential to the theological task?

The starting point of this paper, then, is the question of how the content of other religious traditions is appropriated by Christian theology. The question is here more a methodological question than a historical one. That is, it is possible to study historically the various ways that such material has actually been used by theologians. This question is relevant to, but does not resolve, the methodological question: What is the appropriate use of materials from other religious traditions in Christian theology?

At the outset, it is perhaps important to distinguish this question from the question of the Jewish roots of Christianity. From the beginning, Christian theology has incorporated Jewish content. However, this cannot be construed as the incorporation of content that is somehow foreign to the Christian tradition. As a tradition, Christianity first appears as a form of Judaism. Very quickly, with the pressure of political concerns on the Jewish and Christian communities in the first and early second centuries, the two communities distinguished themselves from each other. It is only at the point of this distinction that one could speak of a borrowing or appropriation of something Jewish by Christian theology. Before that, one can speak only of the Jewish roots of Christianity not as something foreign, but as constitutive of the tradition itself.

Even to raise the question of the use made of the ideas of other traditions in Christian theology immediately invokes the spectre of syncretism. Syncretism refers to the "borrowing" of ideas and practices from other traditions and grafting them into Christian theology. The word "syncretism" is a bad word to most theologians. It is something that theologians are not supposed to do.

To ban syncretism as a theological method is not, however, to make no use of concepts from other religious traditions. The alternative to a syncretistic use of non-Christian concepts is a polemical use of them. That is, concepts of other religious traditions may be introduced into theological discussion as a foil to a "Christian" understanding. The point of this procedure is to contrast the Christian view in order to bring out its distinctiveness (as well as an implied superiority.)

Possibly the most intentional use of syncretism in theology today can be found in the work of Matthew Fox. In attempting to articulate a theology for his "creation centered spirituality," Fox rejects any suggestion that he confine himself to Christian sources. He calls his approach one of "global ecumenism." A creation centered spirituality can be found in many, if not all, of the religious traditions of the world. Thus a Taoist, Buddhist or Sufi insight can be used freely in the articulation of a creation-centered theology. A creation centered approach, according to Fox, removes distinctions between traditions. The creation centered approach is a universalistic approach:

> It is important that religious ecumenism not be limited to dialog among patriarchal religions of the past 5000 years at best. Included must be the more ancient traditions, such as Native American and feminist or matrifocal, and the more recent New Age movements. Creation spirituality can not only dialog with these traditions but move to co-creating with them as well.[1]

An example of a polemical approach to concepts from other religious traditions can be found in Reinhold Neibuhr's classic, *The Nature and Destiny of Man*.[2] Niebuhr, who represents the American face of the so-called neo-orthodox perspective in theology, takes concepts from other religious traditions in order to provide a contrast to what he holds to be the (superior) Christian view.

This paper is concerned to seek an alternative to these two traditional approaches to concepts drawn from other traditions. It seeks a dialogical theology. By "dialogical" is meant an approach to theology which is informed by conversations with other religious traditions but which neither seeks to baptize other traditions nor to treat them as adversaries. A dialogical theology is one in which the articulation of each doctrinal area would show some awareness of the relevance of the insights of other traditions while, at the same time, avoid the radical revisionism of attempting to graft non-Christian concepts into the Christian doctrines themselves. Theology needs to reflect the dialogue without attempting to replicate the concepts of the dialogical partners in a Christian form.

Dialogical theologies are, in fact, beginning to appear. John Cobb has for some time reflected in his theology his experience of dialogue with Buddhism.[3] Through his collaboration with the Buddhist Masao Abe, the so-called "Cobb-Abe group" has involved a number of prominent theologians—Langdon Gilkey, Gordon Kaufmann, David Tracy, Shubert Ogden, Hans Küng, Rosemary Reuther to name the more prominent of the group—in an encounter with Buddhism, an encounter which is being reflected in their theological writings. Hans Küng himself has attempted explicitly to reflect theologically in a dialogical way with four different traditions in his two books, *Christianity and the World Religions*[4] and *Christianity and Chinese Religions*.[5] Jürgen Moltmann has also attempted to write theology which reflects an in-depth dialogue with other traditions. His use of a Jewish-Christian conversation about messiahship in his recent book on Christology is a good example of his approach.[6] Robert Neville's introductory text book on systematic theology[7] presupposes interfaith conversations with various traditions in relation to specific doctrines.

Each of these theologians is writing theology in a dialogical way. As an emerging phenomenon in theology, dialogical theology is a fact. It is the purpose of this paper to contribute to that development and, especially, to reflect on some of the methodological issues that need to be addressed in the intentional development of such a theology.

By "methodology" in theology, we mean those issues centering on questions of the sources used in theology, the authorities recognized by and in theology, and the criteria of meaning and truth used in elaborating a theological position. These are not distinct questions. What is called a question of sources by one theologian may be addressed as a question of authority or of the criteria of theological truth by another. Methodological questions may be addressed explicitly, or they may be included as questions concerning, for example, a doctrine of revelation. It can be granted that questions of theological method cannot be separated from questions of theological content. Nevertheless there are certain decisions that are taken in any theological system which have to do with the sources and/or authority. It is these questions that we need to engage in elaborating a theological method for a dialogical theology.

The question of sources/authority in theology usually involves some mediation of the claims of scripture, tradition, experience and reason. Particular theologians may decide to recognize the claims of one or more of these while excluding the claims of others. Other theologians may attempt to balance the claims of all four. Still others may recognize one or two of these (e.g. scripture, tradition) as sources for the content of theology while treating the others as constituting the context in which theology is done.

When we speak of a "source" of authority, at the back of our minds somewhere lies the model of theology as a discipline that involves the collection and ordering of truths. That is, truth is "out there." It is the theologian's task to locate the truth, to test it, to organize it and defend it. The truths may be discovered in scripture, in tradition, in reason or in experience.

It was, perhaps, possible in pre-Enlightenment theology to have some clarity about what was meant by a source or an authority in theology. Scripture was considered to be such a source/authority. The task of theology was to identify the truths which were contained in scripture and to present them in an ordered and coherent way. Theologians could say that a particular doctrine was "true" because it was "contained in scripture." They could say that other beliefs were not true because they were "contradicted by scripture."

In modern and post modern theology, it is not possible to see theology as basically an affirmation and ordering of "truths" that are "contained" elsewhere.[8] Theology has developed a hermeneutical sophistication. Even the most conservative treatment of scripture cannot help but be aware that the theologian is involved in something more than a mere transfer of truths from a "source" (i.e. scripture) to a doctrinal treatise. The very process of placing "truths" into a new context involves interpretation. In the process, the truth is transformed. It is not identical to what was "contained" in scripture. The very process of selection and ordering makes its own contribution to the meaning of what is affirmed. In no sense can one simply transfer truths from one container to another.

Let me focus my remarks on scripture. However one resolves the question of the relation of reason and revelation, scripture is almost universally acknowledged by Christian theologians as a source/authority for theology. As a Christian theologian, I have some kind of accountability to scripture. This accountability may be kept front and centre in a theology, as it was, for example, by Karl Barth. It may be kept almost hidden in the background, as it was, for example, by Paul Tillich.

Despite the near universality of the acknowledgment of the necessity of scripture as a source/authority for theology, it is not at all clear what that acknowledgment involves. It does not, for example, involve the commitment to treat any and every proposition of scripture as literally true. It does not involve that the simple quotation of a scriptural text can resolve a theological dispute.

If one cannot use scripture in theology by what I would describe as a "cut and paste" method, what is the relationship between theology and scripture? Would it not be appropriate to describe the relation as a conversational one? That is, the responsible theologian is not simply accountable to scripture by replicating it in his or her theology. Rather, the theologian engages scripture by entering a conversation, by putting questions and concerns to the text, by seeing the text through the lens of those questions and concerns, by attending to the questioning of this questioning by scripture, by reformulating the questions and repeating the process, by attempting to gain insight through what he or she sees in the text through this conversational process.[9] If this is a not-unreasonable account or model of what the theologian does in engaging scripture, one would have to say that it is essentially the same process that is involved in interfaith dialogue. If, as a theologian, I am involved in a dialogue with Buddhism, I am involved in conversations with Buddhists and with Buddhist texts. These conversations are structured by the questions and concerns brought by either side. I bring my concerns and questions. I hear the Buddhist responses through the lens of my concerns and questions. I allow my own questioning to be questioned by the concerns and questions and responses of the Buddhist. Under the impact of what I hear, I reformulate my concerns and questions and continue the process, attempting to gain insight by what I see through this conversational process.

What I am attempting to do here, of course, is to shift the methodological metaphor. Instead of speaking of "sources" and "authorities," I am attempting to speak of conversations. Thus, in my work as a theologian, I am involved in a dialogue with scripture. But, again *qua* theologian, I am also involved in other dialogues. I am involved as a theologian, for example, in conversations with history, with culture, with philosophy, with politics. In short, to follow Barth's advice to read the Bible with one hand and the newspaper with the other, is to be involved, *qua* theologian, in a conversation with everything that I can call my context. If I am not involved in this universal dialogue, then I have no recourse but to a sterile replication of old "truths" in the articulating of a theology.

I am not saying anything here that has not been said in thousands of different ways by thousands of different theologians. I do want to call attention to the fact, however, that theology—while engaged in these multilateral dialogues with scripture, tradition and the world—has been notoriously successful in choosing to limit its dialogue partners. There has always been a certain blindness to context by theologians. This blindness has become notorious in recent years. Among the absent dialogue partners that have been named in recent years are women and women's concerns, racial difference, the poor and the concerns of the poor, geographical difference, etc. Since the mid-sixties, life for theologians has been a constant challenge to enter into dialogue with people and concerns which have been formerly ignored, or who have felt to be ignored, in the conversations that constitute the theological endeavour.

Among those groups that have been ignored by theologians are those who belong to other religious traditions. Apart from the occasional syncretistic or polemical engagement of other traditions, usually at second or third hand, the conversation with other religious traditions has only recently become one of the conversations that inform theology. The approach of Karl Barth was symptomatic of the problem. In order to discover in the *Church Dogmatics* a basis for a positive conversation with other religious traditions, one has to go, not to any explicit discussion of religion, or to any engagement with another religious tradition, but to a discussion of secular movements and ideologies.[10] Where Barth does attempt to engage Pure Land Buddhism, he does it only through a second hand account by a European scholar.[11] Barth is hardly alone in his generation. Paul Tillich, for example, only began to move in the direction of significant interfaith encounter in the last decade of his life.

What is involved for theology if other religious traditions enter the theological conversation? What is being assumed? What commitments do theologians make in order to take the conversation with other traditions seriously?

I have attempted to argue elsewhere that conversations with other religious traditions by Christians do not necessarily involve any decision about the "validity" of another tradition.[12] That is, if I, as a theologian, am involved in a dialogue with Buddhists or Muslims, I am not logically bound to hold any particular view of the truth value of the claims of Buddhism or Islam. That "agnostic" view of the validity of a religious tradition other than one's own, however, needs one very important qualification. While, as theologians, many of us may be able to travel with very light metaphysical baggage, I have to assume about any conversation partner that I engage in the process of doing theology that said partner is not totally out of touch with reality.[13] In other words, I may agree with certain Buddhist claims and have trouble with others. I will find some claims of Muslims attractive while others I will find inconsistent with what I, as a Christian theologian, feel that I must defend. I may construe any of my agreements or disagreements with Buddhism or Islam as either apparent or real. In other words, there is considerable room for maneuver in what judgments I make about truth and falsity in the interreligious conversation. But at the root of that flexibility lies a basic metaphysical assumption. I must assume that my partner in conversation is not out of touch with reality. That is, I cannot assume that what my partner represents is, in some fundamental sense, a corporate psychosis. That, in turn, is to say that reality is describable, in general, but not in all its details, in Buddhist or Muslim terms or, indeed, in the language of any living and persisting religious tradition.[14]

To say that, I grant, is not to concede very much to the claims of Buddhism, Islam, or whatever other tradition may enter the theological conversation. My purpose here is not to judge how much can be conceded to other traditions by Christian theology but to indicate how much must be conceded if the conversation is to happen at all. What must be said—namely, that reality is capable of being described, in general, in the terms of other religious traditions—strikes me as a fact with important theological consequences. It is not a trivial conclusion.

In assuming that other religious traditions are in touch with reality, I am attempting to approach the question of truth in a somewhat different manner than is usually taken. Questions of truth claims often focus on questions in which there is an apparently straight forward conflict of claims. Is Jesus Christ the incarnation of God? Christians answer yes. Everyone else answers no. There seems to be clear conflict here in which it would seem that only one side is congruent with reality. The various strategies in dealing with a conflict like this involve taking one side against the other, declaring that both affirmations are a "relative truth" and that the contradiction is made good only in a realm of transcendent truth which is beyond any finite religious position, or by declaring the question to be incoherent or meaningless. In speaking of the various traditions as "in touch with reality" I am neither affirming nor denying that there exist real contradictions between religious traditions. I am attempting to say something more subtle than that.

A conversation of a Christian with a Mahayana Buddhist may provide an example. In this conversation, a Christian will hear an account of reality in which strange words are used. These words will include terms like *sunyata, pratitya samapada, samsara, tathata, upaya*, and the like. As the Christian listens carefully to that language, she or he will discover that the language begins to make sense. That is, in a conversation with Buddhism I discover the appropriateness, although not the necessity, of describing reality in those terms. There will be places, of course, where a Buddhist description of reality rubs against my Christian understanding of reality in a way that the Christian perceives as a "contradiction." At that point, the conversation may become a debate. The debate, however, is only one moment in the conversation. It does not define the conversation itself. In dialogue, then, the Christian learns to see reality in a Buddhist way (and, of course, vice-versa.)

If, as a theologian, I have genuinely engaged a Buddhist or a Muslim or a Hindu view of reality, then my theology will reflect it. The other conversations in which I am involved (with scripture, tradition, culture, economics, etc.) will be informed by the fact that I can and do call upon my encounter with this view of reality in my conversation. I make a beginning at reading scripture, tradition, etc. through Buddhist (or Muslim or Hindu) eyes.[15] A Buddhist view of reality, then, begins to find its place in my Christian theology.

If we move a step farther, and assume that the conversations of which we are speaking are continuing ones, in engaging a Buddhist view of reality I must inevitably engage Buddhist traditions and Buddhist scriptures, Muslim traditions and Muslim scriptures, etc. At that point, I need to admit that the theological conversation that as interlocking conversations with scripture, tradition and the world, becomes much more complex. In particular, by walking on this path we inevitably involve other scriptures and other traditions in the theological conversation. Alongside the Bible, then, the theologian becomes involved in conversations with the Qur'an, various Buddhist sutras, the Upanishads, etc., etc. To speak of the role of scripture and tradition in Christian theology takes on a whole new meaning.

To this point, I have deliberately avoided the question of authority in theology. By avoiding it, I have perhaps created the illusion that, despite my earlier protests to the contrary, I have actually ended up in rampant syncretism. For the Christian theologian, is the Bible only one sacred text among many? Is the Christian tradition only one tradition among many? Can all scriptures and all traditions have equal standing in articulation of a Christian theology?

It is important to remind ourselves again that I am not speaking here of scripture and tradition as "sources" of truths that are incorporated into theology by some kind of "cut and paste" method. Our methodological metaphor is one of the conversations that in-form theology rather than of sources which supplies the raw materials out of which a theology is constructed. Consequently, the problem of how the various conversations informs theology cannot be construed as if it were the same as a question of who owns the territory where the building blocks of theology are quarried.

In raising the question of the authority of a "conversation," then, we are not speaking of a "source" from which authoritative propositions are derived nor through which true propositions are verified. We are asking, however, whether some conversations have a different status than others; whether there are "privileged" conversations.

We need to avoid, at least initially, adopting an authority on the basis of some metaphysical claim. By a "metaphysical claim," I mean a claim that invokes notions of revelation, inspiration, and the like. A "metaphysical claim" is one that imputes to a theological authority some sort of privileged relation to reality. It is not my purpose to impugn or dismiss such claims. In a dialogical theology, claims such as these need to be part of the dialogue. They cannot be permitted to close the dialogue before it begins.

A common basis for speaking of the authority of scripture by many contemporary "main-line" Christians goes something like this: Scripture is authoritative for theology because scripture is a record of revelation. It is the prime witness to those events in which God discloses God's self to humanity. Scripture, while not itself revelation, is a privileged and unique record of God's revelation. This is an account of the authority of scripture with which I, as a not untypical "main-line" Protestant Christian, would be reasonably comfortable. Nevertheless, an account like this could become the pretext for closing the conversation with other religious traditions. That is, I might conclude (not a necessary conclusion, but a common one) that what appears in the scriptures of other traditions is not revelation. I assume that other traditions make analogous claims of their scriptures, but only the Christian claim, in this particular form, is correct. That is, my doctrine of scripture, adopted as an *a priori* in my theological method, might prevent me from listening seriously, or listening correctly, to other traditions. As my acknowledged authority, my doctrine of scripture is not part of the dialogue but becomes the arbiter of what can, and what cannot be heard in the conversation with other traditions.

In elaborating what is meant by a dialogical theology, it is important that something like a Christian doctrine of scripture be a part of the conversation with other traditions. That is, Christian doctrines of scripture need to be informed by Muslim views of the Qur'an, with its very strong understanding of inspiration, by the Sikh understanding of scripture as the Guru, as well as by attitudes such as prevail in Buddhism towards a huge canonical collection, none of which is "revealed" in any sense that would be recognizable by a representative of one of the western monotheistic traditions.[16] In a dialogical theology, the theologian's "doctrine of Scripture" would be informed by, challenged by, enriched by, the very different views of scripture in other traditions. The doctrine of Scripture in a dialogical theology would reflect the conversation, not precede it.

If one brackets the metaphysical claims that are often associated with discussions of authority in theology, then the concept of authority comes to look very much like a privileged conversation. In early church synods that dealt with the canon, for example, the lists produced were represented as lists that were authorized to be read in the liturgy. Underlying those definitions, of course, there may have been one or many "metaphysical claims" for the books of the canon. It was not, however, those "metaphysical claims" that were adopted. What was adopted was a list of writings with a privileged status. They were authorized to be read—and, by implication, heard—in the liturgy.

Christian theologians, I want to argue, are involved in some privileged conversations. Two of those privileged conversations are with scripture and with the Christian tradition.[17] They are privileged because the community to which and for which I speak has been, and intends to continue to be, formed by them. Whether theologians are speaking to a church constituency or whether they are engaged in a conversation with another religious tradition, they are responsible to represent fairly and accurately the tradition and its scriptures in which they stand. If theology is involved in interfaith conversation, however, even these privileged conversations with scripture and tradition will be informed, challenged and enriched by the vision inspired by other traditions. As our theology becomes dialogical, our hermeneutics, both of scripture and of history, becomes dialogical as well. In a dialogical theology, everything is open. Nothing needs to be protected as a "non-negotiable." If scripture and tradition are the central dialogue partners in the family of conversations that constitute theology, they represent a center that is constantly shifting.

To say that the conversation with scripture and with tradition are privileged is only to say that they are at the centre[18] of a circle of conversations, a circle which has no fixed bounds. There is no reason why the stories and the sacred texts of other religious traditions should not also become conversation partners in the work of theology. If, as a theologian, I attempt to speak *with* the Bible in my theological articulation, there is no reason why I should not *also* attempt to speak with the Qur'an, the Guru Granth Sahib or the Lotus Sutra. At first, undoubtedly, I will speak differently in my conversation with the Bible than I do in my conversation with the Lotus Sutra. I will speak differently because, as a Christian theologian, I am "at home" with one, but not with the other. I will begin with where I am, with my expectations and, yes, even the metaphysical claims that I make of my own scriptures but not of others. A dialogical theology will not begin by attempting to read the scriptures of another tradition as if they were one's own. As the dialogue progresses, however, they will increasingly become one's own. The transformative effect of dialogue will be evident even at the centre of the circle of conversations. Even the metaphysical claims about the scriptures will be transformed. The shape of the transformation cannot be predicted.

In advocating a dialogical theology, then, I am not attempting any revolution in theological method. I am only attempting to look from a new perspective at what theology has always done. The code words that have been used by theologians to describe theological method—scripture, tradition, reason, experience, etc.—cannot be interpreted in a static way. They represent parallel conversations that necessarily inform theology. The methodological problem is not why theology should allow itself to be informed by a conversation with other religious traditions. The problem is why theologians ever imagined that these conversations could be excluded from the theological agenda.

NOTES

1.   Matthew Fox, *Original Blessing*, (Santa Fe: Bear and Company, 1983), 16.

2.   Reinhold Niebuhr, *The Nature and Destiny of Man: a Christian Interpretation*, (New York: Scribner's, 1941-43).

3.   Cf. especially John Cobb, *Beyond Dialogue: Toward a Mutual Transformation of Christianity and Buddhism* (Philadelphia: Fortress, 1982).

4.   Hans Küng, et al., *Christianity and the World Religions: Paths of Dialogue with Islam, Hinduism, and Buddhism*, (Garden City, NY: Doubleday, 1986).

5.   Hans Küng and Julia Ching, *Christianity and Chinese Religion* (New York: Doubleday, 1989).

6.   Jürgen Moltmann, *The Way of Jesus Christ: Christology in Messianic Dimensions*, (London: SCM Press, 1990).

7.   Robert Cummings Neville, *A Theology Primer* (Albany: State University of New York Press, 1991).

8.   Although the so-called "biblical theology" movement earlier in this century often gave the impression that the Bible "contained" a theology that could be abstracted from the Biblical writings. Contemporary theology then could be conceived of as a gloss on the abstract and somewhat static Biblical ideas.

9.   It may be objected here, following Paul Ricoeur, that there is no dialogue with a text, that writing intercepts the conversation between a speaker and a hearer, that a text does not "answer" the questions put by a reader. Against such a criticism I would reply (a) that I recognize that the term "conversation" is as much a metaphor as the word "sources" has been in methodological discussions and (b) that in the process of a careful reading of a text, questions are put by the reader and answers received, although not in quite the direct way that it happens in an oral conversation.

10.   Cf. Karl Barth, *Church Dogmatics*, IV/3, First Half (Edinburgh: T & T Clark, 1961), 116ff.

11.   Cf. Karl Barth, *Church Dogmatics*, I/2 (Edinburgh: T & T Clark, 1956), 340ff.

12.   Cf. David Lochhead, *The Dialogical Imperative* (Maryknoll: Orbis, 1988).

13.   That is to say that whatever verbal transactions I may have with someone that I consider to be out of touch with reality, I will not be involved in any significant sense in a dialogue or conversation. At best, such an activity can be described as a "pastime."

14.   This point would need a separate paper to elaborate. If I were to argue it further, I would attempt to make the case that any "living and persisting" religious tradition is engaged in a constant effort to describe reality in terms legitimized by the tradition. The religious community provides its members with a way of speaking of reality that has been produced by this ongoing effort. The language of the religious community is the cumulative deposit of what has worked for the community in the past.

15.   Which is not to say that I would read scripture as a Buddhist would read it. I read it, rather, as a Christian who has begun to feel at home in a Buddhist account of reality. The hermeneutics involved here, as all hermeneutics must, reveals considerable complexity.

16.   A valuable resource to such a conversation is a book like Harold Coward, *Sacred Word and Sacred Text: Scripture in World Religions* (Maryknoll: Orbis, 1988). A work like Coward's highlights the very different models of what a sacred text is in the various traditions of the world.

17. It may seem strange, although it is becoming less so, for a Protestant theologian to speak of scripture and tradition in the same breath. However, when one moves away from the model of authority held by Catholics and Protestants in the Reformation period—that of "authoritative" and divinely guarenteed *sources*, the tension between the two largely disappears. I would not want to confuse the conversation with scripture with the conversation with tradition. As a theologian of the Reformed tradition I would still treat tradition very differently than many Catholic theologians would. Nevertheless, I would agree with a "Catholic" view which held both conversations to be privileged.

18. I am aware that in speaking of "privileged conversations" and of "centres" I am using language that cries out for a deconstructionist critique. Indeed, I would welcome the critique and would see the thesis of this paper as a quasi-deconstructionist one. As a theologian, however, I still need to orient myself with at least the illusion of a centre. The fact, however, that I acknowledge that the centre shifts and is transformed in the interfaith converstation may be taken as evidence that, ultimately, the centre is not a centre at all.

THE EPISTEMOLOGICAL FOUNDATIONS
OF HINDU RELIGIOUS TOLERANCE

Arvind Sharma
McGill University

I

Most philosophical discussions of Hindu religious tolerance connect this feature of Hinduism with its ontology, with the view that according to Hindu thought Reality is one, although it may be formulated or approached in different ways.[1] In this paper I would like to suggest the possibility that Hindu epistemology, as distinguished from Hindu ontology, may have as vital a role to play in the context of Hindu tolerance. In fact, it might be even possible to add, if my presentation is successful, that it plays perhaps an even more vital role in the context of religious tolerance than Hindu ontology.

II

The ontological approach to Hindu tolerance suffers from a basic limitation in the context of Hindu thought in general—namely, that it is based on the ontology of *only one dominant* school of Hindu thought, that of Vedānta. It is only in the Vedānta that the ultimate reality is conceived of as unitary, whether considered absolutistically or theistically. However, according to the conventional view, Hinduism accepts six schools of thought as orthodox and Vedānta is only one of them.[2] Although Vedānta is the one which to this day continues as a living creed,[3] it seems reasonable to suggest that a discussion of Hindu tolerance, to be fully representative of the tradition, should take all the six schools into account as much as possible.

A general observation may serve to indicate the usefulness of such an approach. Schools other than those of Vedānta do not countenance a unitary ontology, and yet as part and parcel of Hinduism they must be viewed as participating in its tolerance. Thus the two schools of Nyāya and Vaiśeṣika are pluralistic in their ontology. On the question of "whether the ultimate reality is one or many" Nyāya maintains "that it is many, and is therefore described as pluralistic to distinguish it from others that are monistic."[4] The same holds true of Vaiśeṣika: the two systems are often hyphenated.[5] The third system, that of Sāṅkhya, is also pluralistic: "The Sāṅkhya is a system of realism, dualism and pluralism. It is a realism because it recognizes the reality of the world independent of spirit; it is a dualism because it holds that there are two fundamental realities distinct from each other, viz. matter and spirit; and it is a pluralism because it teaches a plurality of spirits."[6] Its metaphysics is shared by Yoga,[7] the fourth system with which it is often hyphenated.[8] The fifth system, that of Mīmāṃsā, is comparable to Nyāya-Vaiśeṣika "in that it is pluralistic and realistic."[9]

In sum: the ontology of Nyāya-Vaśeṣika is characterised by a categorial and catagorical pluralism, a view also shared in good measure by Mīmāṃsā. And the ontology of Sāṅkhya and Yoga is characterized by a fundamental dualism of *puruṣa* (spirit) and *prakṛti* (matter). Hence the standard presentation of Hindu tolerance in terms of 'one reality, many paths' poses problems if applied across the Hindu philosophical spectrum.

III

It will now be contended that the epistemologies of all the systems of Hindu thought share a feature in common which is congenial from the point of view of religious tolerance. This point, in our view, has been almost totally overlooked in this context.

To set the stage for introducing it one might begin with the observation that tolerance does not necessarily imply acceptance. If I tolerate another point of view it does not mean that I concede my own; rather it means that I eschew the use of force or coercion in either advocating my point of view or combating another. As the adherent of a particular religion or ideology or philosophy is predisposed to consider his or her position as true or correct, or at least normative, and that of the other party as somehow mistaken or in error, I contend that how "error" is viewed by any religion, or schools of thought within it, has a vital bearing on the extent, nature and degree of tolerance it extends to a point of view other than its own. It turns out to be the case that each school of Hindu thought contains its own theory of error. A survey of these theories, therefore, will provide an important clue to the philosophical basis of religious tolerance in Hinduism.

IV

For reasons of space it will be advisable to treat the theories of error by hyphenating the allied systems of Nyāya-Vaiśeṣika and Sāṅkhya-Yoga. Those of Mīmāṃsā and Vedānta, then, could be treated on their own.

The theory of error in Nyāya-Vaiśeṣika may be summarized as follows: "the error is not in respect to the presented object as such, but is confined to its predicative (or attributive) elements."[10] If, for instance, a rope is mistaken for a snake, the rope is real, it is the predication of snake which is erroneous. The details of the process by which such erroneous perception occurs need not detain us, for from our point of view the "essential point for us to remember is that *error always has an objective basis* and that its erroneous character lies in transferring to what is presented some feature which does not belong to it, no matter whether that feature is now being, or has in the past, been experienced."[11]

According to the theory of error in Sāṅkhya-Yoga, error arises because our knowledge "only *selects* certain aspects and omits the rest. According to this theory of selective apprehension all the characteristics that can ever be known of an object actually belong to it; and, if only some of them are apprehended by a particular person at a particular time, it is entirely due to subjective limitations."[12] It is on account of such subjective apprehension that an individual sees a rope as a snake, omitting to apprehend those features of the rope inconsistent with its being a snake. The main point to be kept in mind from our view is the fact that although "men obtrude their personalities into their judgements, and subjective prejudices undoubtedly affect their knowledge of things; yet they *never create the things they perceive.* But our knowledge, though pointing to an external universe, is one-sided. This is a fundamental defect of human experience."[13]

The two sub-schools of Mīmāṃsā have their own theories of error; very briefly, that of one school bears a close resemblance to that of Nyāya-Vaiśeṣika and the other to that of Sāṅkhya-Yoga. As for Vedānta—all the three major schools of it also have their own theories of error. Advaita Vedānta believes that even in erroneous perception "an illusory object . . . endures so long as its knowledge lasts"[14] but only for so long, that is to say, for the time that the rope is mistaken as a snake, a snake must be assumed to exist in some sense for the duration. This view is hard on one's common sense and relies on the doctrine that the Advaitin "accepts an objective factor or counterpart in all knowledge *completely* corresponding to its content, and error is no exception to this rule."[15] This view, however, is very significant from the point of view of this paper for it demonstrates that even an absolutistic school of philosophy such as Advaita posits an objective counterpart to error. In other words, error cannot be baseless according to it. Viśiṣṭādvaita Vedānta has a view of error which takes even a more indulgent view of it: "all knowledge is true necessarily, although it may not be true enough. . . . When a torch held in the hand is turned round rapidly, we see a circle of fire. This is an illusion, and Rāmānuja says that it is quite correct so far as it goes. He means that it is right in comprehending the fact that the point of the torch occupies every possible position on the circumference; it only omits to note that the occupation takes place successively and is not simultaneous, as it should do to form an actual circle."[16]

Finally, Dvaita Vedānta also possesses a theory of error which it regards as an "improved version"[17] of the Nyāya-Vaiśeṣika theory discussed earlier.

V

The reader would by now have noticed one common feature underlying *all* these theories of error: *that even while committing an error one is never completely out of touch with reality according to any school of Hindu philosophy.* It seems to me that this aspect of Hindu epistemology provides as secure a basis for religious tolerance as Hindu Vedantic ontology. In fact, it might provide an even more secure basis for it as it is more broad-based: it covers all the schools of Hindu philosophy and is not confined to one of them.

NOTES

1.   S. Radhakrishnan, *The Hindu View of Life* (New York: The Macmillan Company, 1927), 22, 34; *Eastern Religions and Western Thought* (New York: Oxford University Press, 1959), 318-19; T.M.P. Mahadevan, *Outlines of Hinduism* (Bombay: Chetana Limited, 1971), 16-21; etc.

2. *Outlines*, Chapter Seven.

3. M. Hiriyanna, *The Essentials of Indian Philosophy* (London: Allen & Unwin,1949), 152.

4. *Essentials*, 86.

5. *Essentials*, 84.

6. Mahadevan, *Outlines*, 116.

7. *Outlines*, 124.

8. Hiriyanna, *Essentials*, 106.

9. *Essentials*, 130.

10. *Essentials*, 97.

11. *Essentials*, 98, emphasis added.

12. *Essentials*, 117.

13. *Essentials*, 117-18, emphasis added.

14. *Essentials*, 166.

15. *Essentials*, 166, second emphasis mine.

16. *Essentials*, 183.

17. *Essentials*, 196.

CONTRIBUTORS

Bruce Alton is Professor of Religious Studies, Trinity College, University of Toronto.

Gregory Baum is Professor of Theological Ethics, Faculty of Religious Studies, McGill University, Montreal.

Maurice Boutin Is McConnell Professor of Philosophy of Religion, Faculty of Religious Studies, McGill University, Montreal.

Richard Cooper holds a Ph.D. in Philosophy of Religion from McGill University and resides in Montreal.

Donald Evans is Professor of Philosophy, University of Toronto.

Edward Furcha is Professor of Church History, Faculty of Religious Studies, McGill University, Montreal.

Douglas J. Hall is Professor of Christian Theology, Faculty of Religious Studies, McGill University, Montreal.

Morny Joy is Professor of Religious Studies, University of Calgary.

David Lochhead is Professor of Systematic Theolgoy, Vancouver School of Theology.

Alister McGrath is Professor of Historical and Systematic Theology, Oxford University.

Alastair McKinnon is Emeritus Professor of Philosophy, McGill University, Montreal.

Arvind Sharma is Birks Professor of Comparative Religion, Faculty of Religious Studies, McGill University, Montreal.

Wilfred Cantwell Smith is Emeritus Professor of World Religions, Harvard University.